I0803274

IMAGES
of America

FILIPINOS IN GREATER BOSTON

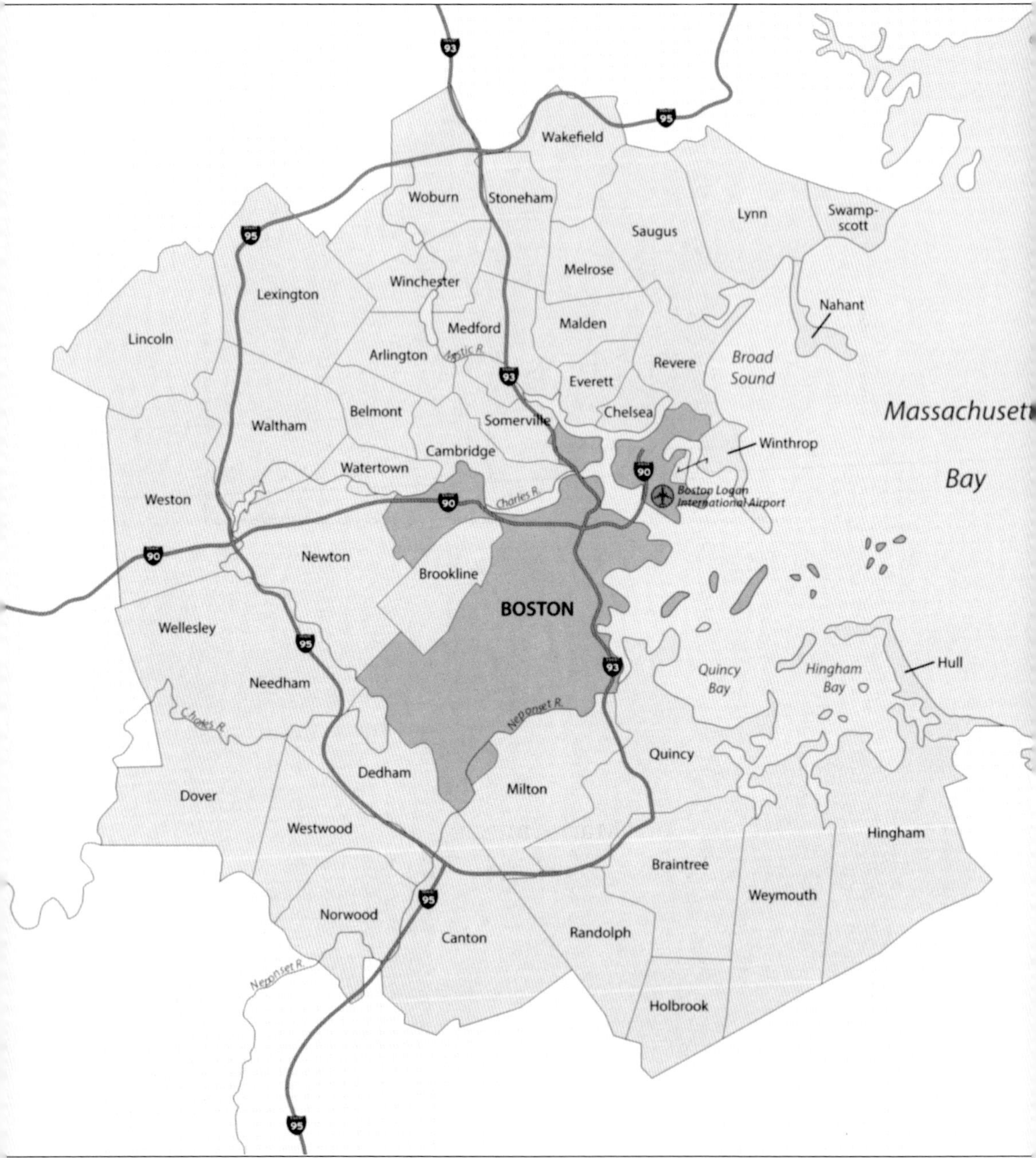

This map shows the cities and towns of Greater Boston. During the 1960s, many Filipino medical professionals and military personnel settled in Cambridge, Quincy, Randolph, and other towns and cities. Today, their children and grandchildren as well as new immigrants from the Philippines settle in and around Greater Boston and beyond. (Courtesy of Rainer Lesniewski.)

ON THE COVER: Filipino American cultural dancers dressed in traditional attire perform to crowds at Boston City Hall Plaza as part of the Philippine Centennial Celebration in Boston. (Courtesy of Francisco Celazo.)

IMAGES
of America

FILIPINOS IN GREATER BOSTON

Mary Talusan
Foreword by Grace Talusan

ARCADIA
PUBLISHING

ISBN 978-1-4671-0960-4

Published by Arcadia Publishing
Charleston, South Carolina

Printed in the United States of America

Library of Congress Control Number: 2022946989

For all general information, please contact Arcadia Publishing:
Telephone 843-853-2070
Fax 843-853-0044
E-mail sales@arcadiapublishing.com
For customer service and orders:
Toll-Free 1-888-313-2665

Visit us on the Internet at www.arcadiapublishing.com

For the immigrant generation who left their families and homeland to build a future for us in Boston

Contents

Foreword

Filipinos in Greater Boston brings together, within one book, the dreamers, innovators, and brave souls who sacrificed and built for a future they might never see. As new immigrants, they were constantly in motion, working toward their unique American Dream. For a brief moment, when the camera pointed its lens, centering them for once, they stopped what they were doing. They posed; sometimes, they smiled. They said, "I was here."

A book is not complete without its reader. You may not immediately recognize every face, but if you listen to their stories, you will come to know them as family.

—Grace Talusan
Author of *The Body Papers: A Memoir*
Lecturer, Nonfiction Writing Program, Brown University

ACKNOWLEDGMENTS

This book would not exist without the help of my mother, Araceli "Arcel" Gamalinda Talusan. To gather photographs, we tapped into our family's network of friends, or *barkada*, and then cast a wider net on social media. Fifty people responded, and we visited thirty-eight people in fourteen towns. Thank you to everyone who welcomed us into their homes as they dug into their photo albums and memories. We gathered 550 wonderful photographs but, unfortunately, could not use them all.

Thank you to past and present members of the following organizations who participated: Filipino Association of Greater Boston, Philippine Medical Association of New England (PMANE), Pilipino-American Association of New England (PAMAS), Philippine Nurses Association of New England (PNANE), Iskwelahang Pilipino (IP), Philippine Dance and Culture Organization (PDCO), the Facebook groups BOS Filipinos and Filipinos IN Massachusetts, Boston Filipino American Book Club (BFAB), Filipino Apostolate of Boston, Bagong Kulturang Pinoy (BKP), and the Philippine-American Mainstream Advocacy for Nonpartisan Associations (PAMANA).

I honor the work of Lourdes Avena Javier, who documented our community through 1982 in the self-published book *Montage*. I appreciate the advice of my *kababayan* and fellow authors in the Images of America series: Theo Gonzalves and Rod Labrador of *Filipinos in Hawaii*, Christy Panis Poisot and Jenah Maravilla of *Filipinos in Houston*, and Florante and Roselyn Ibanez of *Filipinos in Carson and the South Bay*.

I owe an *utang na loob*, or debt of gratitude, to Grace Talusan, Barbara Gaerlan, Christi-Anne Castro, Myra Liwanag, Bernadette Bague, Joanie Cordova, Fr. Cyriac Mattathilanical, Leila Amarra, Linda Ott, Fritz Friedman, Ben Manzano, Bill Solar, PhilJay Solar, Felipe Tolentino, Norma Bucal, Alice Layug, Mimi Strickland, Patty Yusah, Cher Agular, Mary Rose Ezpeleta, Joju Bautista, Marietta Felina Sable, Richard Chu, Nelly Lichauco Fung, Celine de Leon Young, Myrna Lacson, Flor and Medi Hipona, Dolly Marmol, Linda Ty-Casper, Rudy Hermosa, Bernard Ellorin, Chit Abriam, Susan Cid-Espanola, Lito and Esther Santos, Fe and Nestor Festin, Gary and Lina Angeles, Ofelia Villanueva, Frank Celoza, Virginia Jacildo, Aida Kalb, Nida Prado, Pia McCusker, Fanny and Peping Valencia, and all the hands who lightened the weight of my work. Please forgive any unintentional omissions or errors. Photographs without a note were supplied by the author.

All my love goes to John Patrick, Gavin, and Norhanna for their patience and constant support.

INTRODUCTION

The connection between the Philippines and Boston has had a long history. Filipinos enlisted from the Boston area to fight in the Civil War (1861–1865). An anti-imperialist movement protesting President McKinley's annexation of the Philippines held its first meeting at Boston's Faneuil Hall on June 15, 1898. As that movement failed to stop US colonization, American colonialists created the Philippine Constabulary Band to promote the successful assimilation of Filipinos by obscuring the Philippines' centuries-old heritage of European music. The band traveled to Boston to perform three concerts at Boston's Symphony Hall. Several years later, a Philippine band from the USS *Georgia* performed at an event hosted by the Manila Society of the "Gota de Leche, an organization of Boston-based Filipinos," according to the *Boston Daily Globe*. In 1924, the Filipino Collegians of Greater Boston, made up of students attending Harvard, Tufts, Massachusetts Institute of Technology, Boston University, Northeastern University, and Gordon Bible School, held an event to celebrate Philippine national hero José Rizal along with the raising of the Philippine flag. A prominent family from the Philippines, the Lichaucos, lived in Boston during the 1920s and sent their daughters to the Academy of the Sacred Heart in Newton. Their son Marcial became the first Filipino to complete an undergraduate degree at Harvard in 1923. Other Filipinos who made a mark in Boston include Dr. Fe del Mundo, who founded the first pediatric hospital in the Philippines and furthered her graduate work at Harvard Medical School through an appointment at Boston's Children's Hospital from 1936 to 1940. During the 1950s, a group of Filipino students and professionals formed the Philippine-Bataan Club of Boston and New England, Inc., and socialized at the Touraine Hotel, located at the corner of Boylston and Tremont Streets.

After the Immigration and Nationality Act of 1965 lifted a federal quota system that restricted immigration from Asia, Filipino immigrants arrived in large numbers during the 1960s and 1970s as medical professionals, military personnel, and engineers. They settled in suburbs and cities throughout Greater Boston to raise their American-born children. In the 1960s, they founded several organizations, such as the Philippine Medical Association of New England and the Filipino Association of Greater Boston, a collaboration of "medical personnel, educators, engineers, lawyers, servicemen, scientists, musicians, artists and businessmen," according to Lourdes Javier. The Philippine Dance and Culture Organization, formerly the Philippine Dance Company of Boston, and Iskwelahang Pilipino were founded in 1976. Filipino American students, mostly from the West Coast, studied United States–Philippine relations at the Goddard-Cambridge Graduate School under instructor Dr. Daniel Boone Schirmer from 1974 to 1977. They participated in several Boston-based anti–martial law organizations. A Filipino apostolate was formed under the Archdiocese of Boston in 1977, and the Pilipino-American Association of New England was established by military families in 1978. The Philippine Nurses Association of New England was incorporated as a nonprofit in 1990, and the Philippine-American Mainstream Advocacy for Nonpartisan Associations, Inc., was established in 1998 during the Philippine Centennial to foster cooperation among a variety of Filipino American organizations in New England and to hold Philippine Independence Day celebrations. Several other groups are mentioned in this book.

The Aquino family lived on Commonwealth Avenue across from Boston College from 1980 to 1983 during the exile of opposition leader Benigno S. Aquino Jr. Upon his return to the Philippines, he was assassinated. After snap elections, his wife, Corazon "Cory" Aquino, became president of the Philippines, and she returned to Boston during a state visit in 1986. Years later, their son Benigno S. Aquino III served as president, and he visited Boston in 2014.

Today, Filipino immigrants are drawn to Greater Boston and add their contributions to this diverse community. According to APIAVote.org, the Filipino American population in Massachusetts has grown steadily over the years to 25,842 as of 2020.

One

Exchange Students and Visitors 1920s–1950s

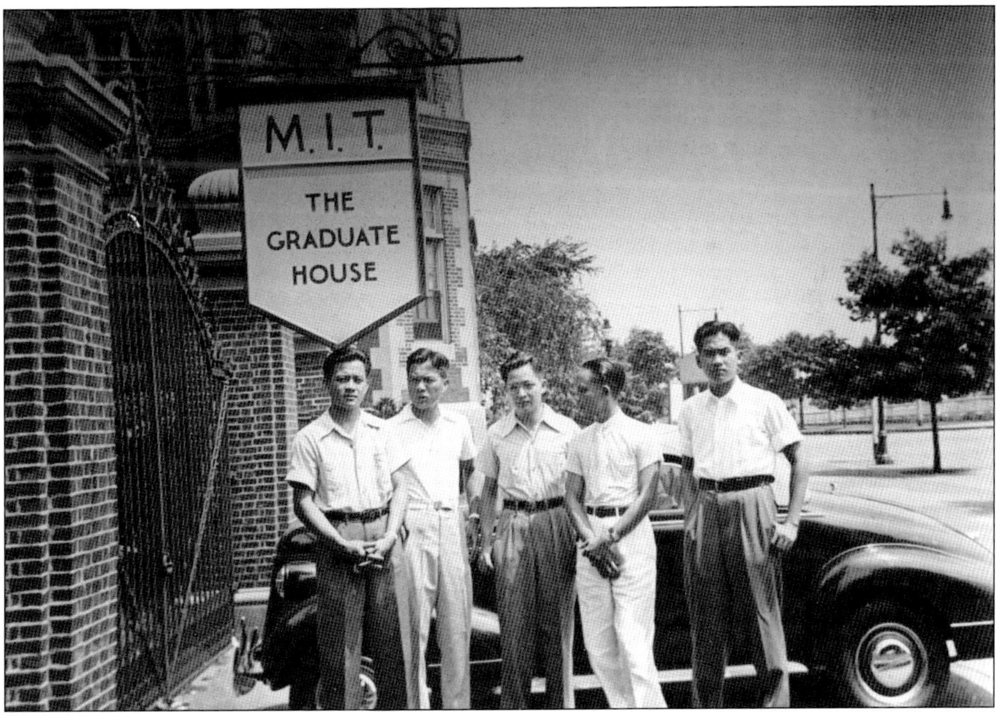

Posed in front of MIT, from left to right, are graduate students Luis Hidalgo Lim and Mike Unson and visitors Roberto Lim, unidentified, and Mamerto Cruz. Luis and Roberto were the sons of Gen. Vicente P. Lim, the first Filipino to graduate from West Point, and Pilar Hidalgo Lim, an organizer for Philippine women suffragettes. Luis's daughter Patricia settled in Lexington. (Courtesy of Patricia Lim Yusah.)

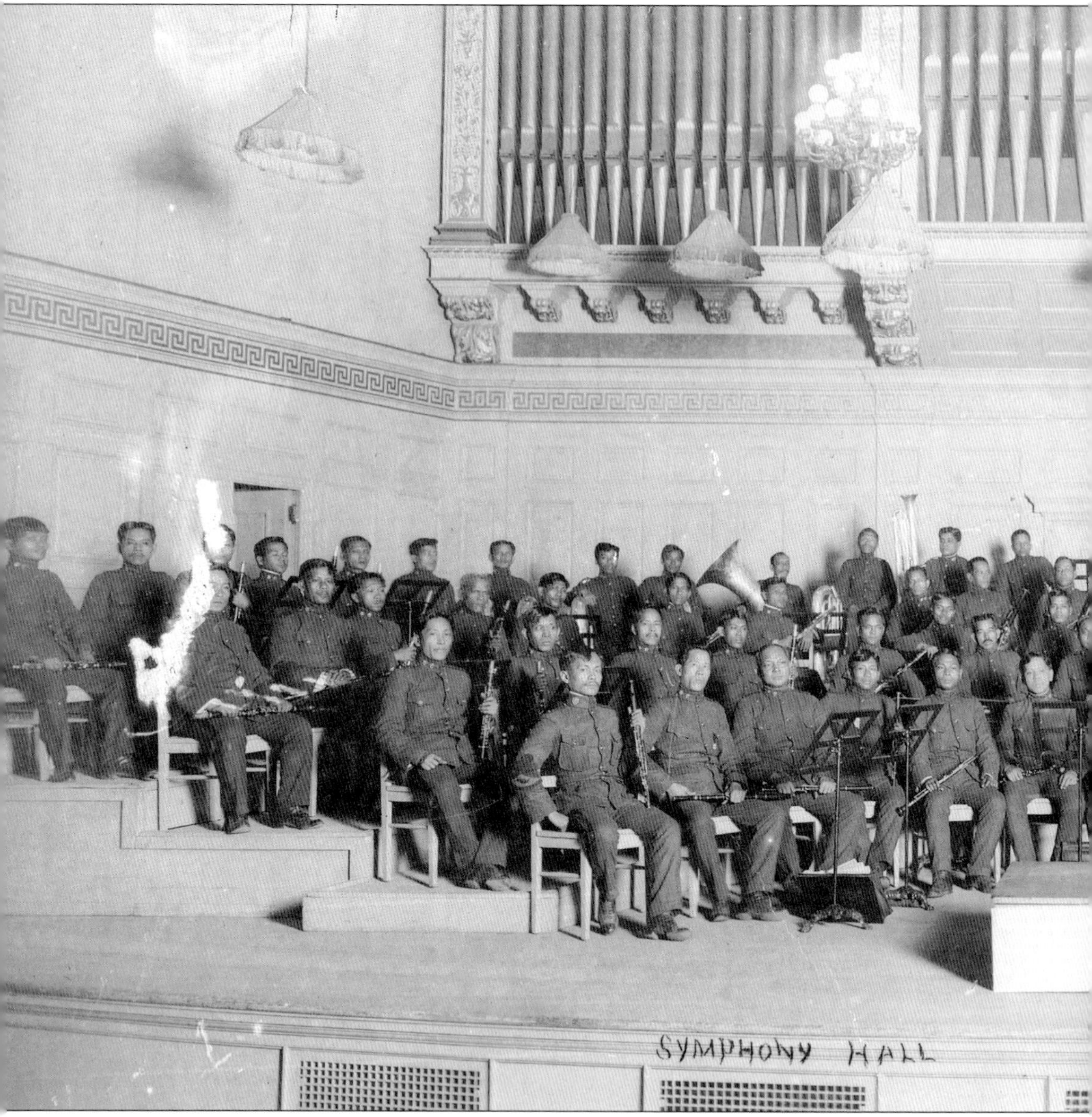

The world-famous Philippine Constabulary Band performed three concerts at Boston's Symphony Hall in 1909 after they marched at Pres. William H. Taft's inaugural parade in Washington, DC. The 80-plus members of the band impressed Boston audiences by playing both as a concert band and orchestra. Their conductor, African American officer Lt. Walter H. Loving (far right), attended the New England Conservatory of Music but left to serve in the Philippines in 1899. He

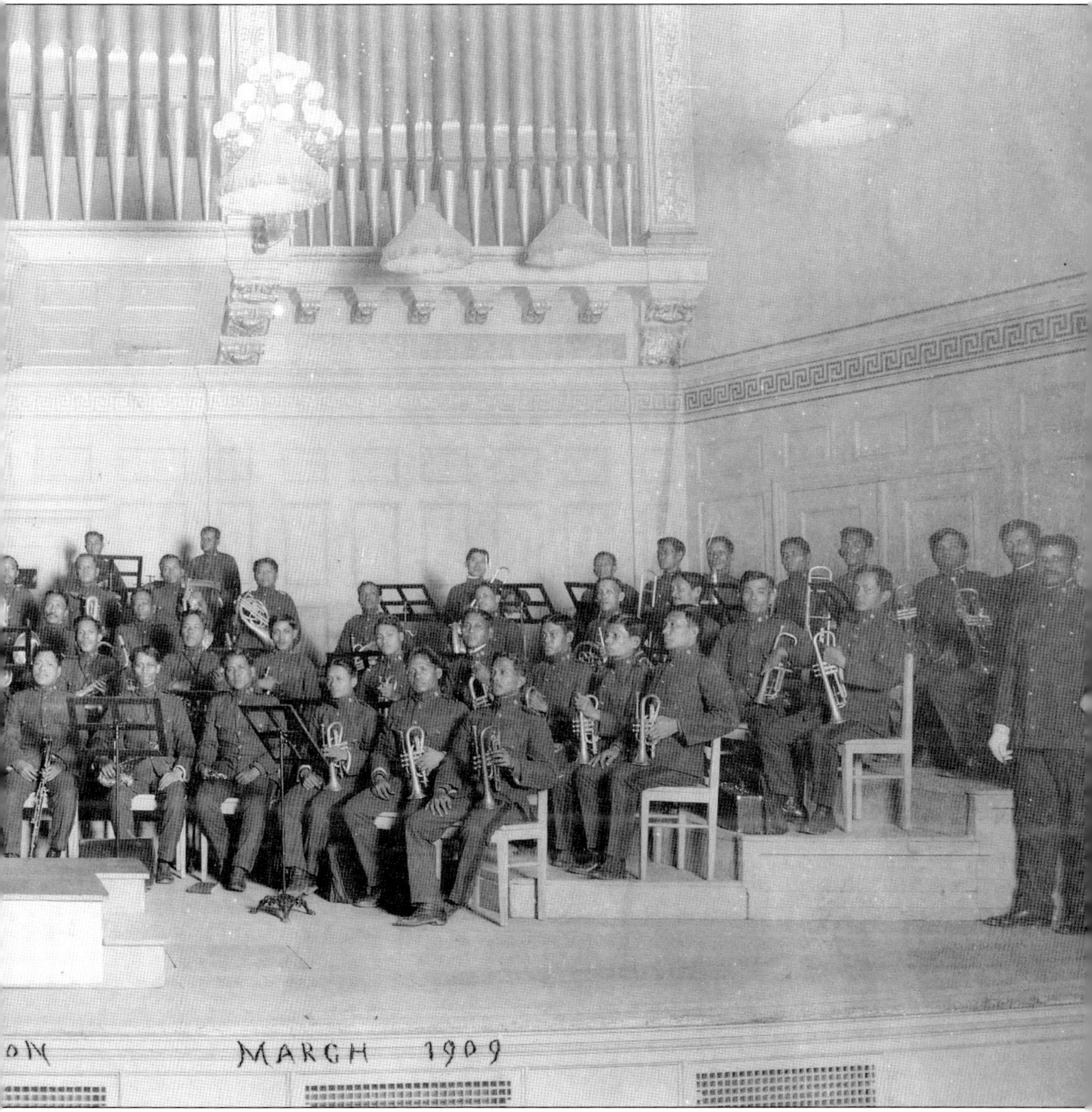

worked with the band for 40 years and was appointed lieutenant colonel. Capt. Pedro B. Navarro (front left), who became the band's first Filipino conductor, is the maternal grandfather of Araceli Gamalinda Talusan and great-grandfather of Mary, who played on the same stage at Symphony Hall some 80 years later as a cellist with the Greater Boston Youth Symphony Orchestra. (Courtesy of the Moorland-Spingarn Research Center, Howard University.)

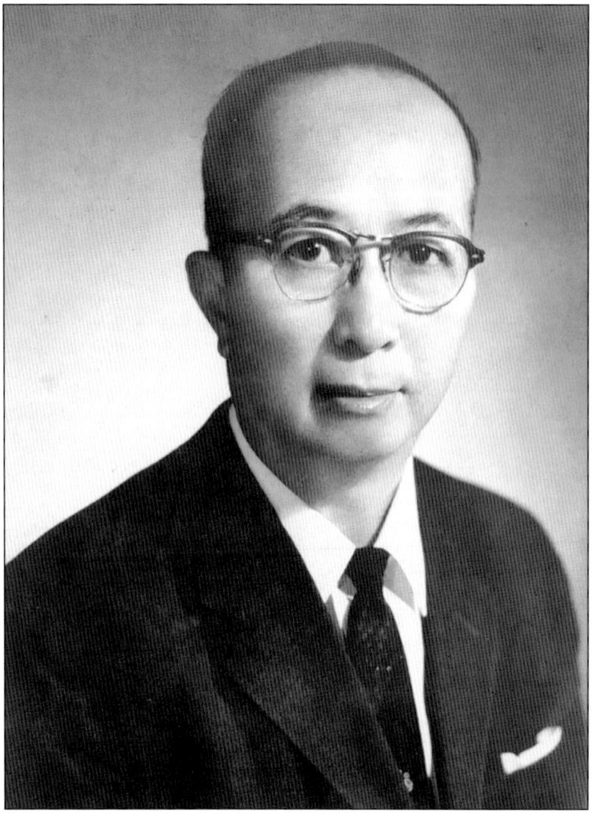

Marcial P. Lichauco was the first Filipino to graduate from Harvard College in 1923. He coauthored *The Conquest of the Philippines by the United States, 1898–1925* with American lawyer and anti-imperialist activist Moorfield Storey. Marcial married Jessie Coe, an American who lived in the Philippines until the age of 109. His nephew Alejandro Lichauco, an economist, graduated from Harvard Law School in 1951. (Courtesy of the Marcial P. Lichauco family.)

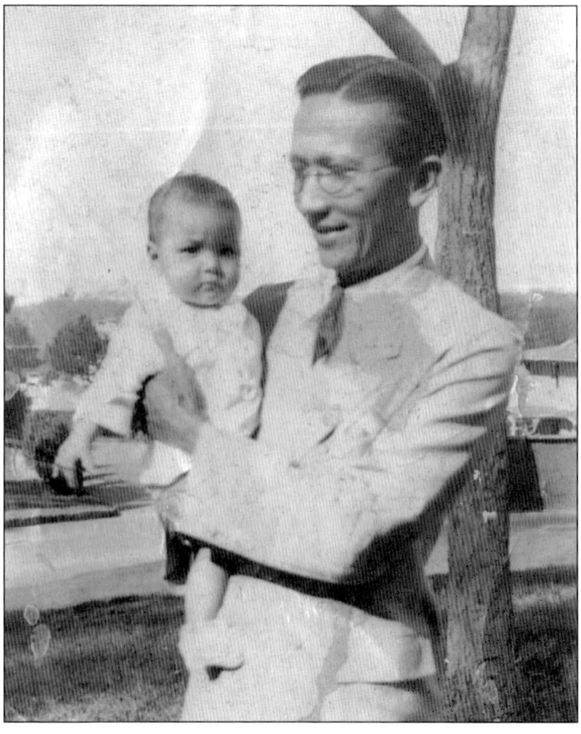

Marceliano R. Montemayor was the first Filipino to receive a master of law degree from Harvard Law School in 1924. He was appointed to the Supreme Court of the Philippines as an associate justice in 1948. Marceliano is pictured here in 1935 with his eldest child, Myrna. (Courtesy of Myrna Lacson.)

Exchange scholars, medical professionals, and military personnel formed a small community of Filipinos in Boston. Photographed here from left to right in the mid-1950s are CPO R. Epi (US Navy), Mrs. M. Epi, D. Mata, Dr. B. Lacsamana, Lourdes Javier, and Sgt. N. Llaneta (US Army). (Courtesy of Filipino Association of Greater Boston, Inc.)

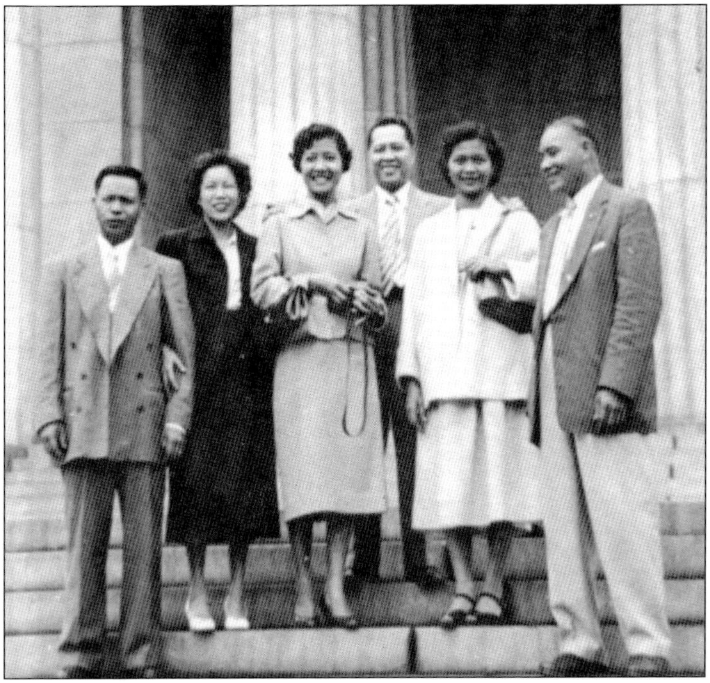

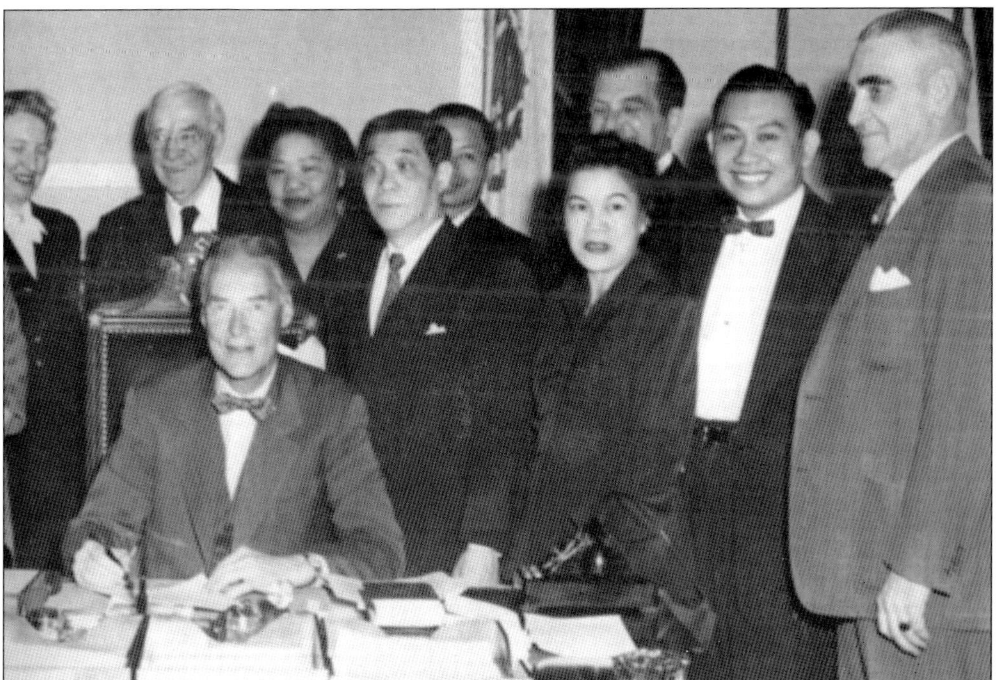

The Philippine Bataan Club was formed in Boston in the early 1950s to share their experiences during World War II. They met with Massachusetts governor Christian Herter (sitting), who served from 1953 to 1957, on the proclamation of Philippine-Bataan Day. Included in this photograph are club members B. Rosales, president and CPO R. Epi, and Mrs. M. Epi. (Courtesy of Filipino Association of Greater Boston, Inc.)

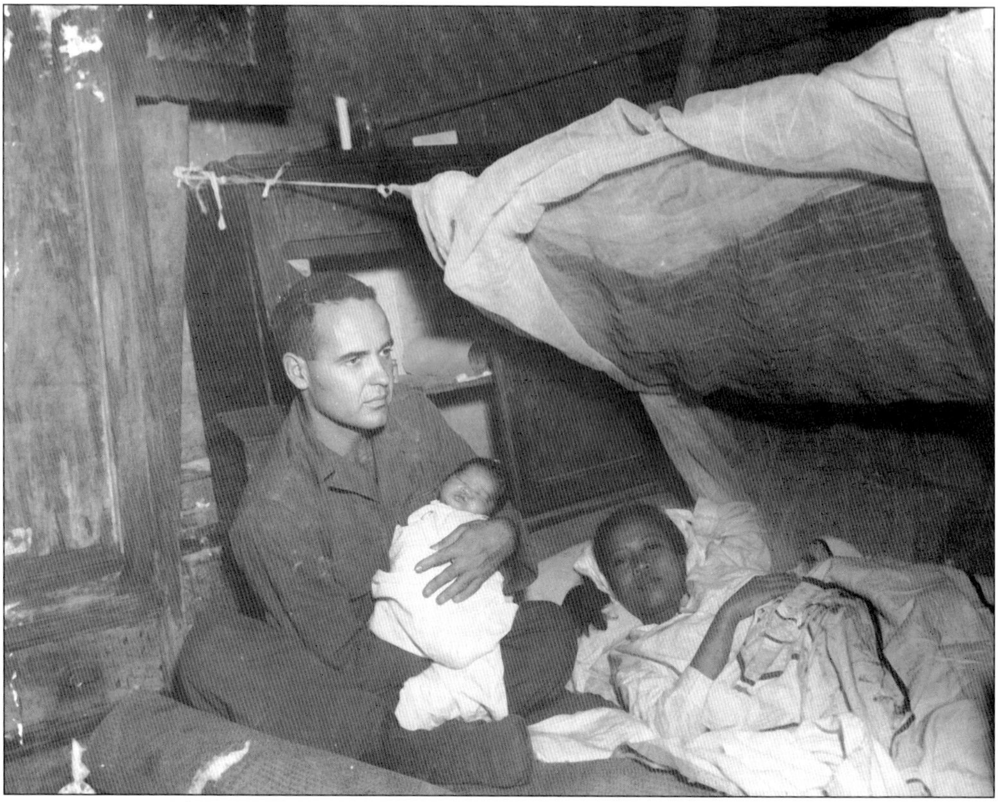

Capt. James C. Fisher, son of American author and social activist Dorothy Canfield Fisher, graduated from Harvard Medical School. He served in the US Army Medical Corps in the Philippines during World War II and is pictured holding a baby that he delivered. Below, Fisher, third from left, carries the newborn baby to be baptized by a priest. During a rescue operation that freed hundreds of POWs in what is known as the "Great Raid," Fisher was critically injured. A married couple, Drs. Julita and Carlos Layug, worked diligently to save him, but Fisher ultimately died on January 31, 1945. (Both, courtesy of the Layug family.)

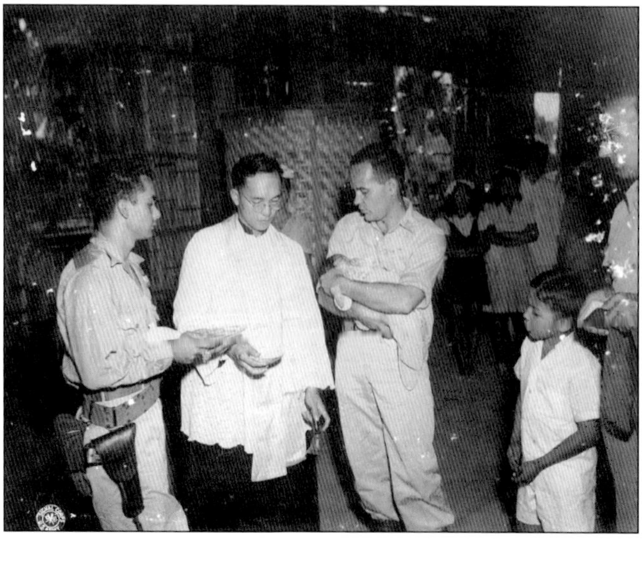

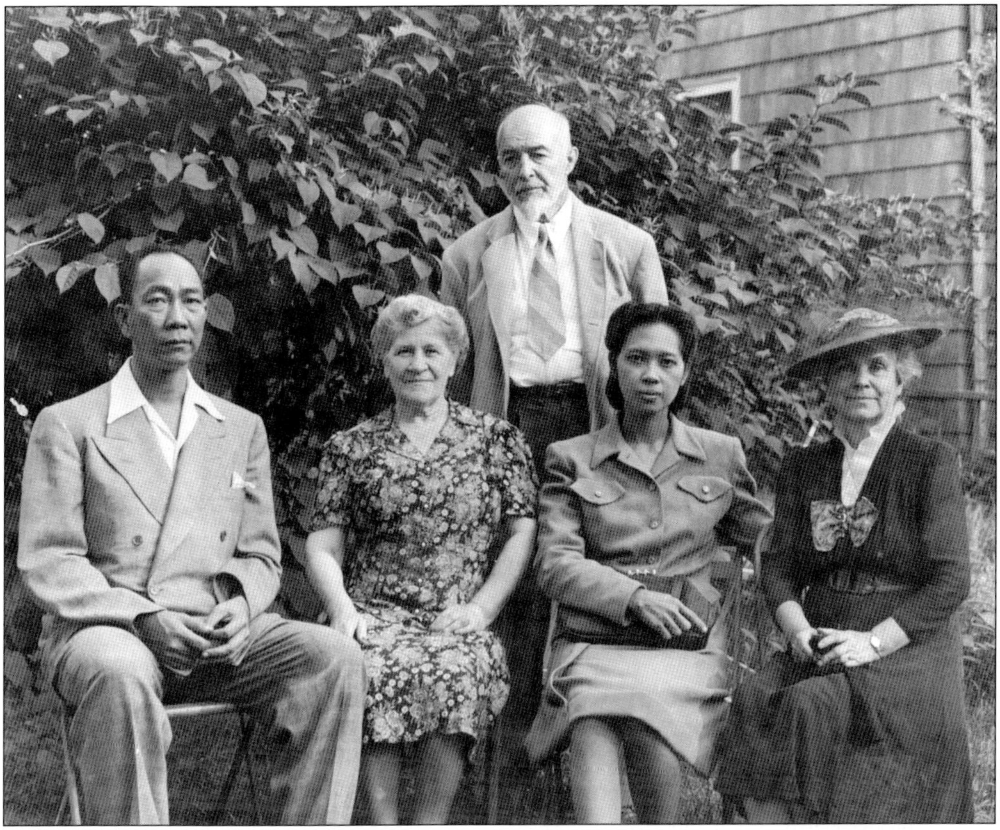

After James died, Dorothy Canfield Fisher (right) was grateful to the Layugs for caring for her son. She supported Drs. Carlos (left) and Julita Eugenio Layug (third from left) while they trained at Harvard Medical School. The Layugs lived in Captain James's former apartment in Wellesley Hills during their yearlong stay in Boston. (Courtesy of the Layug family.)

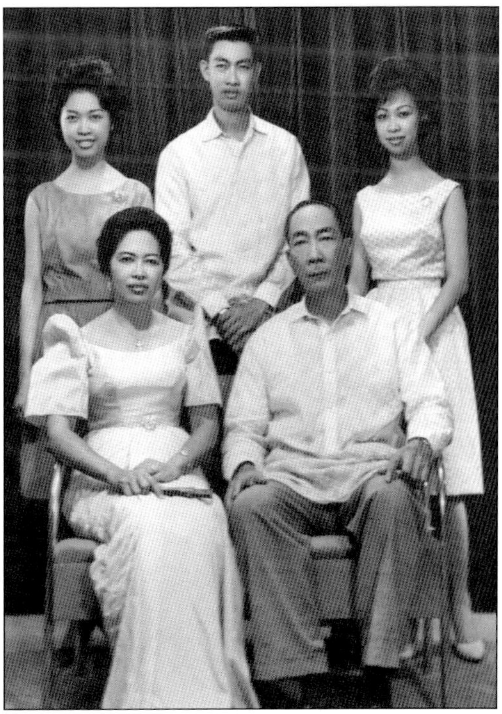

Dr. Julita Eugenio Layug (seated left) and Dr. Carlos Layug (seated right) are pictured with their children. Their son, Dr. Antonio Layug (standing center), settled in Massachusetts with his wife, Dr. Alicia Layug, and two children, Larissa and Anthony. (Courtesy of the Layug family.)

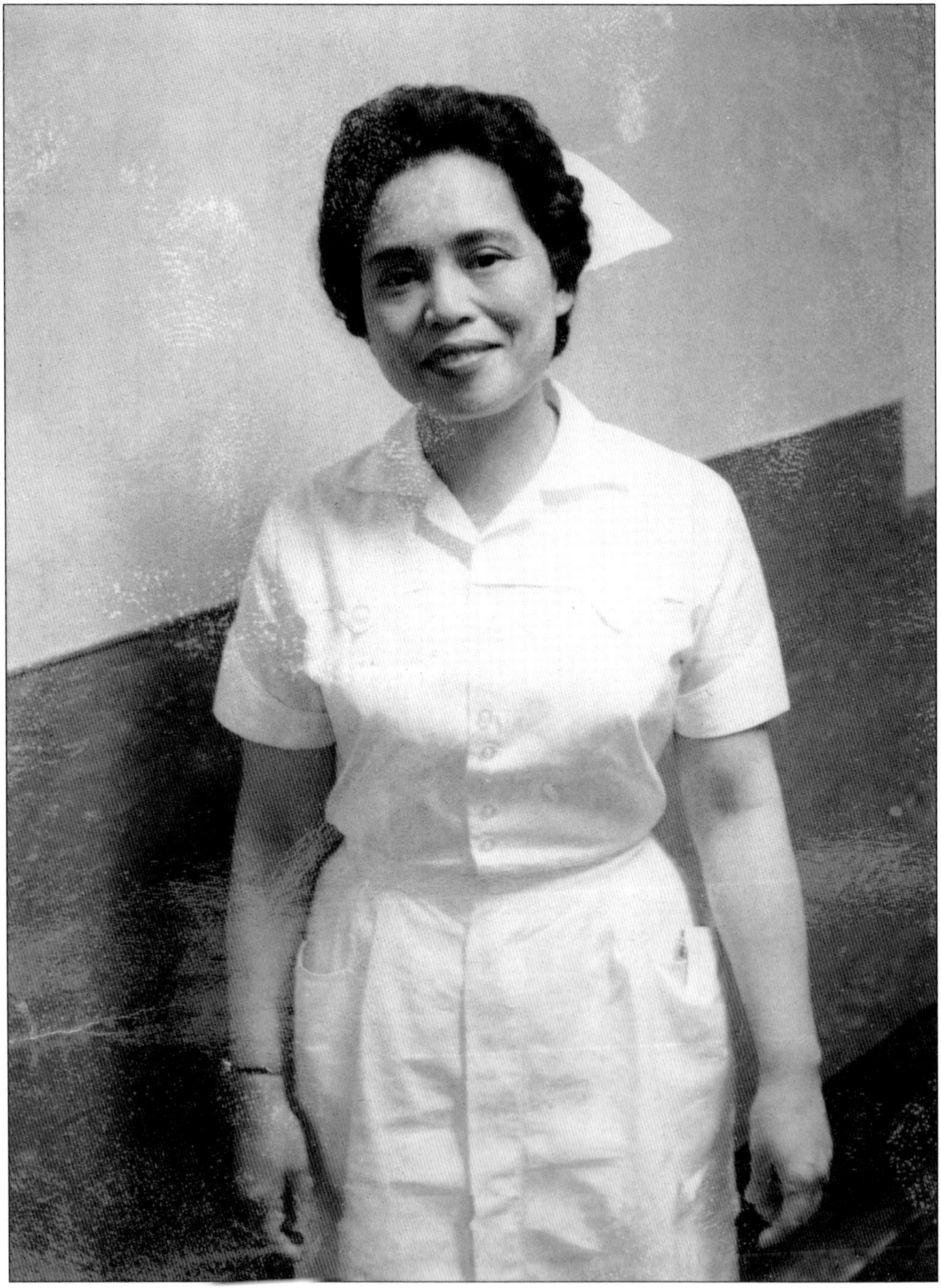

Catalina "Nena" Cornista Friedman immigrated to the United States with her husband, Dr. Frederick Friedman, and two sons in 1956. She worked as a nurse at the University Hospital, located in the South End neighborhood of Boston. Many students from the Philippines were welcomed into her home. She was active in the Filipino Association of Greater Boston, the Philippine Medical Association of New England, and other organizations. (Courtesy of Fritz Friedman.)

Two

Early Immigrants and Communities 1960s

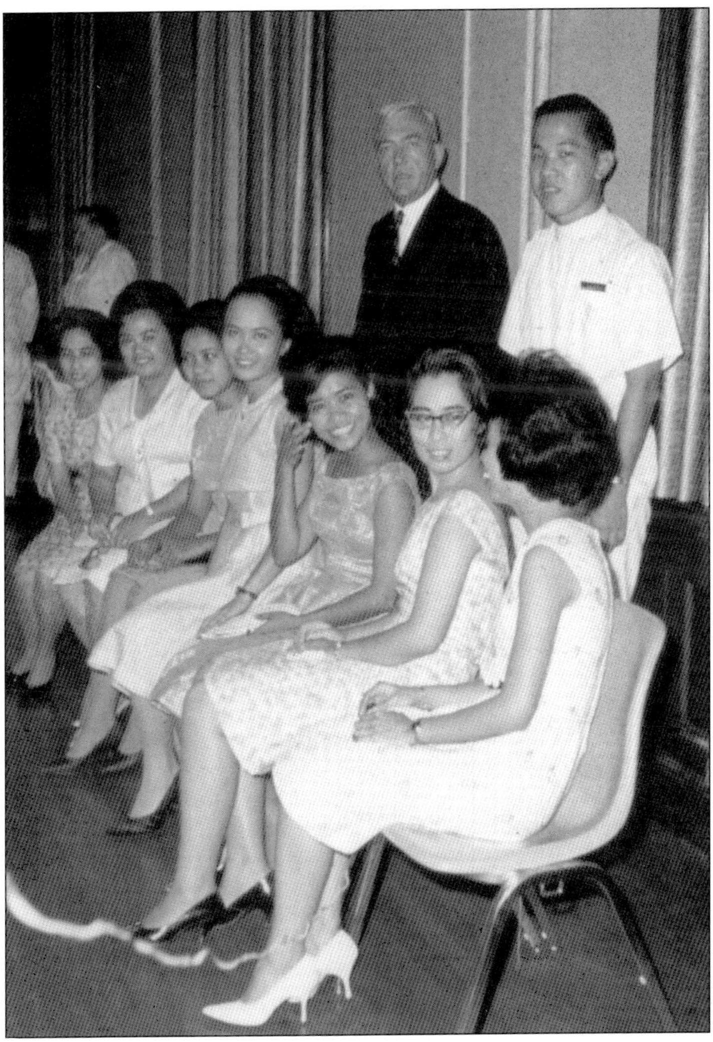

In 1960, about 1,300 Filipinos lived in Massachusetts, according to the US Census. The population grew as medical professionals from the Philippines were encouraged to immigrate. These physicians, training at Cambridge City Hospital in 1965, pose with hospital administrator Theodore Austin. Standing is Carlos Say, and seated from left to right are Carmen Aquino, Alenei Estrellato, Rosalinda Judan-Ott, Felocelia Deladisma, Violeta Andres, Susan Cid-Espanola, and Priscilla B. Alanguilan. (Courtesy of Dr. Rosalinda J. Ott.)

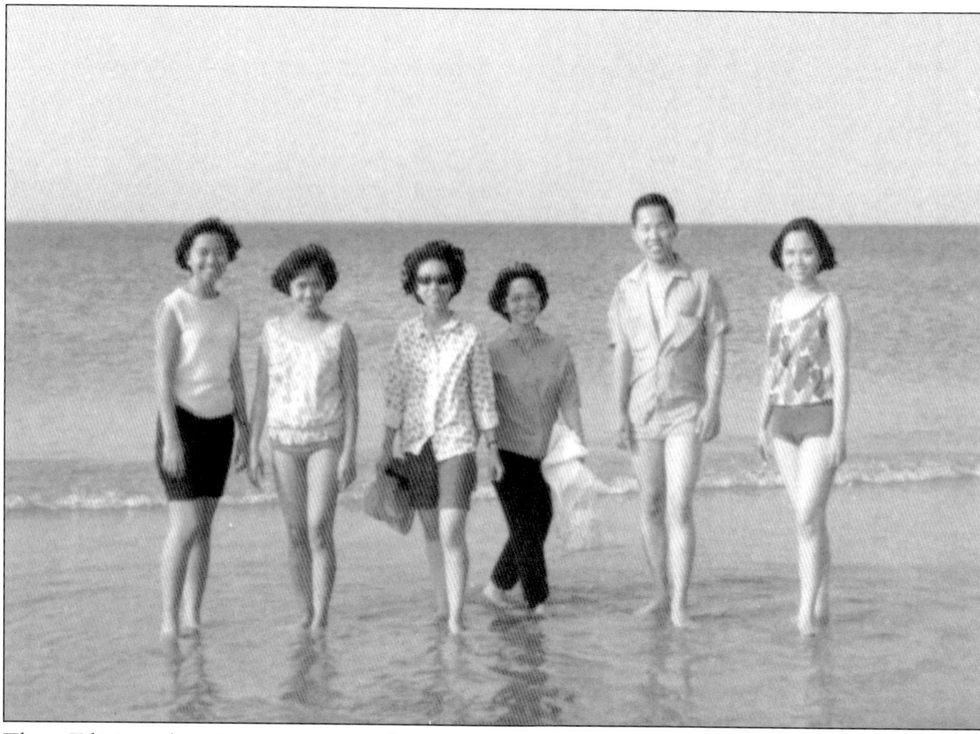

These Filipino physicians, enjoying a day at Nantasket Beach, were classmates at the University of Santo Tomas in the Philippines. They arrived in Boston in June 1964 to train at Cambridge City Hospital. Several of them settled permanently in Massachusetts to raise their families. (Courtesy of Dr. Rosalinda J. Ott.)

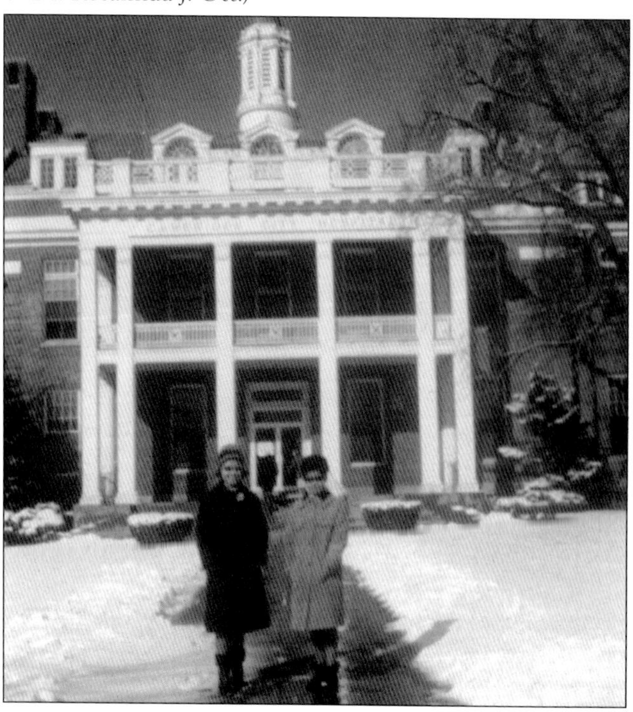

Dr. Rosalinda J. Ott (left), who specialized in pediatrics, and Dr. Violeta Andres-Kelley (right), who trained in OBGYN, pose in front of Cambridge City Hospital. They came to work as interns at the hospital in 1964 and subsequently settled in the Greater Boston area. (Courtesy of Dr. Rosalinda J. Ott.)

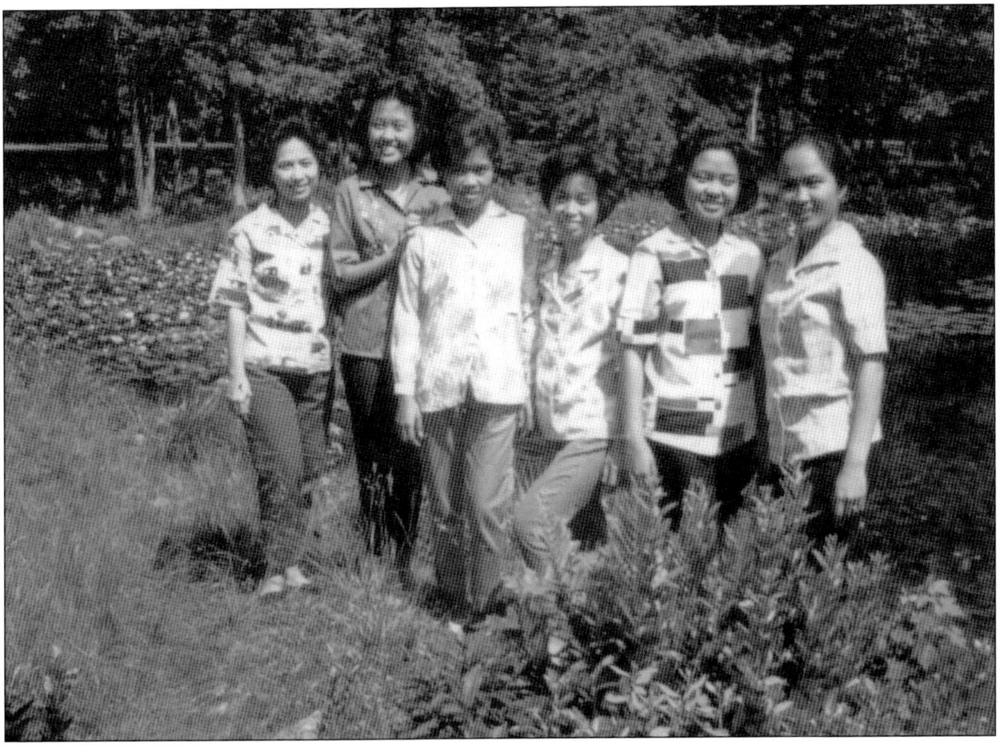

Physicians training at Cambridge Hospital visit a park in Brockton in 1964 just before they began their internship. From left to right are Carmelita Aquino-Belen, Aleni Estrellado-Araullo, Violeta Andres-Kelley, Priscila Alanguilan, Rosalinda Judan-Ott, and Felocelia Deladisma-Alcid. (Courtesy of Dr. Rosalinda J. Ott.)

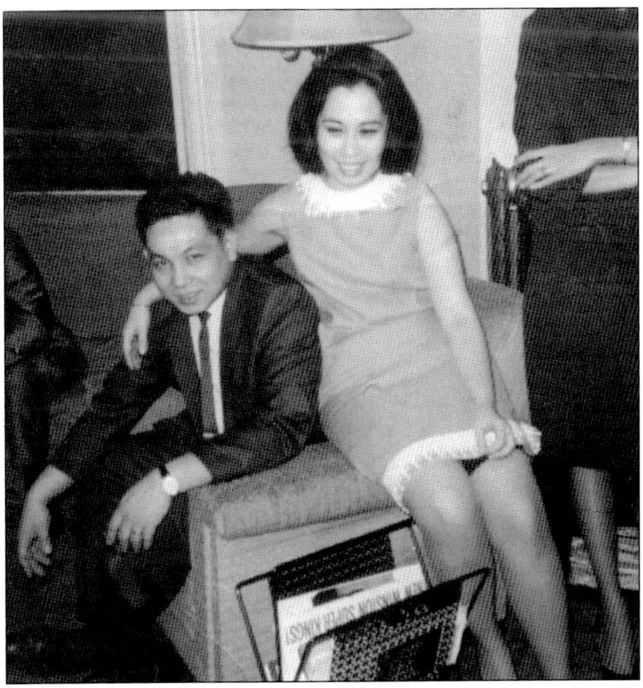

Dr. Susan Cid-Espanola and her husband, Wilfrido R. Espanola, met while students at the University of Santo Tomas in Manila and married in 1961. Wilfrido attended the Massachusetts Institute of Technology for graduate studies while Susan was an intern at Cambridge City Hospital. They are pictured here at a party in Boston in 1964. (Courtesy of Dr. Susan Cid-Espanola.)

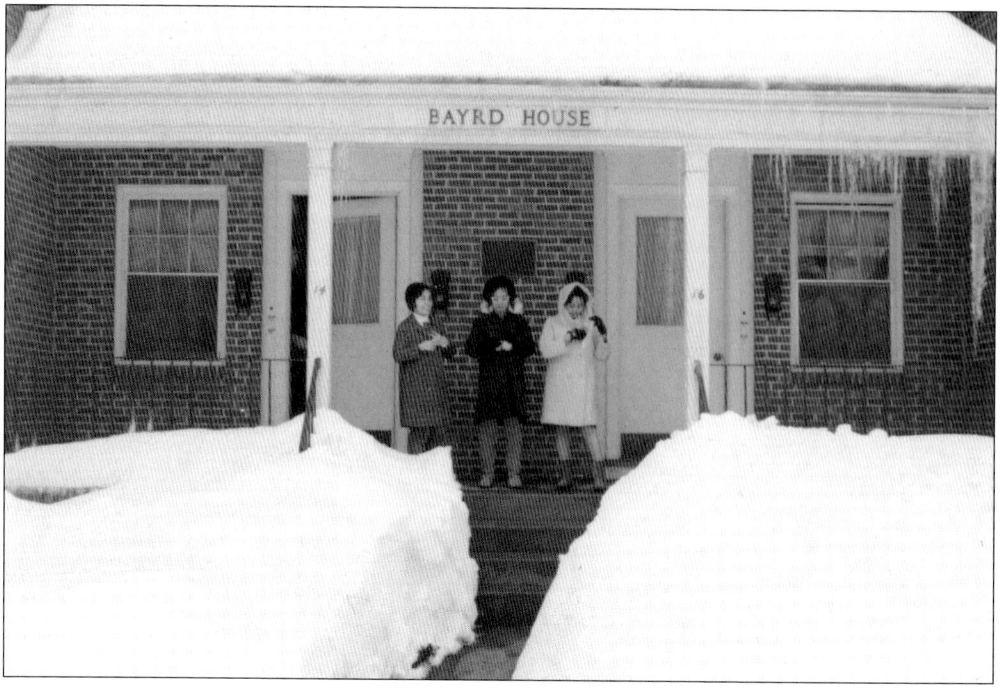

This photograph was taken in January 1968 in front of the Bayrd House at Malden Hospital, where Filipino medical professionals were housed. They came directly from the tropical Philippines to face New England's harsh winters. Pictured from left to right are Jenny Banigan, Dr. Marietta Bague, and Dr. Alicia Layug. Below, Drs. Marietta and Ceferino F. Bague are pictured inside their apartment at the Bayrd House. (Both, courtesy of Bernadette M. Bague.)

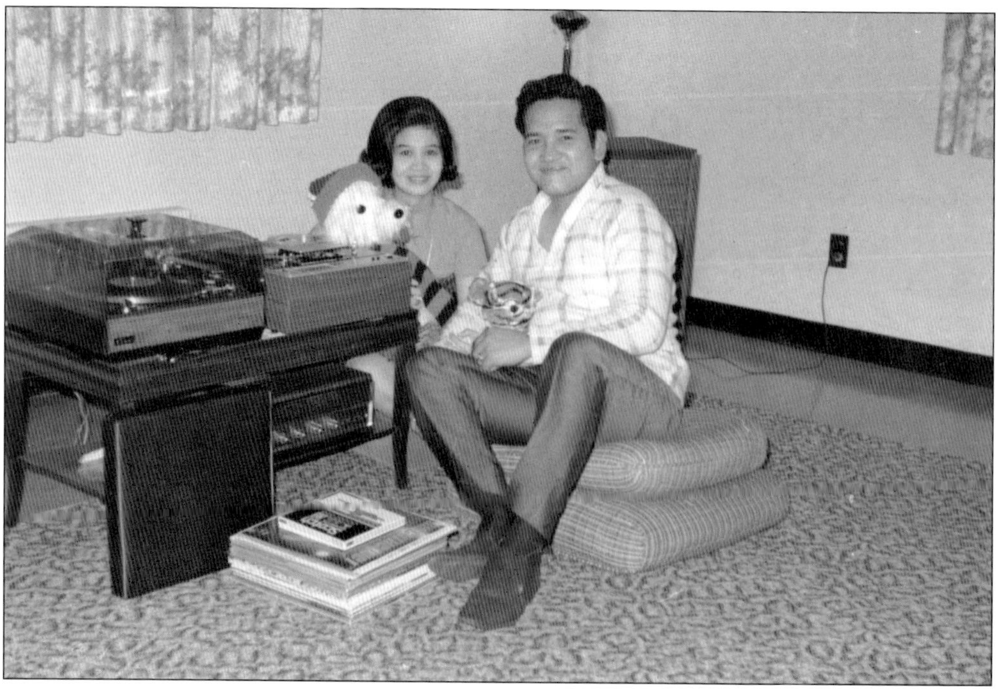

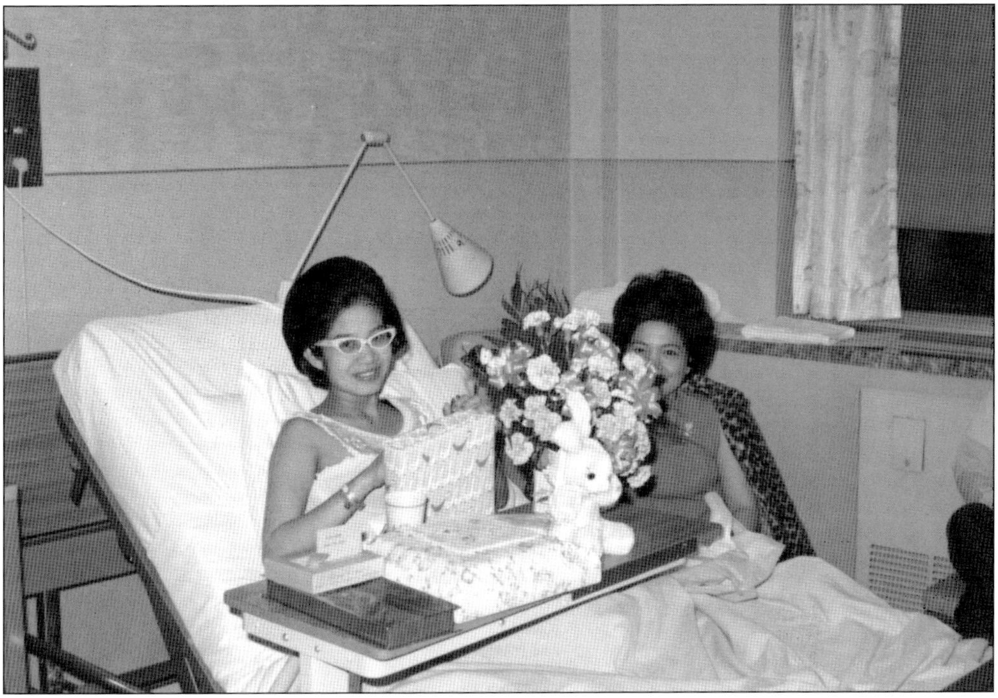

Dr. Marietta Bague is pictured while giving birth to her first American-born child at Malden Hospital in 1970. Below, Dr. Bague and baby Bernadette enjoy a summer afternoon in front of the Bayrd House in Malden. (Both, courtesy of Bernadette M. Bague.)

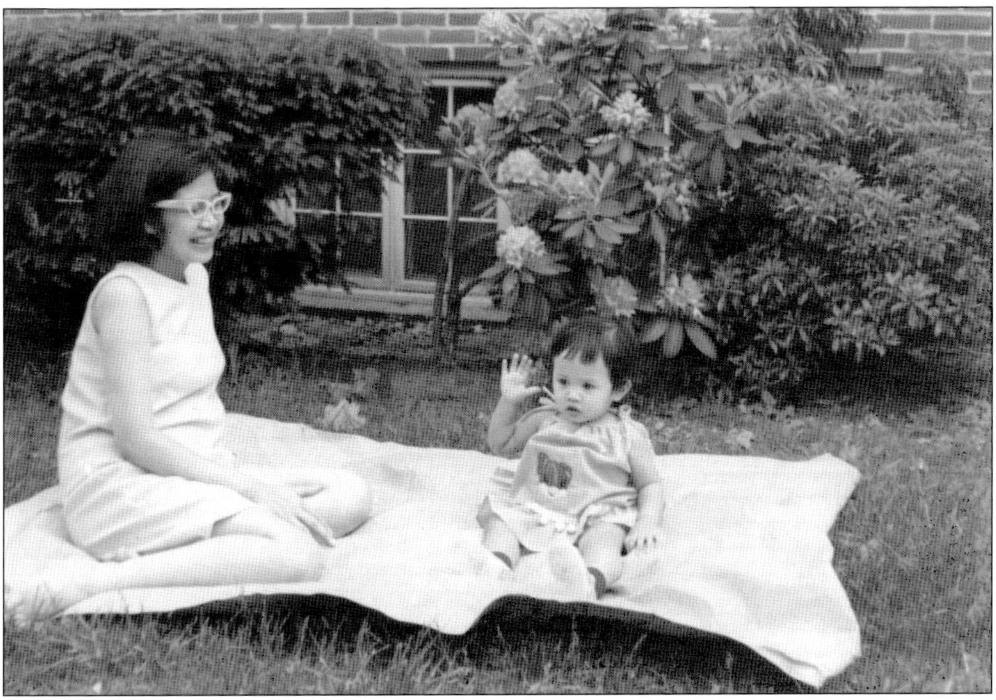

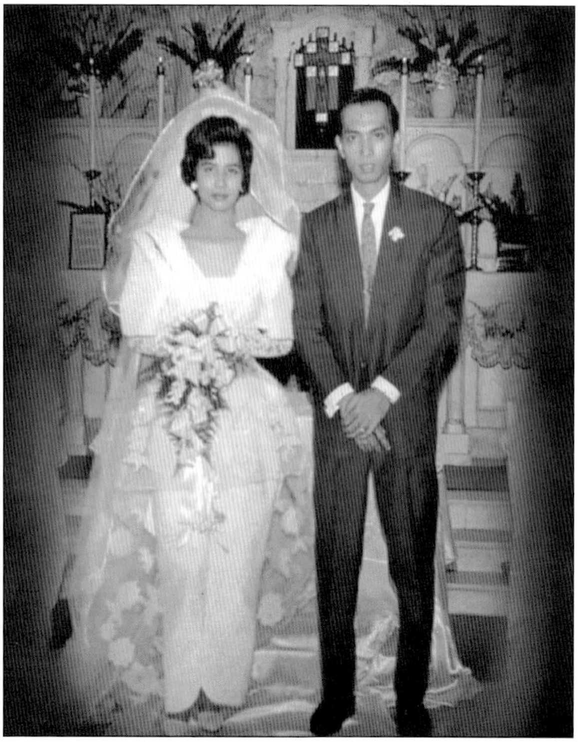

Dr. Almario "Mai" Bucal first came to the United States with his wife, Norma, in 1962 for an internship at a New Jersey hospital before they moved to Pittsburgh, where Mai did his specialty in pathology. They returned to Manila before Mai was recruited in 1972 by Bioran, then a small pharmaceutical company based in Cambridge. He was the director of pathology at Somerville Hospital. (Courtesy of the Bucal family.)

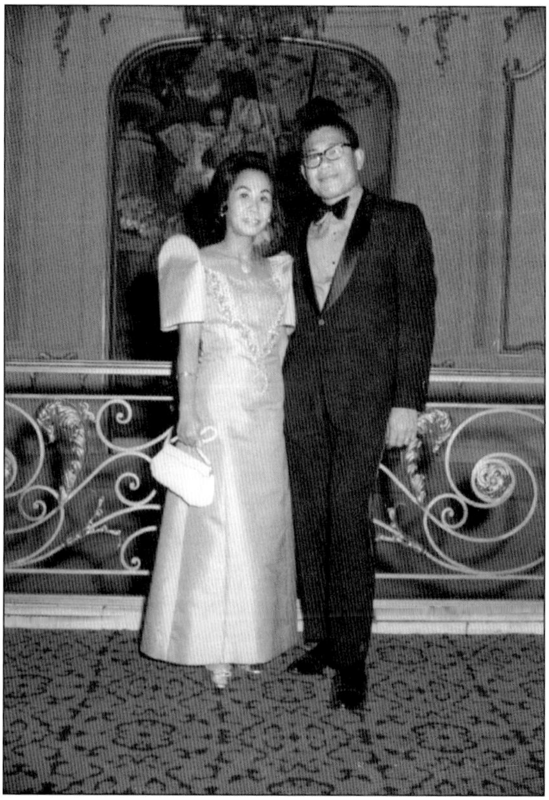

Dr. Florencio A. Hipona and his wife, Almeda, arrived in New Haven in 1960 when he was a cardiovascular radiology fellow at Yale University. In 1966, Harvard Medical School offered him a job. They lived in Wellesley for 45 years and raised five boys. Dr. Hipona was instrumental in founding the Philippine Medical Association of New England in 1966 and served as president. (Courtesy of the Hipona family.)

Dr. Frederick Friedman was the son of a Jewish American who went to the Philippines in 1917 and married a Filipina. He and his wife, Catalina Cornista Friedman, moved to Boston in 1956. Dr. Friedman became an anesthesiologist at Boston City Hospital, and Catalina became a nurse at the University Hospital. This photograph was taken in 1964 at the wedding reception of Dr. Lucy Lee. (Courtesy of Fritz Friedman.)

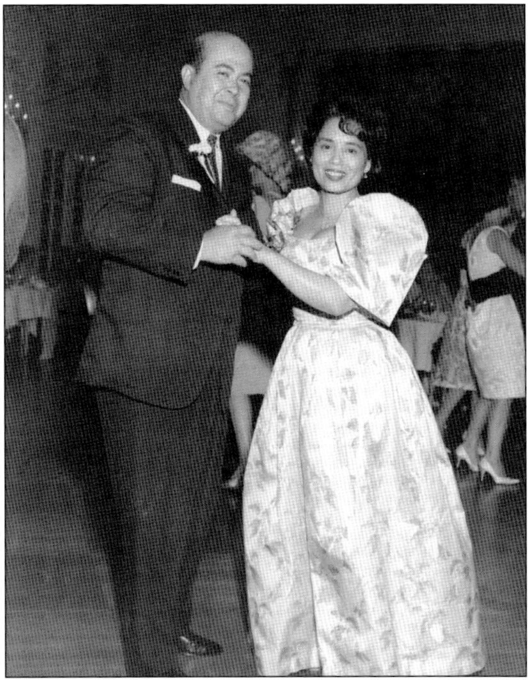

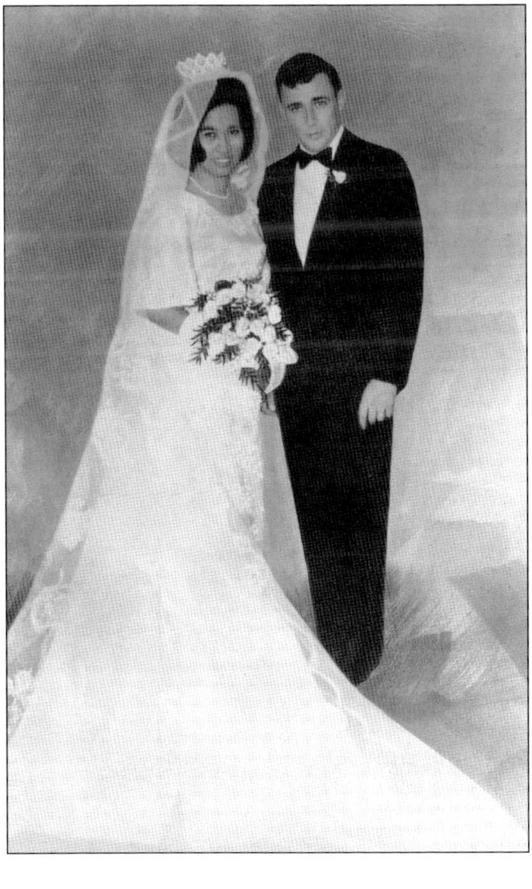

Dr. Remedios Yap moved to the United States in 1964 to work as a pathologist in Boston-area hospitals. Robert Strickland, an American marine serving in the Vietnam War, was sent to Subic Bay as a patient of Yap's brother Jesse. He introduced the couple, and they married in 1966. (Courtesy of Dr. Remedios "Mimi" Strickland.)

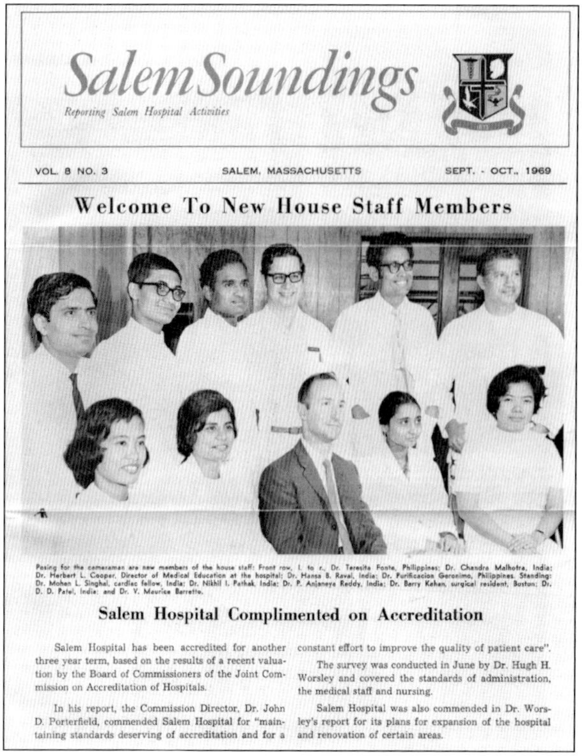

Salem Soundings

Reporting Salem Hospital Activities

VOL. 8 NO. 3 SALEM, MASSACHUSETTS SEPT. - OCT., 1969

Welcome To New House Staff Members

Posing for the cameraman are new members of the house staff: Front row, l. to r., Dr. Teresita Fonte, Philippines; Dr. Chandra Malhotra, India; Dr. Herbert L. Cooper, Director of Medical Education at the hospital; Dr. Hansa B. Raval, India; Dr. Purificacion Geronimo, Philippines. Standing: Dr. Mohen L. Singhal, cardiac fellow, India; Dr. Nikhil I. Pathak, India; Dr. P. Anjaneya Reddy, India; Dr. Barry Kehan, surgical resident, Boston; Dr. D. D. Patel, India; and Dr. V. Maurice Barrette.

Salem Hospital Complimented on Accreditation

Salem Hospital has been accredited for another three year term, based on the results of a recent valuation by the Board of Commissioners of the Joint Commission on Accreditation of Hospitals.

In his report, the Commission Director, Dr. John D. Porterfield, commended Salem Hospital for "maintaining standards deserving of accreditation and for a constant effort to improve the quality of patient care".

The survey was conducted in June by Dr. Hugh H. Worsley and covered the standards of administration, the medical staff and nursing.

Salem Hospital was also commended in Dr. Worsley's report for its plans for expansion of the hospital and renovation of certain areas.

In 1969, Salem Hospital welcomed medical professionals from India and the Philippines. Two Filipina doctors, Dr. Teresita Fonte (first row, far left) and Dr. Purificacion Geronimo (first row, far right), are featured in this newsletter welcoming the new staff. (Courtesy of Dolly Carluen Marmol.)

Ildephonso Torres Lauron came to the United States to study at the prestigious New England Conservatory of Music. This is a flyer for his artist's diploma recital in 1964. After graduating, he became a flutist for the Boston Pops Orchestra and performed as a soloist on several works from 1967 to 1979. (Courtesy of the Lauron family.)

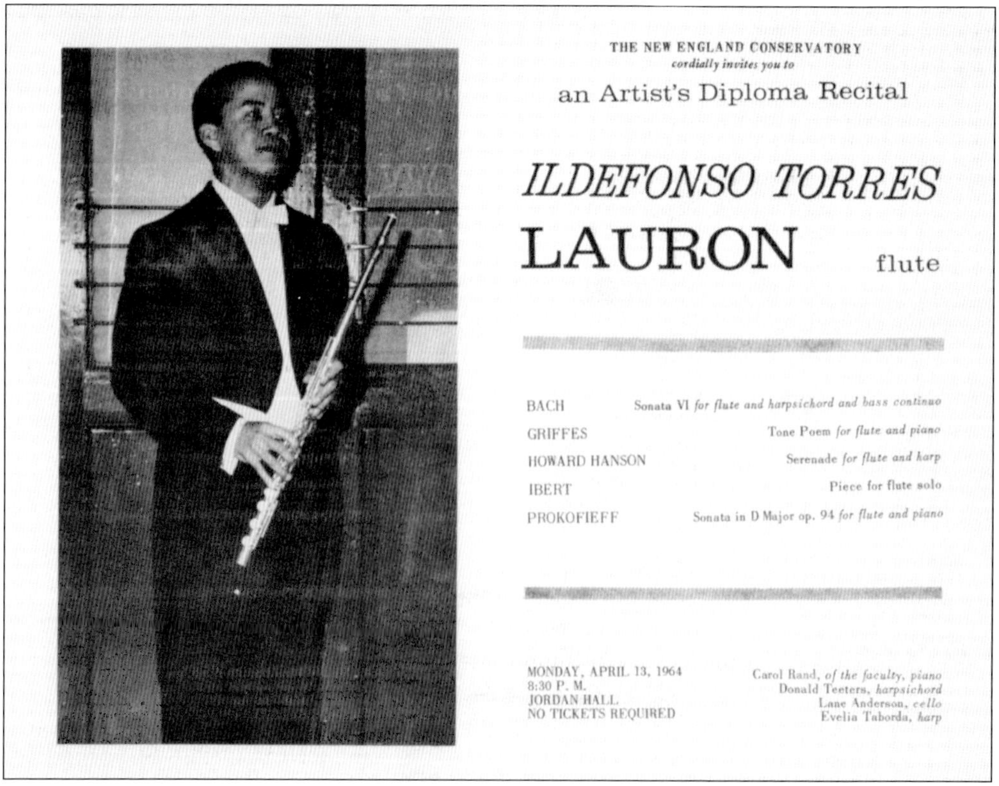

THE NEW ENGLAND CONSERVATORY
cordially invites you to

an Artist's Diploma Recital

ILDEFONSO TORRES
LAURON flute

BACH	Sonata VI *for flute and harpsichord and bass continuo*
GRIFFES	Tone Poem *for flute and piano*
HOWARD HANSON	Serenade *for flute and harp*
IBERT	Piece for flute solo
PROKOFIEFF	Sonata in D Major op. 94 *for flute and piano*

MONDAY, APRIL 13, 1964
8:30 P. M.
JORDAN HALL
NO TICKETS REQUIRED

Carol Rand, *of the faculty, piano*
Donald Teeters, *harpsichord*
Lane Anderson, *cello*
Evelia Taborda, *harp*

José "Jesse" Jacin Marmol joined the US Coast Guard in 1966 and lived in Hyde Park. Non-naturalized Filipinos were recruited to serve in domestic and food service positions until 1971, when the policy was discontinued, and all positions were opened to Filipinos who were qualified. In 1982, Marmol became the first Filipino in the Coast Guard to be chosen as a warrant officer in the medical field. (Courtesy of the Marmol family.)

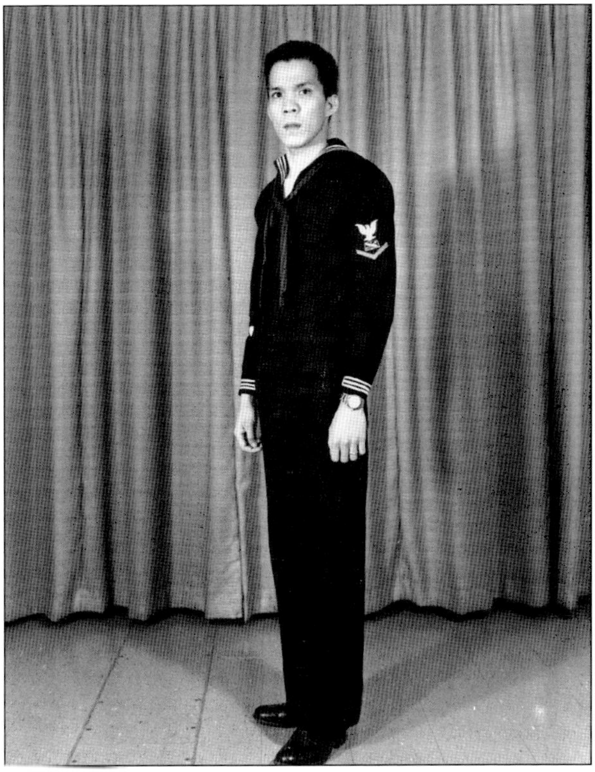

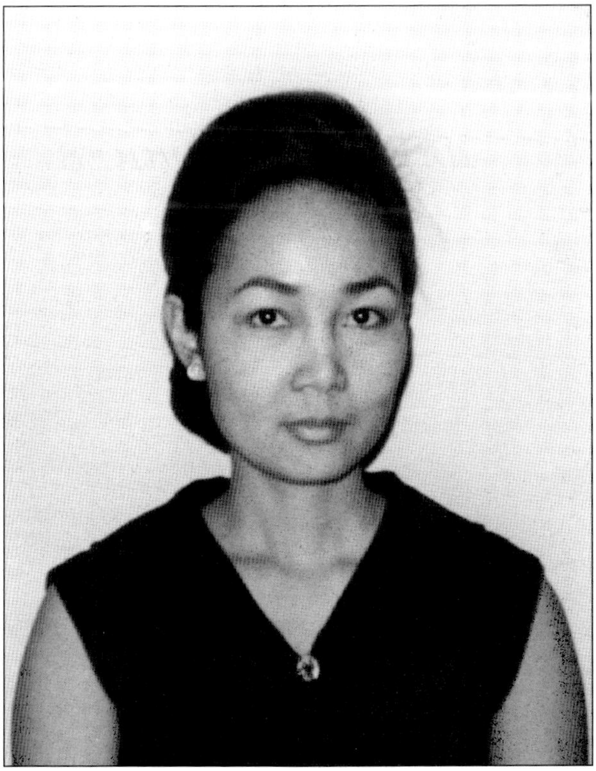

Linda Ty-Casper came to Boston in 1956 and earned a master's degree from Harvard Law. She married Leonard Casper, professor emeritus at Boston College. She authored 16 novels and received numerous awards, including Filipino-American Women Network Award for Literature, Massachusetts Artists Foundation, and UNESCO/PEN Short Story. (Courtesy of Linda Ty-Casper.)

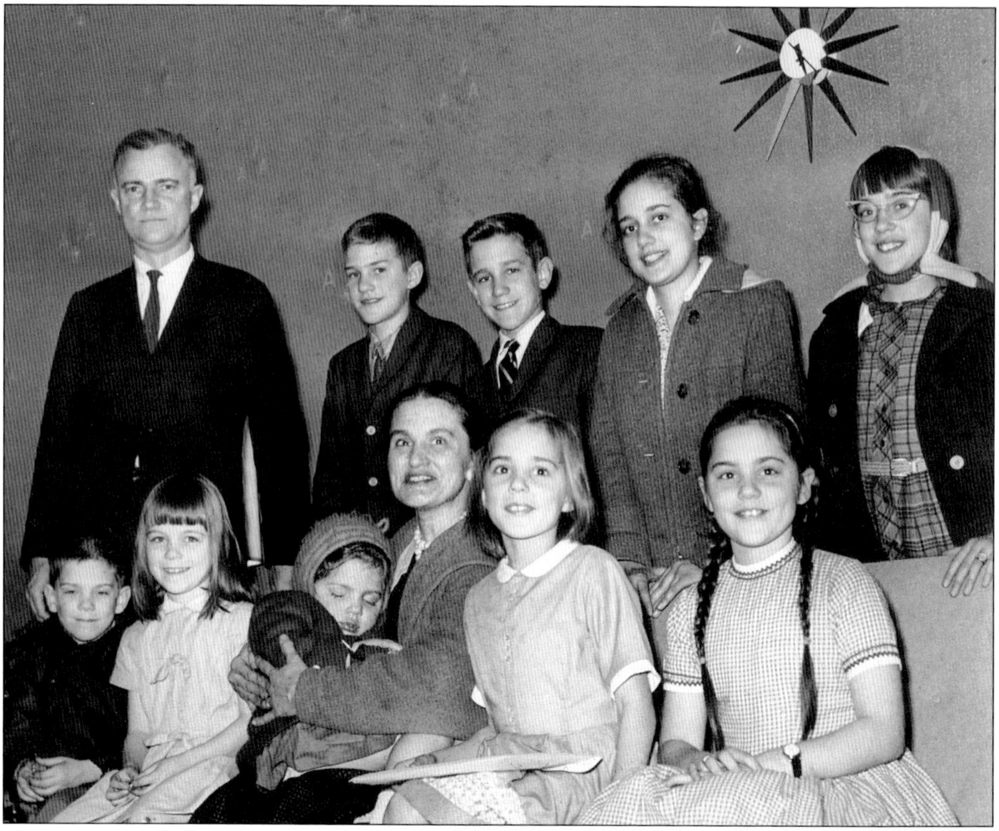

The Cort family is pictured at Logan Airport just before they departed for the Philippines in February 1962. The Philippines was one of the first 10 countries to accept Peace Corps volunteers from the new Kennedy administration in September 1961. The inaugural director, Prof. Lawrence Fuchs of Brandeis University, selected an entire staff that came from Boston. The departure of deputy director John Cort was delayed, however, while Congress debated the fiscal responsibility of sending a family with nine children. From left to right are (first row) David, Alice, Susan, Helen (wife), Mary Elizabeth, and Lydia; (second row) John, Nicholas, Paul, Barbara, and Rebecca. They lived in Cubao, Quezon City, until June 1964. Below, the Cort family waves from the plane. (Both, courtesy of the Cort family.)

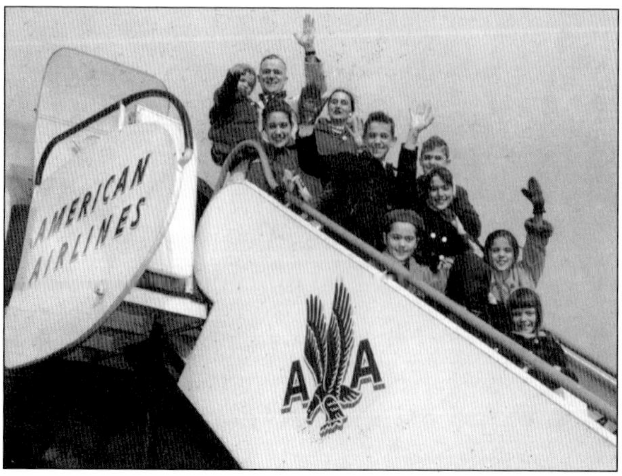

Three

Building Organizations and Raising the American-Born Generation

1970s

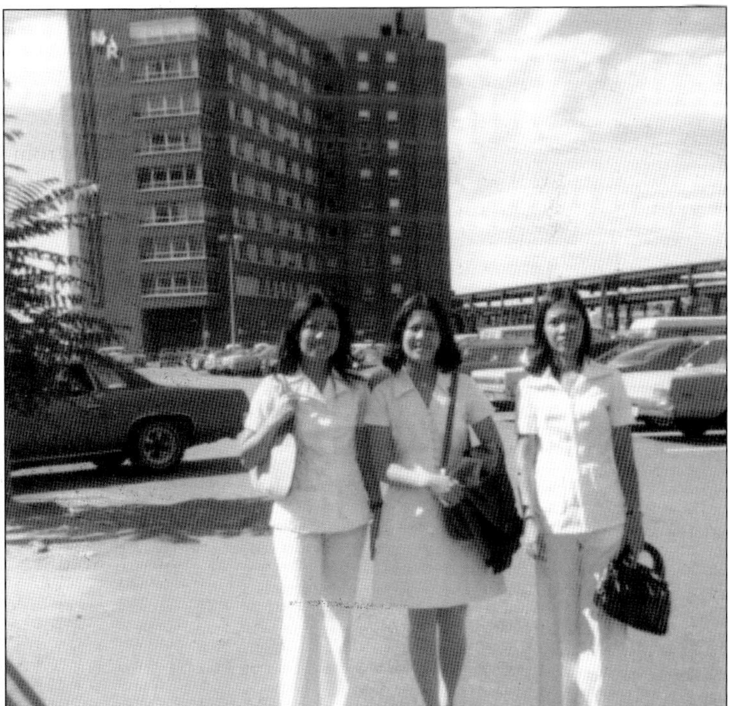

In 1970, the Filipino population of Massachusetts was 2,361, according to the US Census. These nurses were recruited from the Philippines to work at the Massachusetts Rehab Hospital (later Spalding) in 1976. When recruits came from the Philippines, the established nurses helped them to get settled. This informal network became the Philippine Nurses Association of New England, which was incorporated as a nonprofit in 1990. (Courtesy of Virginia Jacildo.)

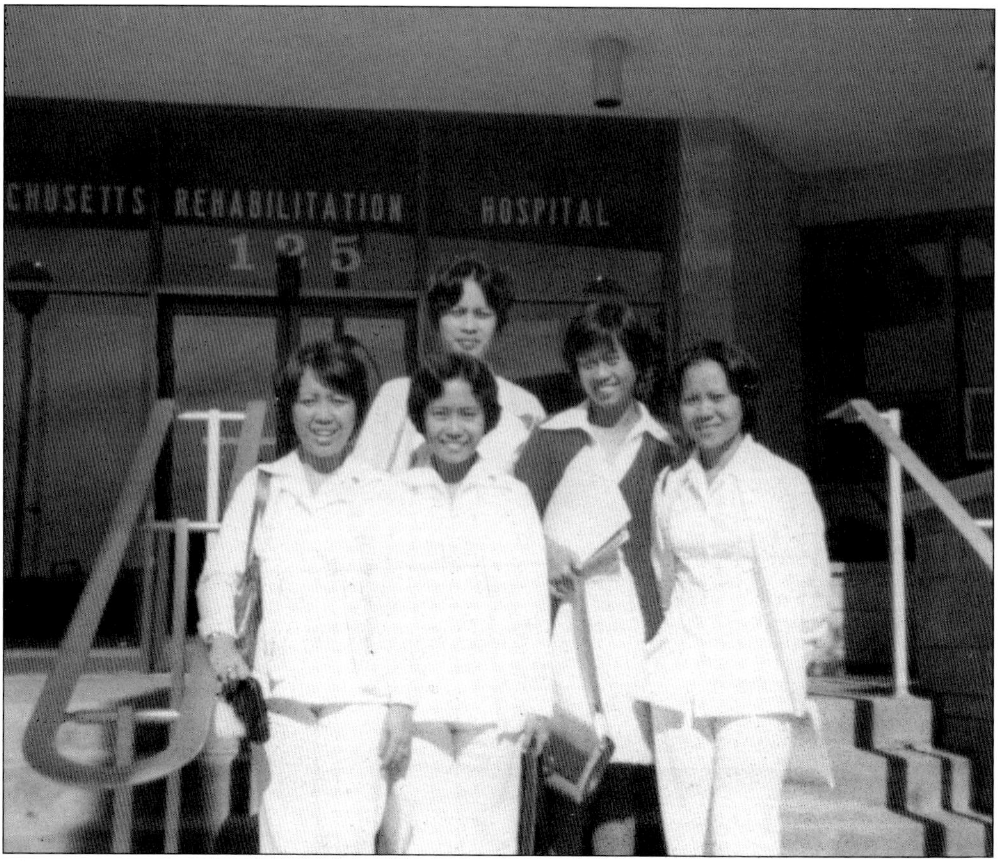

These Filipina nurses were recruited in 1977 to work at Massachusetts Rehab Hospital. In the first row, from left to right, are Verna May Catedral Gonzales, Arme dela Cruz Gallanaro, Esther Acosta Santos, and Gloria Espino Diaz. Behind them is Leila Caparanga Amarra. Due to nursing shortages in the United States, Amarra and other nurses started a recruitment agency of their own in 2002. (Courtesy of Leila C. and Gregorio A. Amarra.)

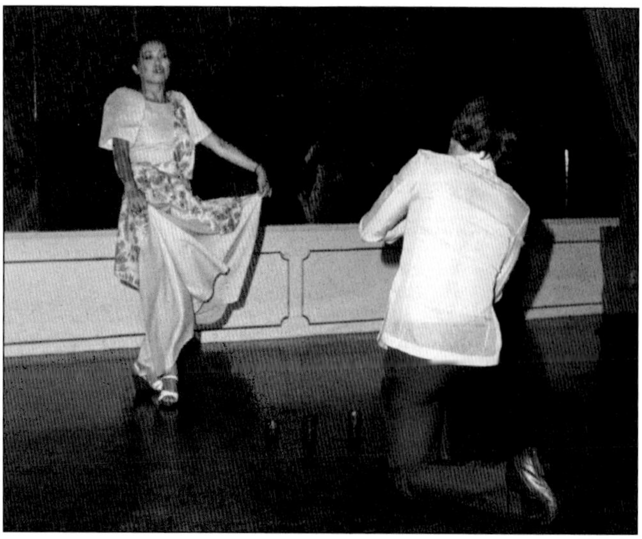

Christmas was a special time for the predominantly Catholic Filipina nurses to share their culture. Virginia Jacildo is pictured in traditional dress performing a Filipino folk dance with a male coworker at the Massachusetts Rehab Hospital in 1976. (Courtesy of Virginia Jacildo.)

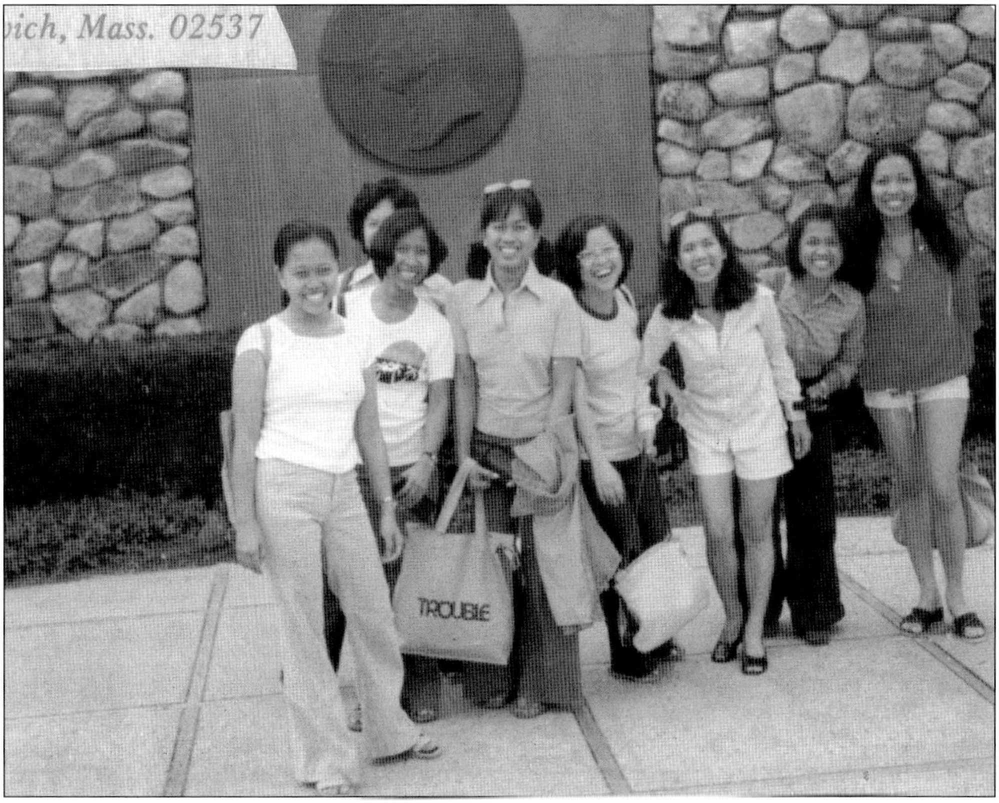

These nurses from the Philippines are on their day off visiting the John F. Kennedy Memorial in Hyannis on Cape Cod in 1979. From left to right are Suzette Oglesby, Nelda Galan, Esther Acosta Santos, unidentified, Elvie Fuertes, Aida Armas, and Virginia Jacildo. (Courtesy of Esther Acosta Santos.)

Filipina nurses who arrived a year before and recruits from the Philippines take in the fall foliage in 1978. From left to right are Rodela Parolanan Fernandez, Maria Rosario Escareal, Virginia Jacildo, Marie Sano, and Cecilia Maquiling. (Courtesy of Cecilia Maquiling.)

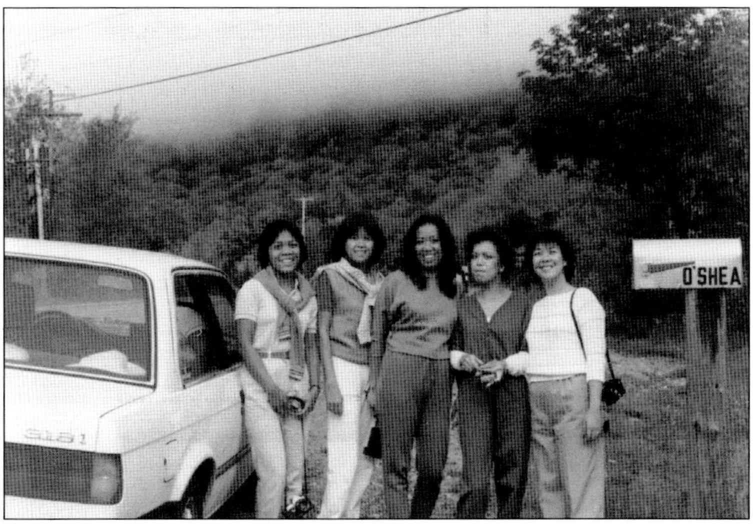

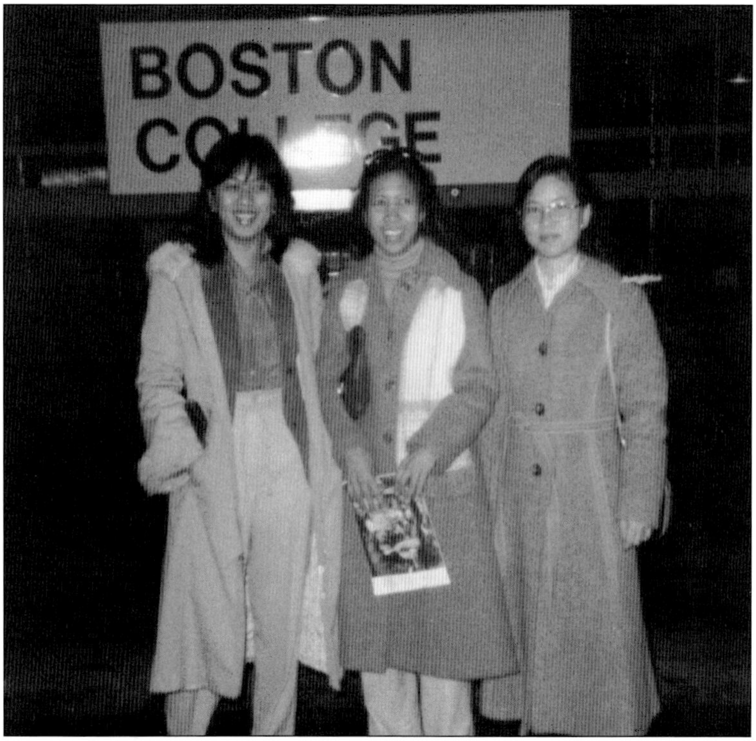

These Filipina nurses take a day off to sight-see, posing in front of Boston College in 1979. From left to right are Esther Acosta Santos, Nelda Galan, and Elvie Fuertes. (Courtesy of Esther Santos.)

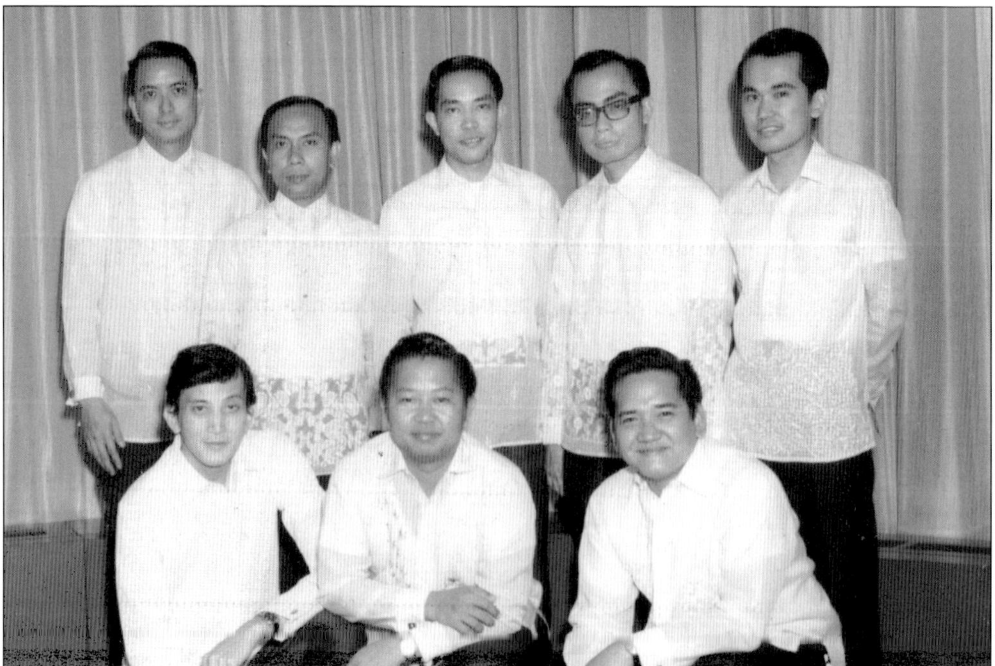

Filipino physicians pose in traditional formal wear called *barong tagalog* during an event in Brookline in 1971. From left to right are (kneeling) José "Pepito" Villanueva, Leoni Banigan, and Cerefino Bague; (standing) Sergio Garces, Marci Malapira, Vicente Banigan, Rudy Dollede, and unidentified. (Courtesy of Bernadette M. Bague.)

In 1970, Sen. Edward Kennedy visited the Salem Hospital lab where several Filipino medical technologists worked. From left to right are Rudy Castro, Leah Obligacion, Tessie Manalo, Dolly Carluen Marmol, Alicia Alpuerto Belisle, and Uraiwan Patiyuth (an exchange student from Thailand). (Courtesy of Dolly Carluen Marmol.)

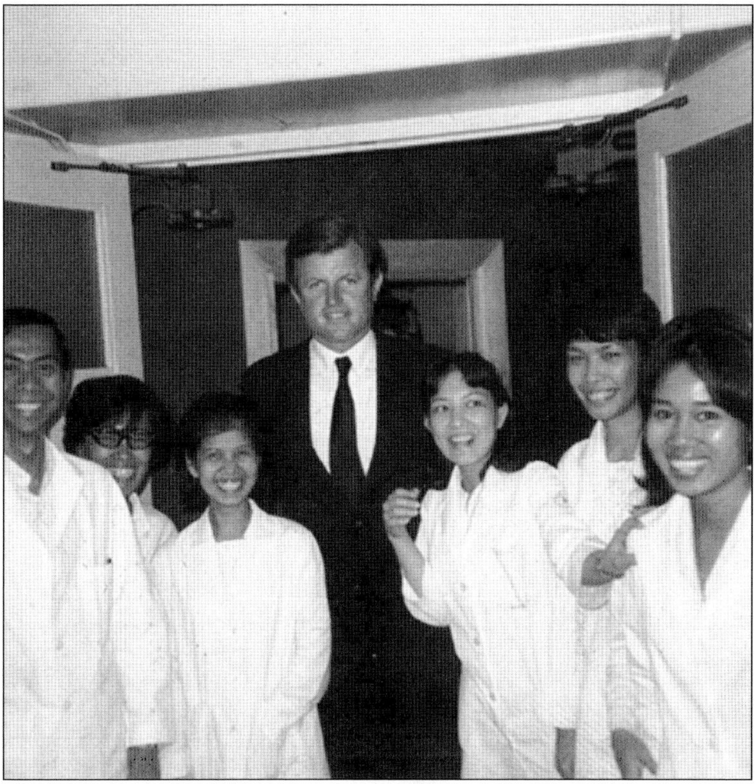

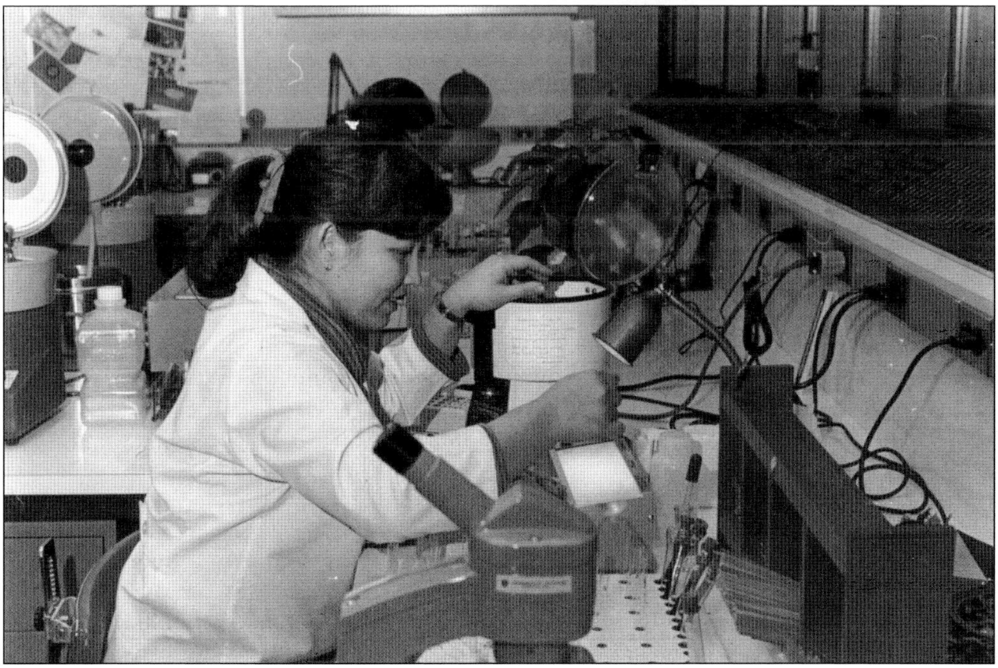

Pictured here in 1978, Dolly Marmol was the first blood bank technologist hired to work at Faulkner Hospital in 1975. Before this new requirement, the job was formerly done by registered nurses. (Courtesy of Dolly Carluen Marmol.)

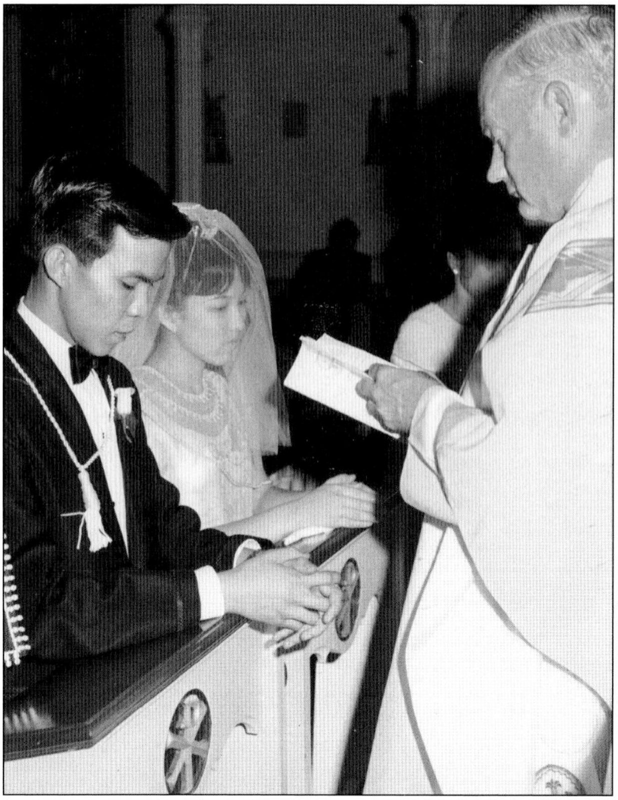

Dolly Carluen Marmol and José Jacin Saulog Marmol made the pages of the *Boston Globe* on October 4, 1970, when they had a traditional Filipino wedding in Salem. The article noted that since traditional *sampaguita*, or Philippine jasmine flowers, were not available, their gold convertible was decorated with "American popcorn." The couple had their reception at the China Sails restaurant in Salem, where they were toasted by Filipino friends with "Mabuhay!" for health and long life. (Both, courtesy of the Marmol family.)

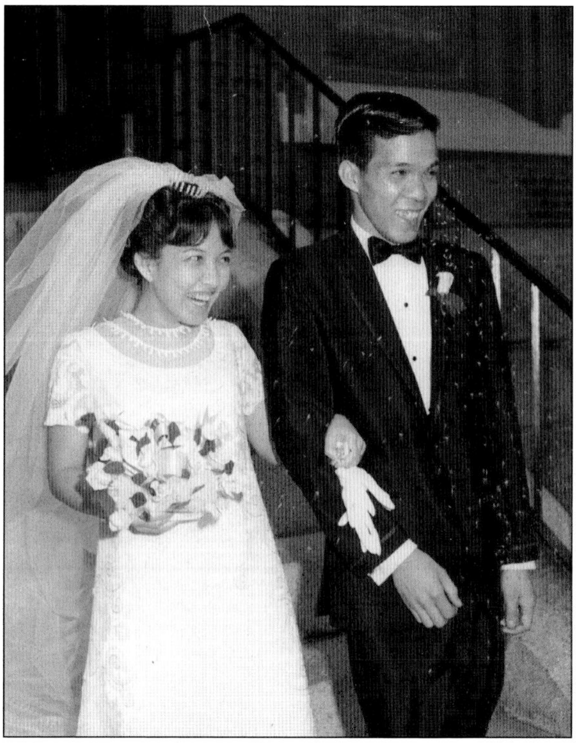

Severina "Bobin" Felina immigrated to Boston in 1971. The photograph to the right was taken in 1973 outside of the University Hospital, where she worked. There, she met Catalina "Nena" Cornista Friedman, a nurse, who connected her with others in the Filipino community. Below, friends within the Filipino community gathered at the house of Ponce de la Cruz in 1975. From left to right are Manuel and Severina Felina with baby Emmanuel, Nena Friedman, and Fely Villarino. (Both, courtesy of Manuel and Severina Felina.)

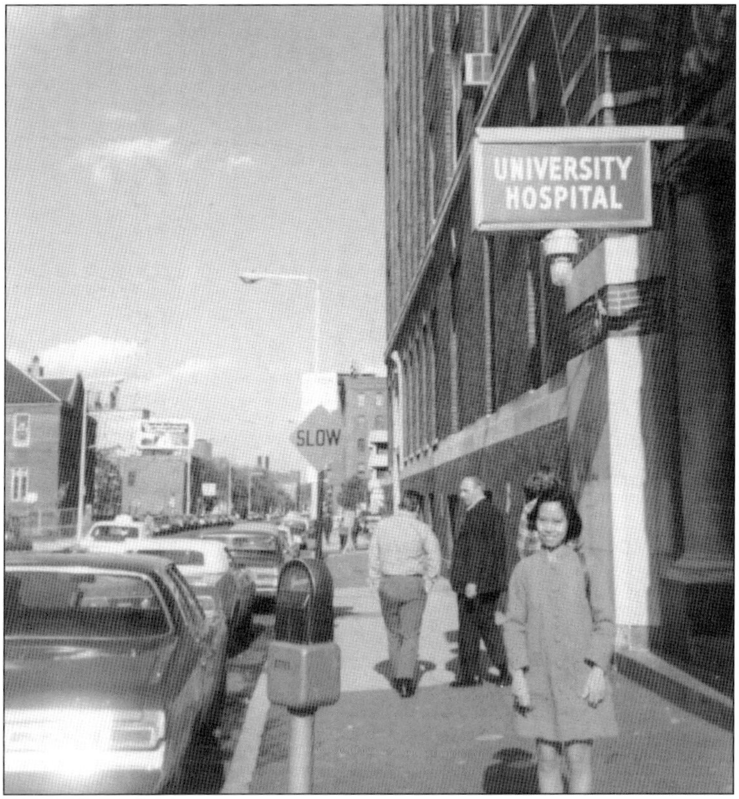

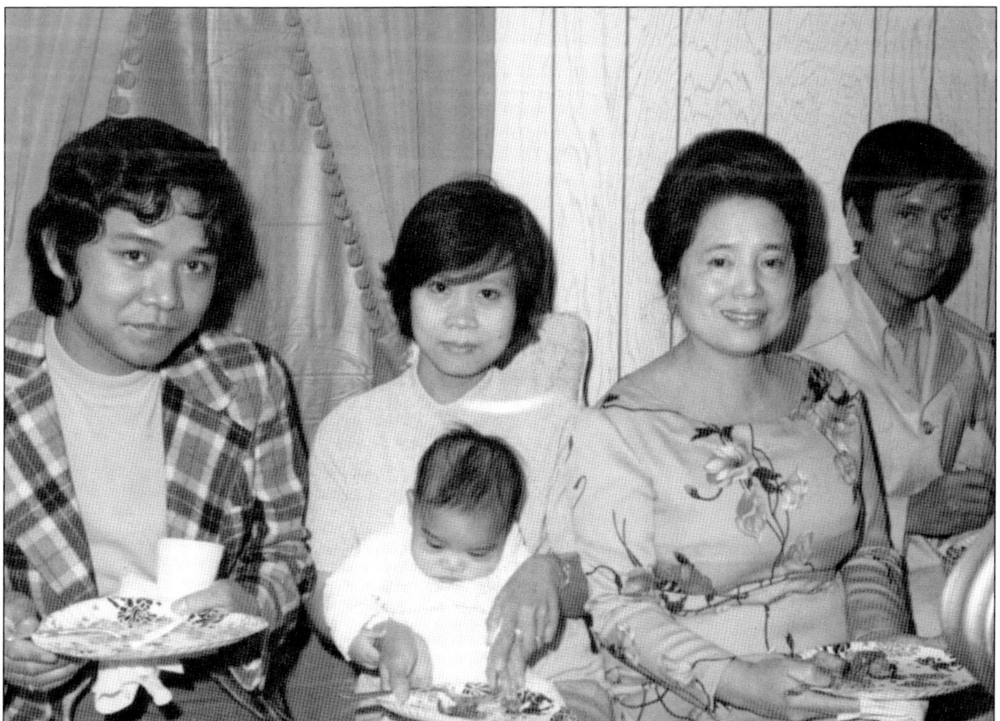

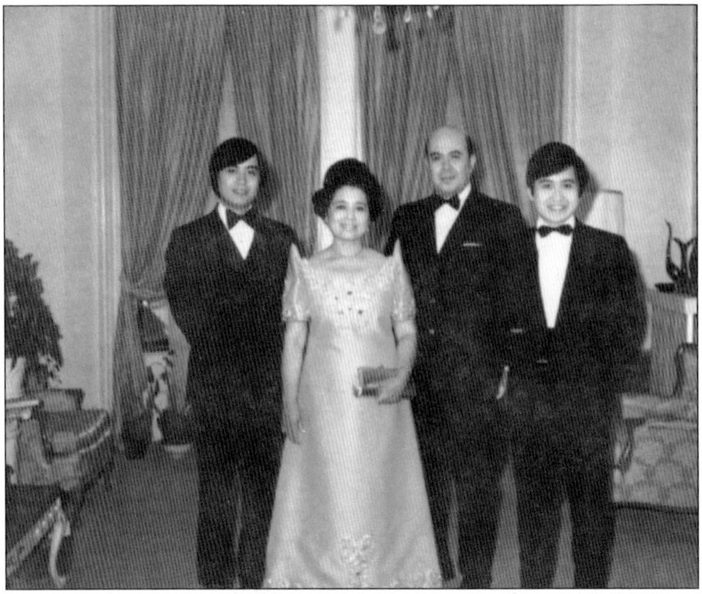

Nena Friedman and her husband, Dr. Frederick Friedman, pose with their two sons, Aaron (far left) and Fritz (far right), at their home in the South End neighborhood of Boston. Fritz graduated from Boston College High School in 1968 and serves on the board of trustees. The Friedmans hosted exchange students from the Philippines who found a home away from home and a tight-knit community. (Courtesy of Manuel and Severina Felina.)

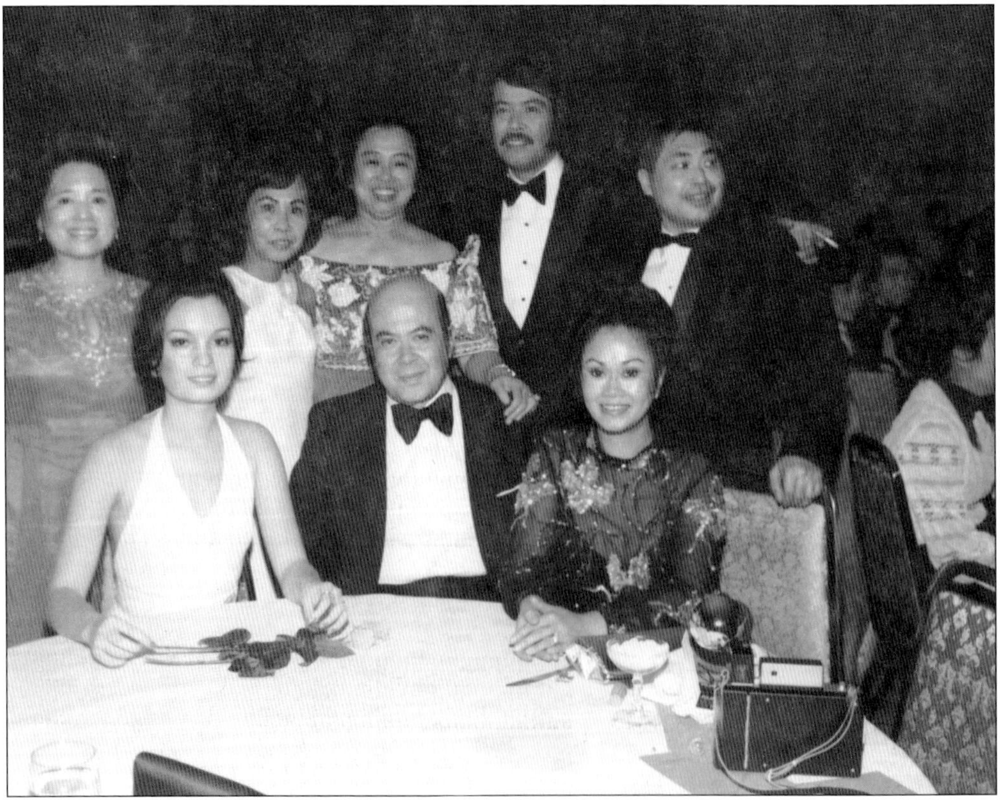

This photograph was taken at the Philippine Medical Association of New England ball in the mid-1970s. From left to right are (seated) Boston University student Margarita "Margie" Moran (who won the second Miss Universe crown for the Philippines in 1973), Dr. Fred Friedman, and Linda Wixon; (standing) Nena Friedman, Medy Hipona, Dr. Lucy Lee, Fred Friedman Jr., and Albert Y. Chin. (Courtesy of Fritz Friedman.)

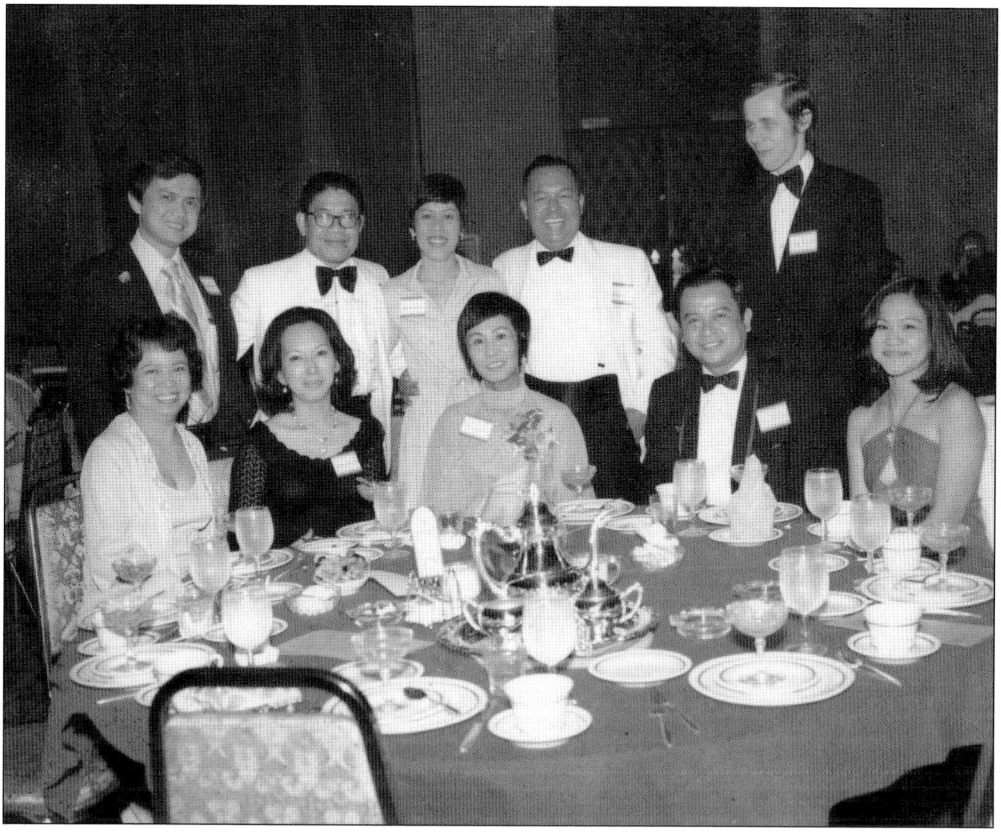

This photograph was taken at the Philippine Medical Association of New England ball in 1975. From left to right are (first row, seated) Louise Larraga, unidentified, Medy Hipona, unidentified, and Gerrie Korten; (second row, standing) unidentified, Dr. Flor Hipona, unidentified, Liloy Larraga, and Dr. Klaus Korten. (Courtesy of Geraldine B. Korten.)

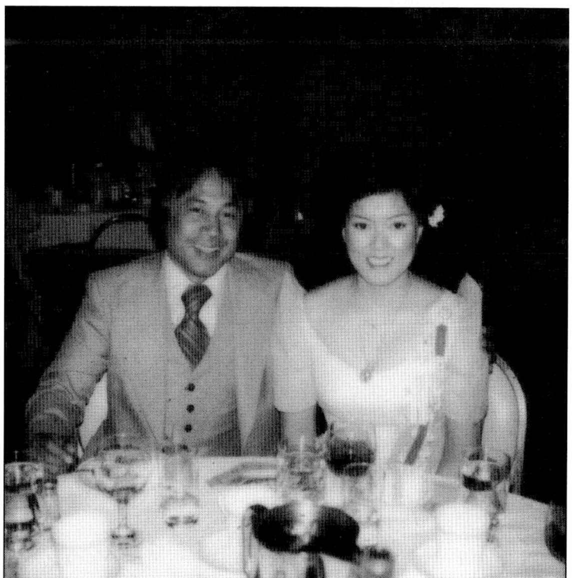

Patricia Aldaba Lim and Dr. Darwish Rasul "Winnie" Yusah attended the Philippine Medical Association of New England ball in 1977. Yusah is originally from Jolo, Sulu, and arrived in Boston in 1962. He had a private practice in obstetrics and gynecology. Lim graduated with a master's in communication for TV broadcasting from Boston University in 1976. They are married and have three sons. (Courtesy of Patricia Lim Yusah.)

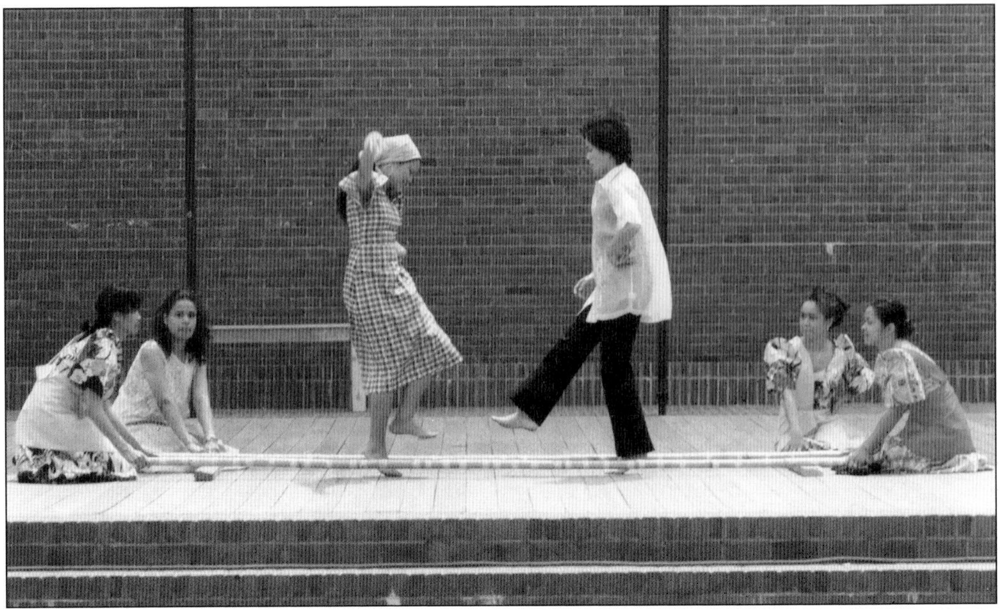

The Philippine Dance Company of Boston was formed in 1976. The group participated in the New England Folk Festival in Natick every spring. Gerri Korten (left) and Patricia Yusah (right) choreographed and taught folk dances. Here, they perform at the Boston City Hall Stage with students of the company. (Courtesy of Geraldine B. Korten.)

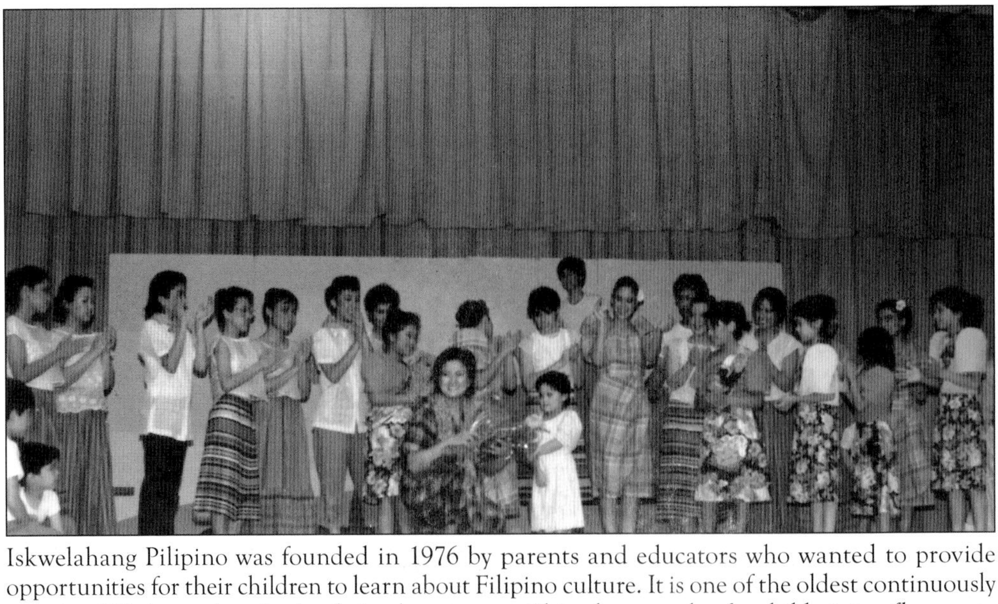

Iskwelahang Pilipino was founded in 1976 by parents and educators who wanted to provide opportunities for their children to learn about Filipino culture. It is one of the oldest continuously running Filipino cultural schools in the country. This photograph of a child giving flowers to Patricia Yusah was taken at the 1980 commencement. (Courtesy of Linda J. Ott.)

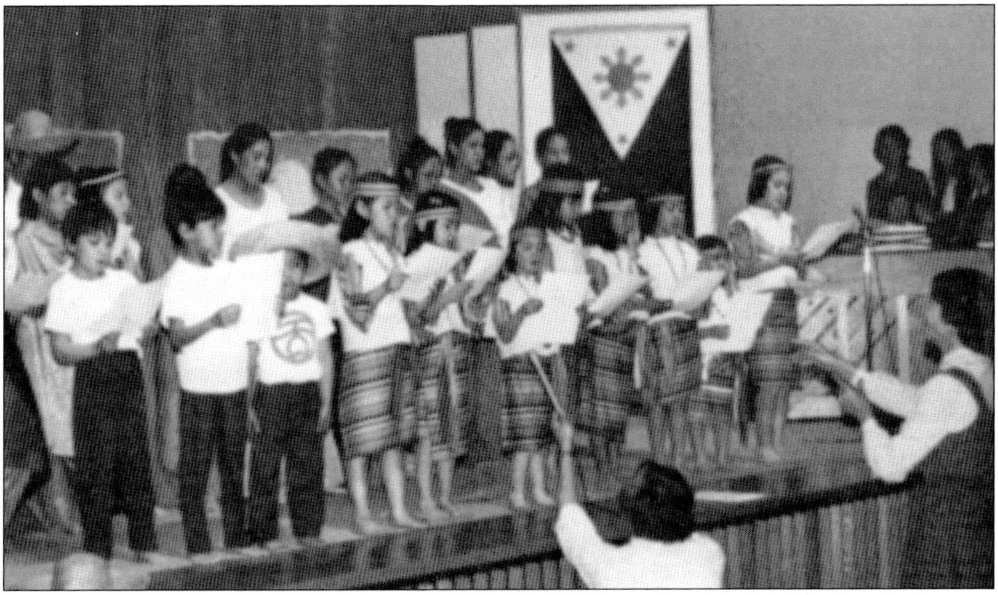

These are photographs of the Iskwelahang Pilipino commencement in 1978. Above, a group of active parents sings with their children. Below, students sang "I Love the Philippines" and "America, the Beautiful." Still active today, the organization's mission is to "strengthen Filipino American children, families and community by celebrating the rich Philippine cultural heritage in a structured and nurturing environment." (Both, courtesy of Filipino Association of Greater Boston.)

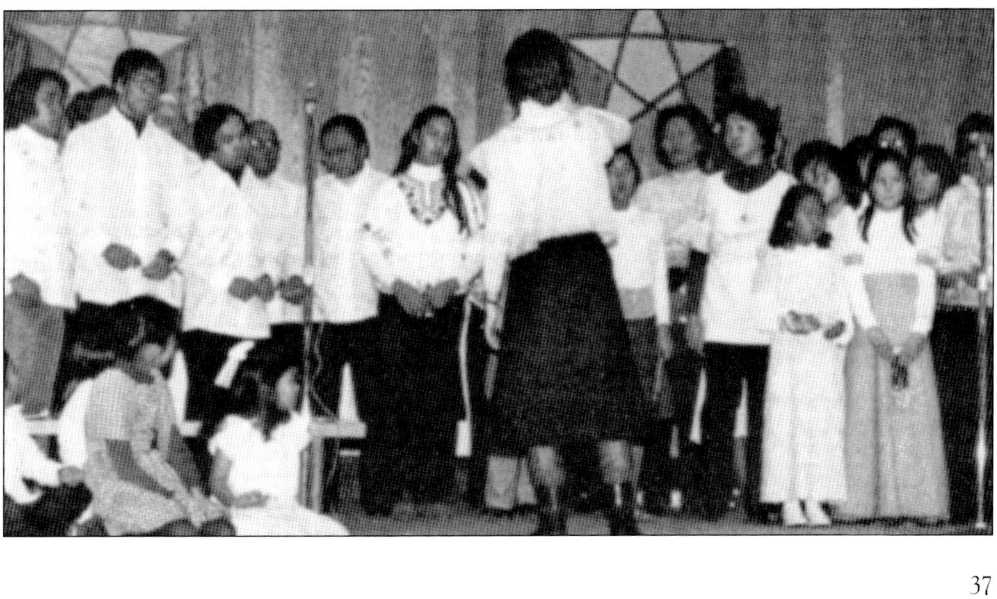

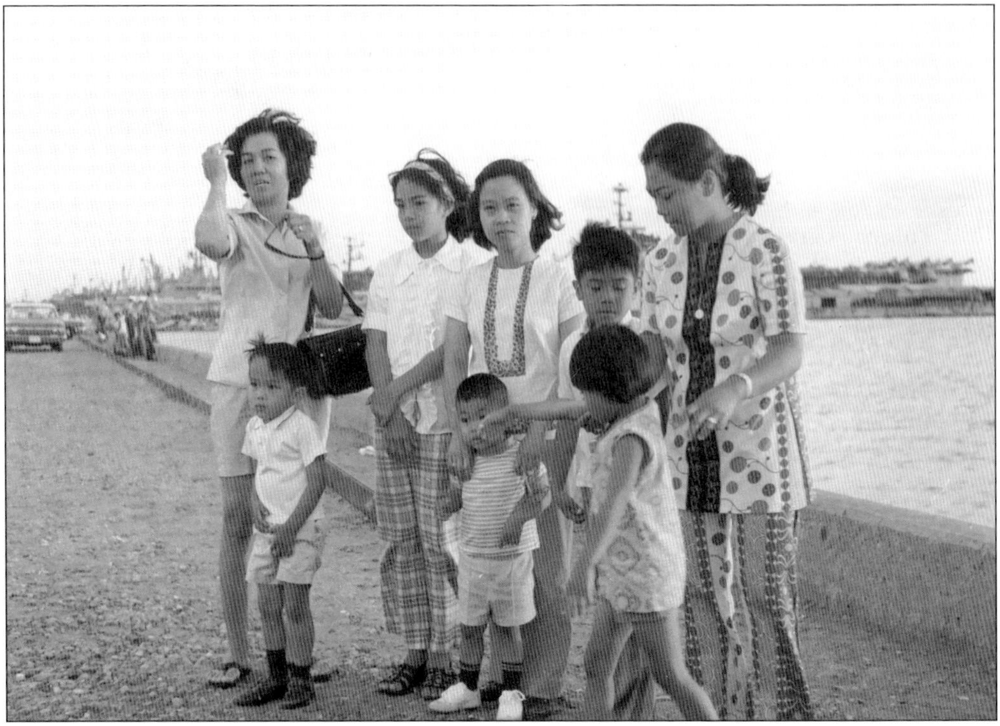

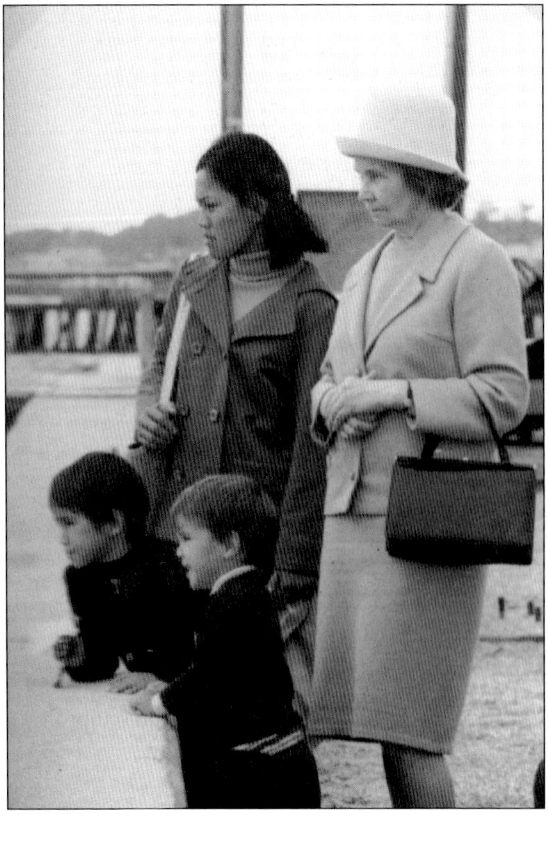

In addition to teaching their American-born children about Filipino heritage, immigrant parents provided opportunities for their kids to make connections to their Bostonian identity by visiting historically significant destinations. Members of the Felina family are pictured here touring Plymouth in 1978. (Courtesy of Manuel and Severina Felina.)

Gerrie Korten (left) is pictured with her mother-in-law (right), who was visiting from Europe, and her sons Carlos (left) and Dino on a trip to Provincetown. Gerrie and her husband, Dr. Klaus Korten, an anesthesiologist at the Peter Bent Brigham Hospital, arrived in Boston from Germany in 1974. (Courtesy of Geraldine B. Korten.)

Behind members of the Felina family is the *Mayflower II*, a reproduction of the original *Mayflower* ship that brought the pilgrims to the New World in 1620. This photograph was taken in 1978 during a visit to the historic sights of Plymouth. (Courtesy of Manuel and Severina Felina.)

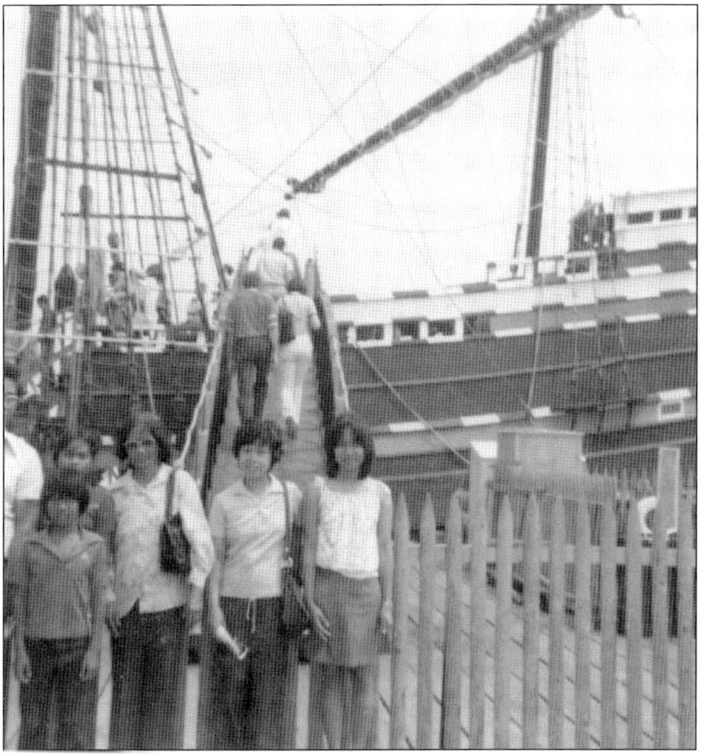

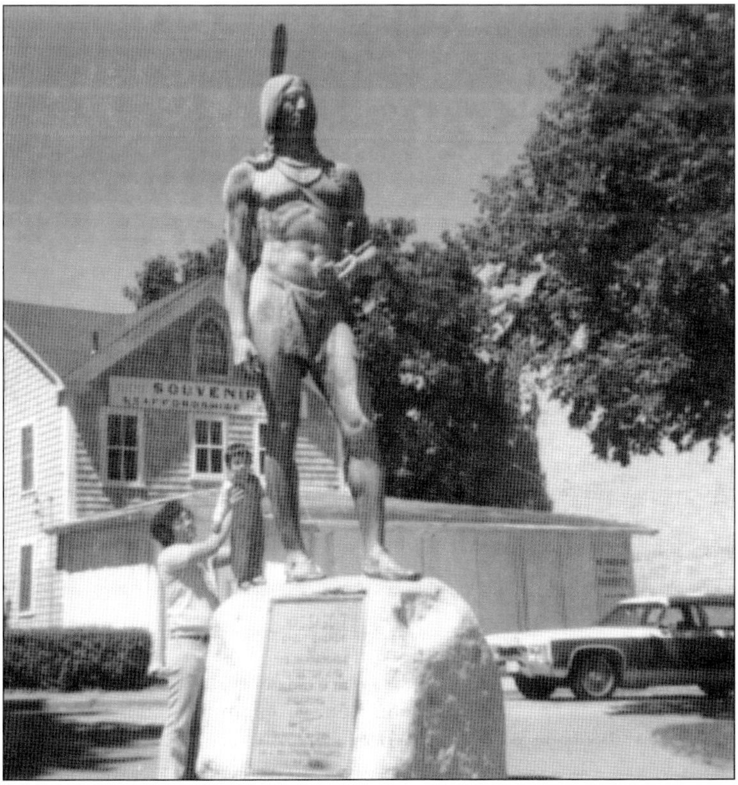

The Felina family poses with the grand statue of Massasoit (c. 1581–1661), leader of the Wampanoags, in Plymouth. The statue was created by American sculptor Cyrus Edwin Dallin. (Courtesy of Manuel and Severina Felina.)

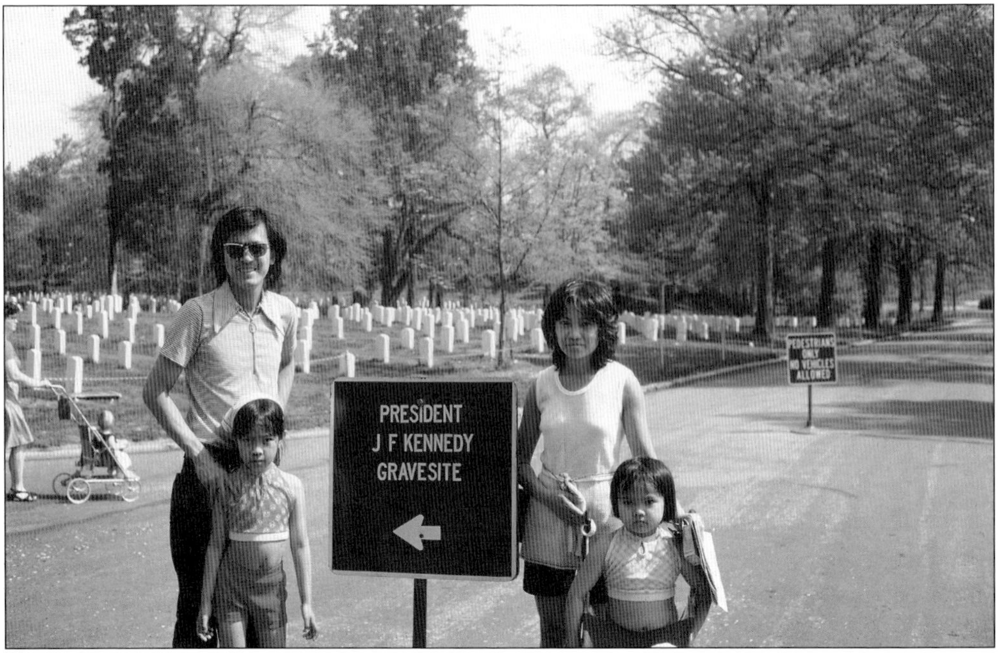

Pictured here at the gravesite of John F. Kennedy in the mid-1970s are Drs. Eduardo and Arcel G. Talusan with their two children, authors Mary and Grace. At the time, they were medical fellows at the Tufts Medical Center. The family eventually settled in Easton, where three more children—Liza, Paul, and Jonathan—were born.

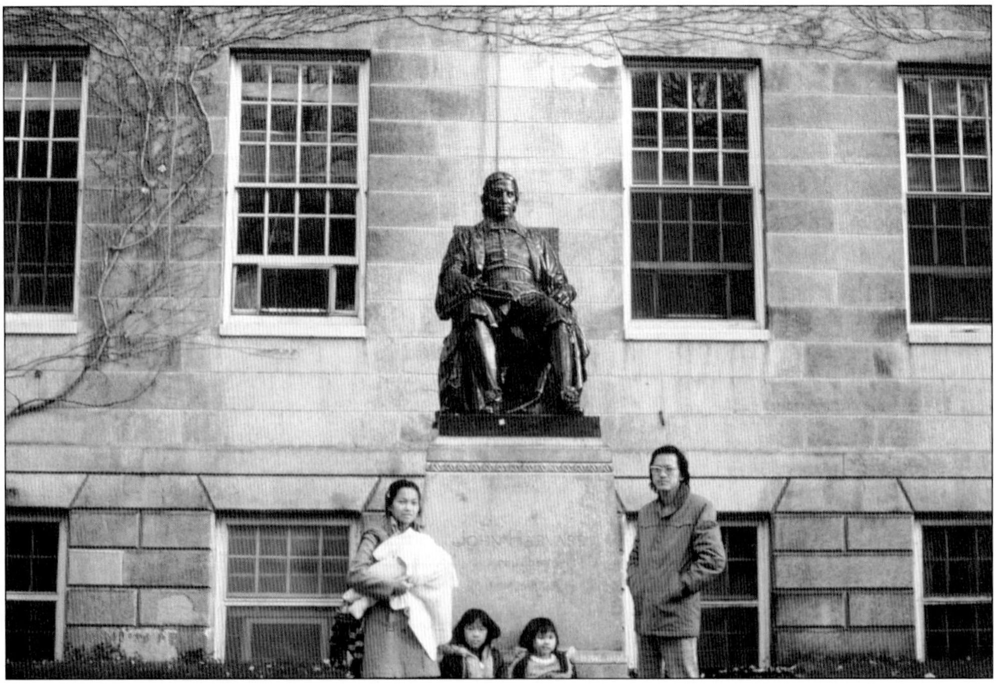

This photograph of the Talusan family was taken in 1976 at the John Harvard statue in Harvard Yard. Because of Harvard's prestige in the Philippines, Filipinos still visit this historic statue. The family poses with their first American-born child, baby Liza.

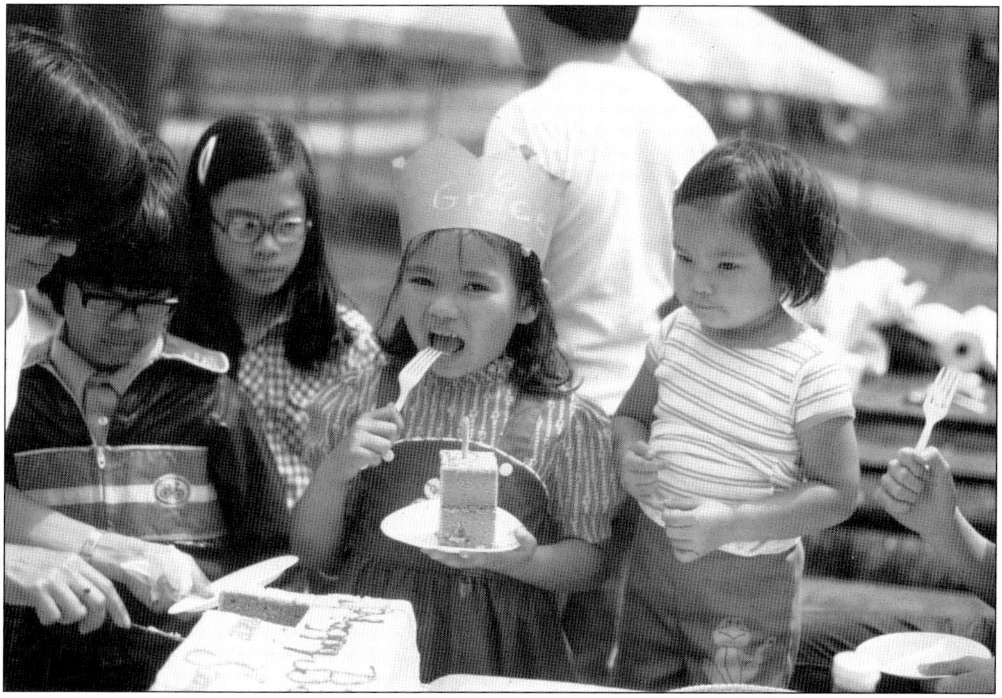

Both photographs were taken at Grace Talusan's birthday party in 1977 at Lars Andersen Park in Brookline. Since most Filipino immigrants left behind their relatives in the Philippines, their children referred to each other as "cousins" even though they were not blood-related. Below is Edgardo "Sonny" Gamalinda (standing), who migrated to Boston to live with his sister Arcel (center) and nieces for several years before rejoining his own family in California. One day, he recalled seeing another Filipino, a rare sight during the early 1980s, inside a bank in Boston. Suddenly he realized that he recognized him. Not believing his eyes, he asked the man, "Excuse me, sir, are you Ninoy Aquino?!"

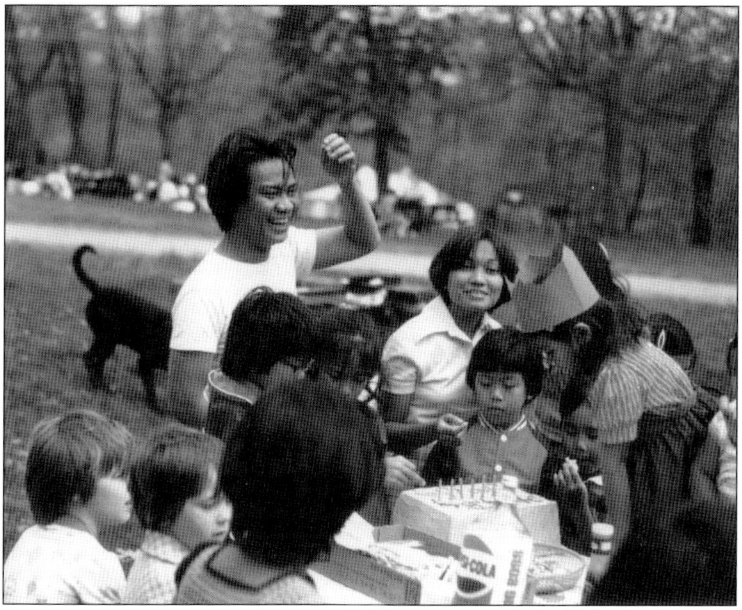

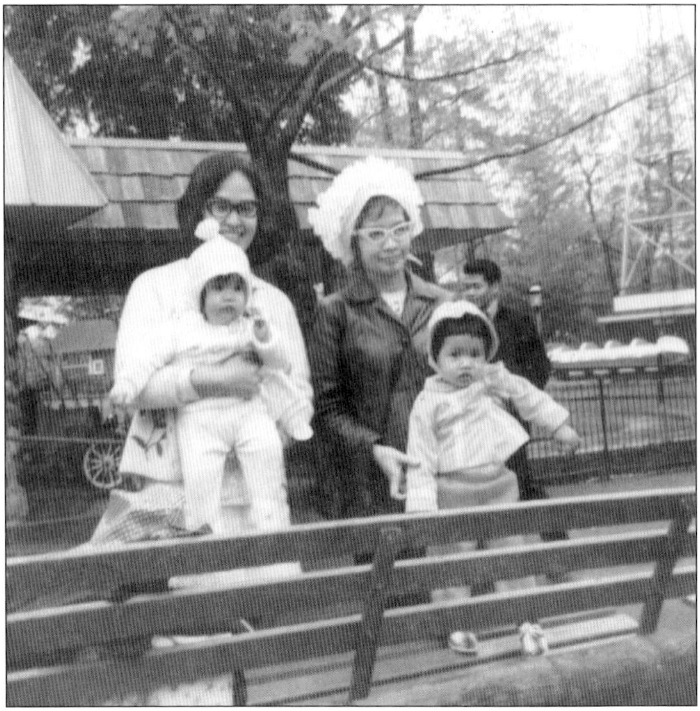

Filipino immigrants enjoyed taking their American-born children to New England amusement parks. This photograph of Myrna Liwanag with her daughter Myra (left) and Dr. Marietta Bague with her daughter Bernadette (right) was taken at Canobie Lake Park in Salem, New Hampshire, in 1970. (Courtesy of Myra O. Liwanag and family.)

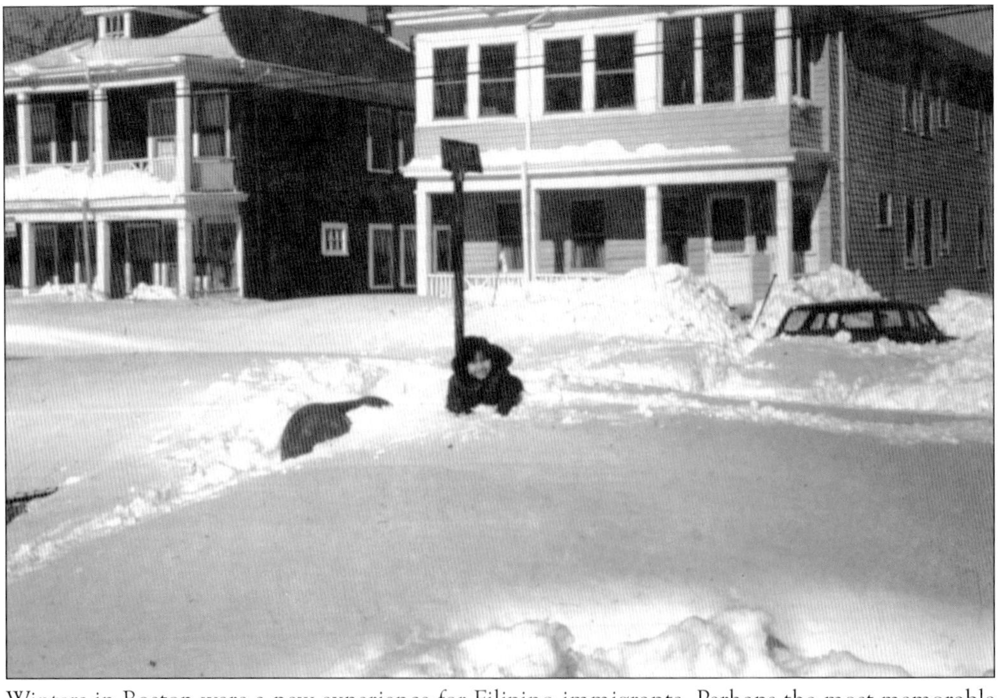

Winters in Boston were a new experience for Filipino immigrants. Perhaps the most memorable winter was the Blizzard of 1978, in which a record-breaking 27 inches of snow shut down the Boston area. The National Guard was called in to help people stranded during a power outage. In this photograph taken in Mattapan, Grace Talusan shows the height of the snow that reaches past the mailbox.

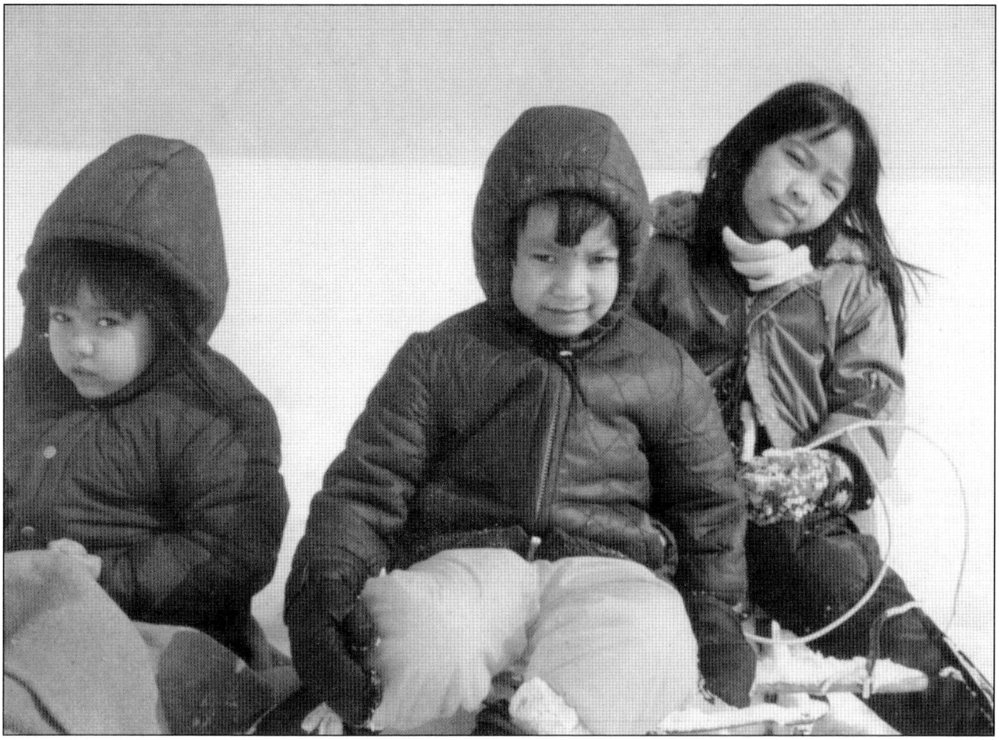

Children acclimated well to Boston winters. In this photograph, Mary (right) and Grace (left) enjoy a day of sledding with neighbor Emix Dial (center) in 1979. The Talusans, along with the Dial, Alday, Raagas, Francisco, and de la Paz families, lived in the same apartment building in Mattapan when they first immigrated to Boston to work as physicians in area hospitals.

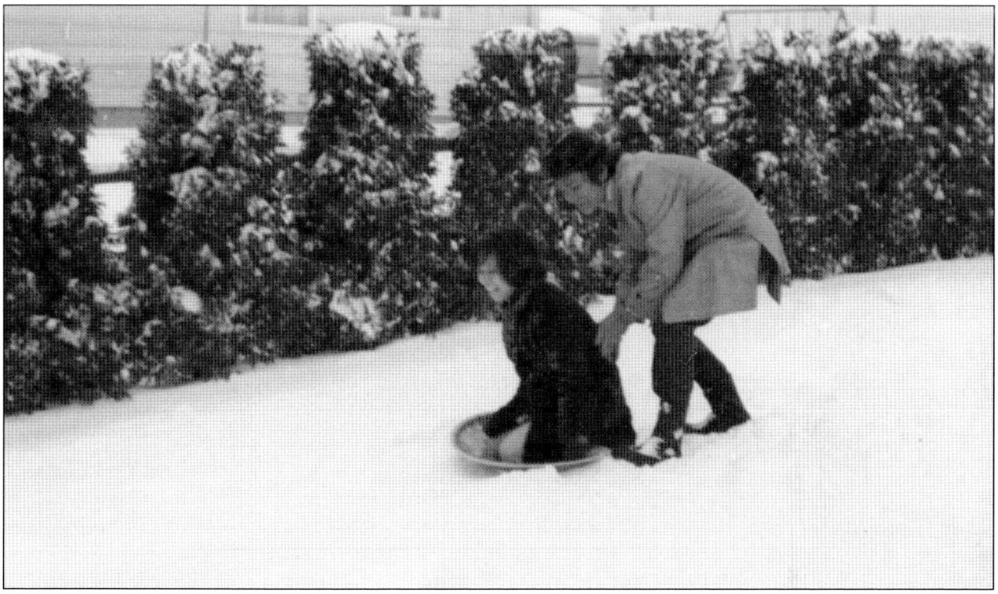

Filipino immigrants also delighted in taking part in winter activities. This photograph, taken around 1974, shows Bobin and Manny Felina enjoying the winter pastime of sledding. (Courtesy of Manuel and Severina Felina.)

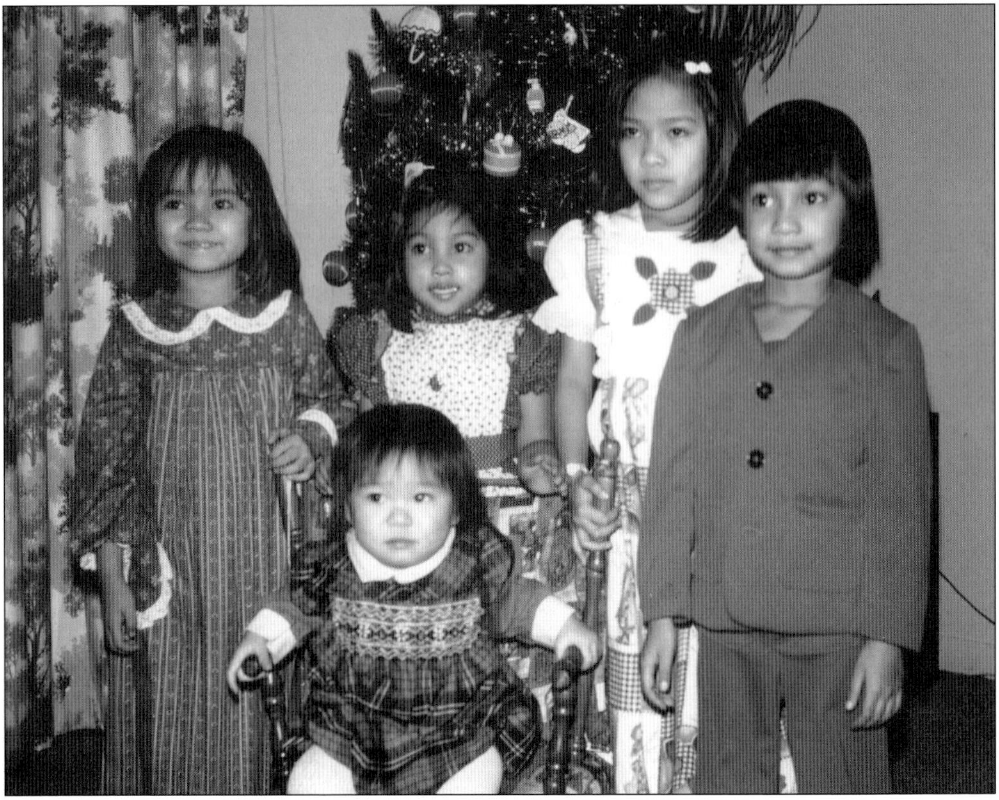

Pictured in 1976, the Talusan family celebrated Christmas with their neighbors Emix (right) and Ruth Dial (standing second from left), who lived in the same apartment building in Mattapan. They referred to each other's parents as "auntie" and "uncle" and to each other as "cousins," even though they were not blood-related.

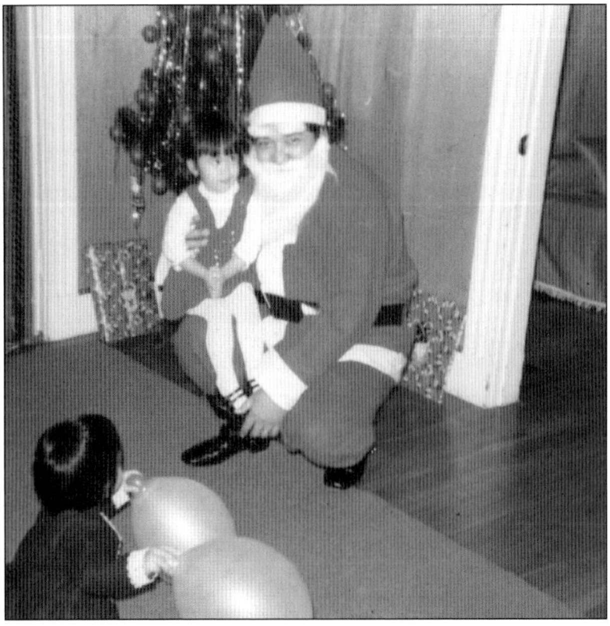

Christmas was an important holiday for Filipino immigrants, who were mostly Catholic. They celebrated Filipino Christmas traditions along with newly adopted American traditions such as believing in Santa Claus. Dr. Fer Bague poses as Santa in 1972 for the Bague and Liwanag children. (Courtesy of Myra O. Liwanag.)

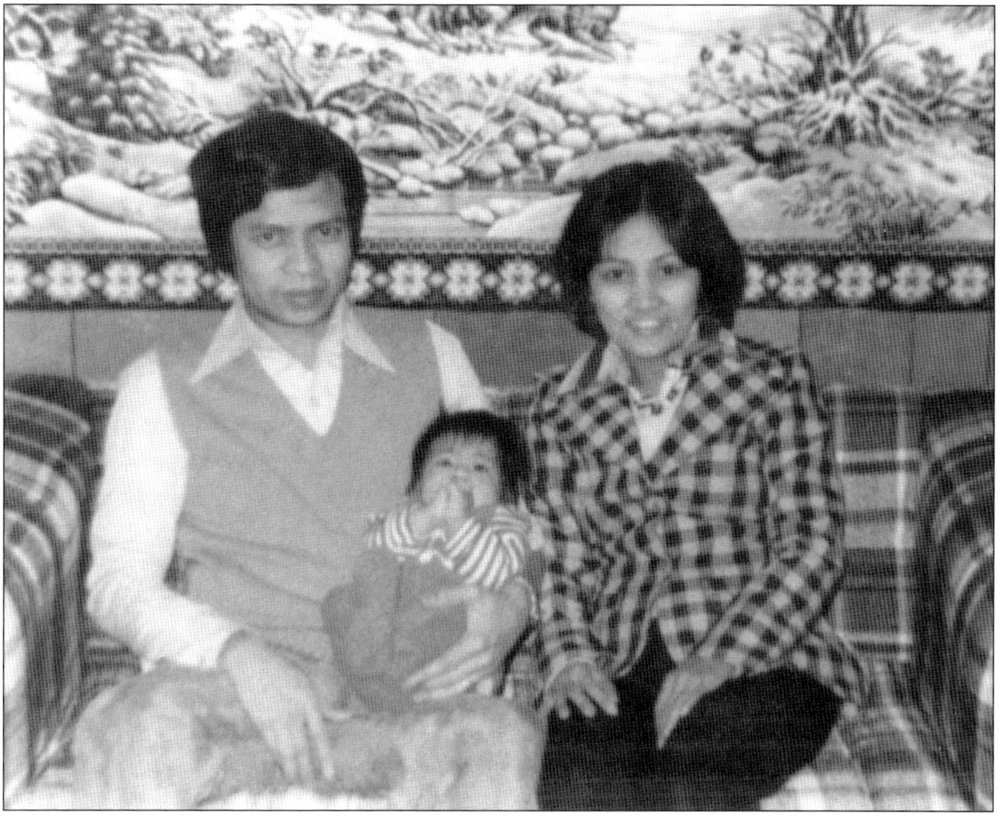

José "Peping" and Fanny Valencia pose with their firstborn child, Christine, in Charlestown in 1978. Peping worked at the Cole Hersee Company in South Boston before transferring in 1980 to Tufts Medical Center, where he worked until his retirement in 2015. They are active in the Filipino Apostolate of Boston and live in Medford. (Courtesy of the Valencia family.)

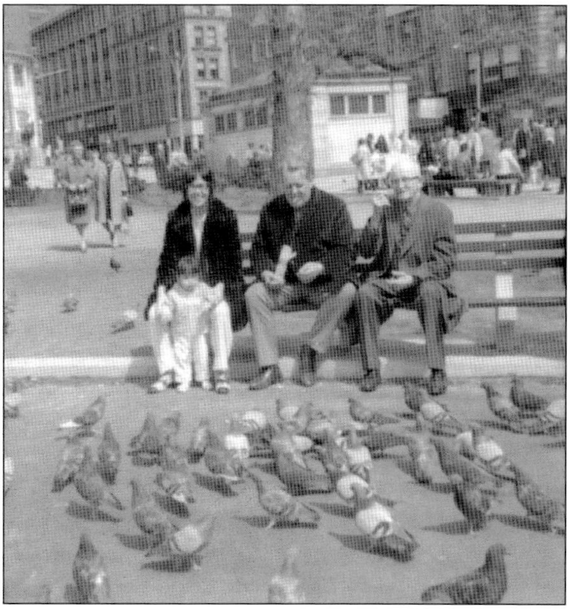

Baby Myra and her mother, Myrna Liwanag, sit on a park bench to feed the pigeons at the Boston Commons in 1971. Behind them is an entrance to the MBTA (Massachusetts Bay Transportation Authority) train station, commonly known as the "T." (Courtesy of Myra O. Liwanag.)

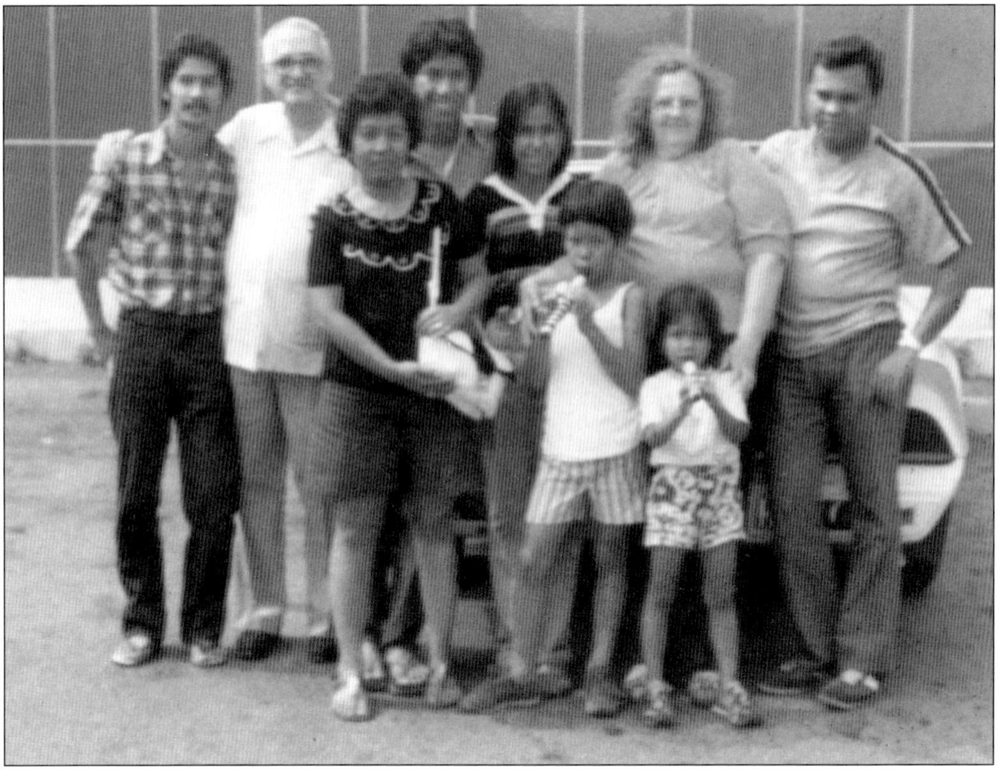

Many Filipino military families lived in Charlestown. In the photograph above, taken in the 1970s, Ronnie Puzon (boy in the center), his younger sister, Melinda (right of Ronnie), and his mother, Esther (left of Ronnie, holding her purse), pose with friends. Ronnie's father, Ricardo Puzon (not pictured), came to Boston in 1969 to serve in the US Navy. Esther taught in Boston public schools for 35 years. Below, the Puzon family poses with friends in Charlestown. According to the National Park Service, the Charlestown Navy Yard serviced ships from 1800 until it closed 174 years later in 1974. Today, there is a visitor's center at the Boston National Historical Park. (Both, courtesy of Ronnie Puzon.)

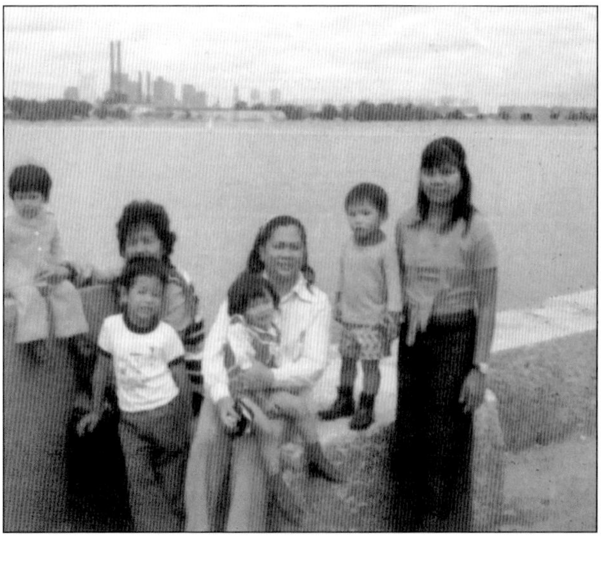

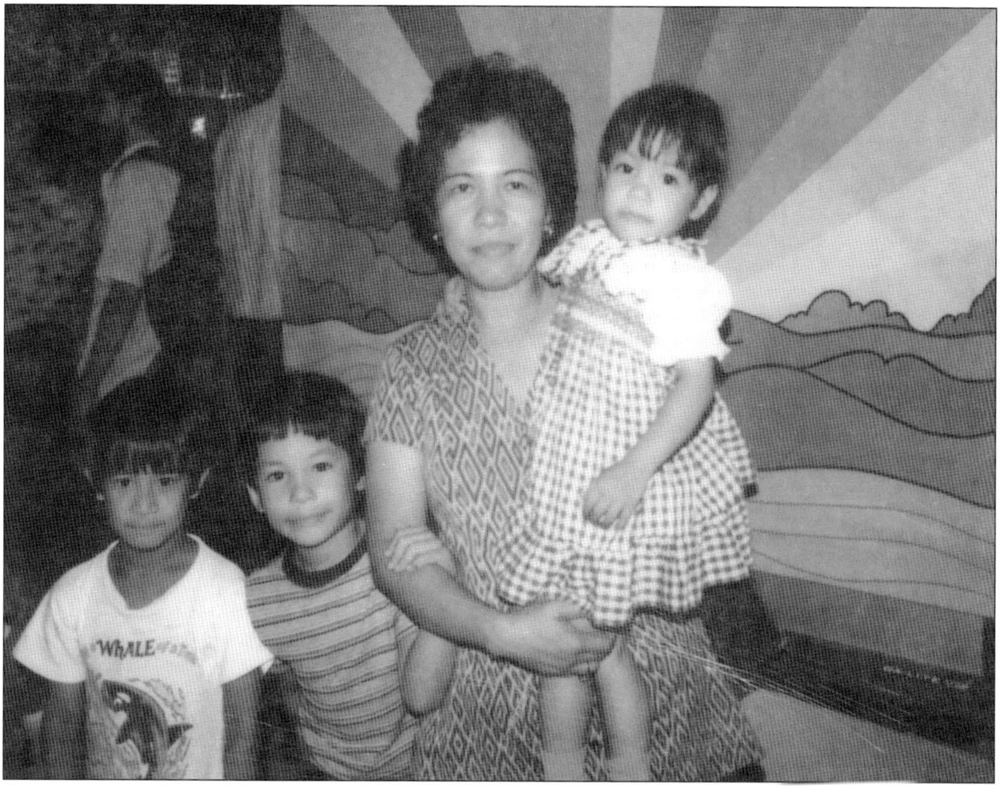

The two boys on the left are Ronnie Puzon and his friend Ray Calimlim. Their fathers, Ricardo Puzon (Navy) and Loreto Calimlim (Coast Guard), grew up together in the Philippines and reunited in Boston. The above photograph including Ronnie's mother, Esther, and sister, Melinda, was taken around 1974. Below, the Puzon children celebrate Melinda's birthday with friends in their home in Charlestown in 1979. (Both, courtesy of Ronnie Puzon.)

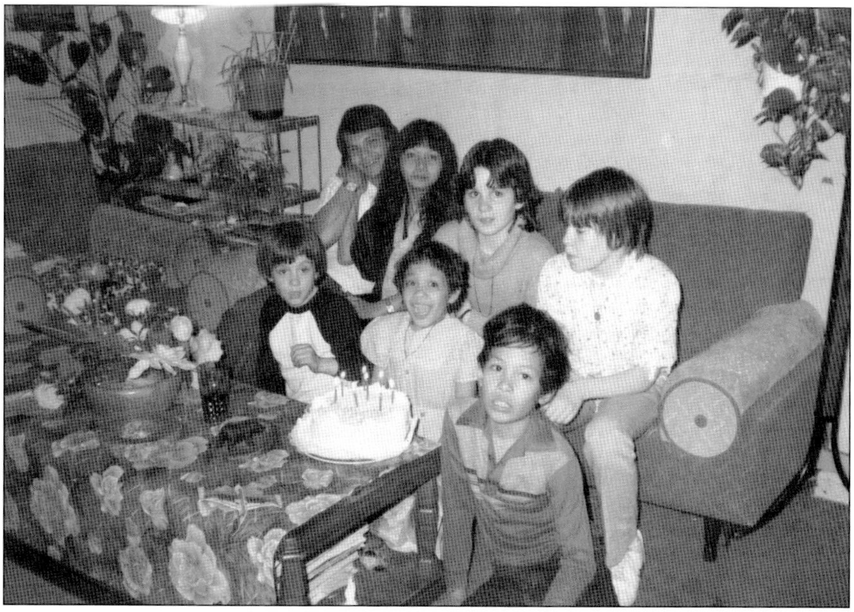

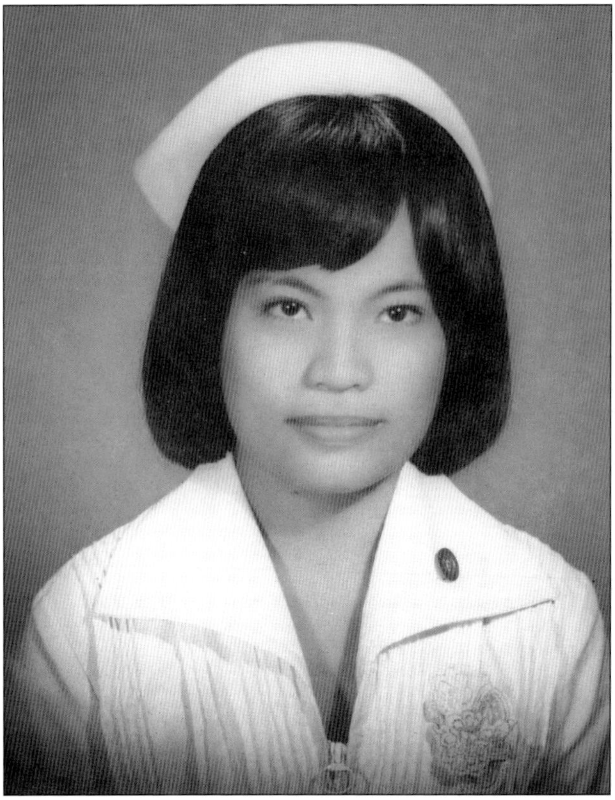

This photograph of Fracel Somera Solar was taken in 1974. She came to the United States to work as a nurse at the Jamaica Plain Veteran's Affairs Medical Center starting in 1981. She was one of the founders of the Philippine Nurses Association of Massachusetts (PNANE). Fracel finished her bachelor of science degree in nursing at Simmons College in 1991 and graduated with a master of arts degree from Regis College in 2000. (Courtesy of the Solar family.)

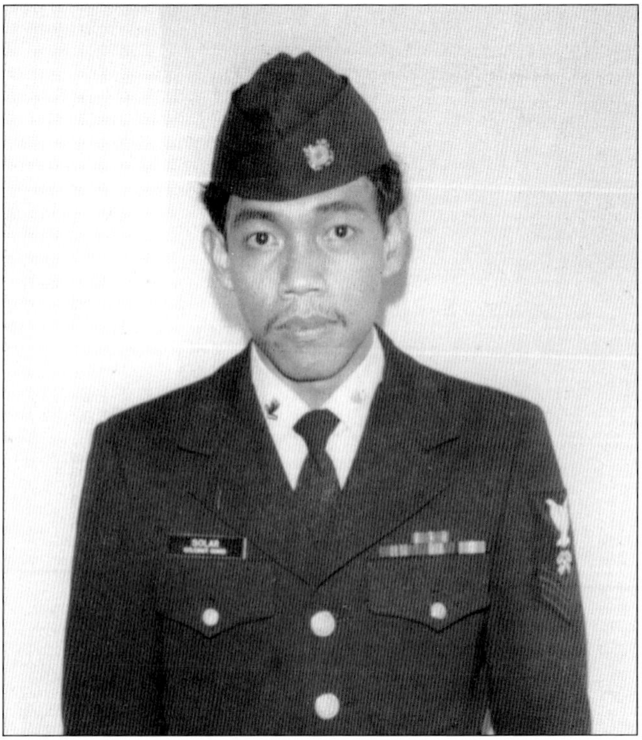

Isobelo "Bill" Sistoza Solar enlisted as a first-class petty officer in the Coast Guard in 1981. When he arrived in Boston, he joined fellow Filipinos Jesse Marmol, Tony Mateo, and Ben Manzano, who already lived in Coast Guard housing in Hyde Park. He worked at the VA (Veterans Affairs) until he retired in 1996. Bill earned a bachelor of science degree in business administration from Northeastern University in 1998. (Courtesy of the Solar family.)

This photograph was taken at the wedding of Fracel Somera Solar and Isobelo Sistoza Solar in 1977. They are active in many of the Filipino American organizations featured in this book. Their children, Judy, Lozel, and PhilJay, were born and raised in Massachusetts. (Courtesy of the Solar family.)

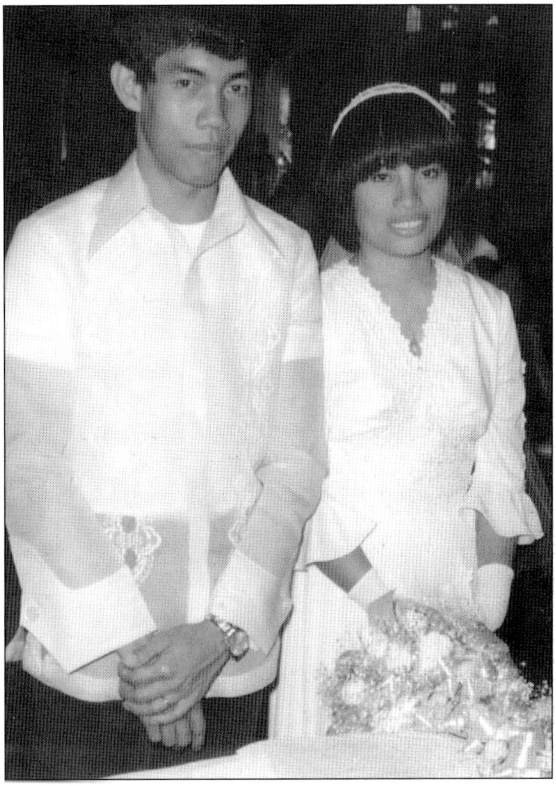

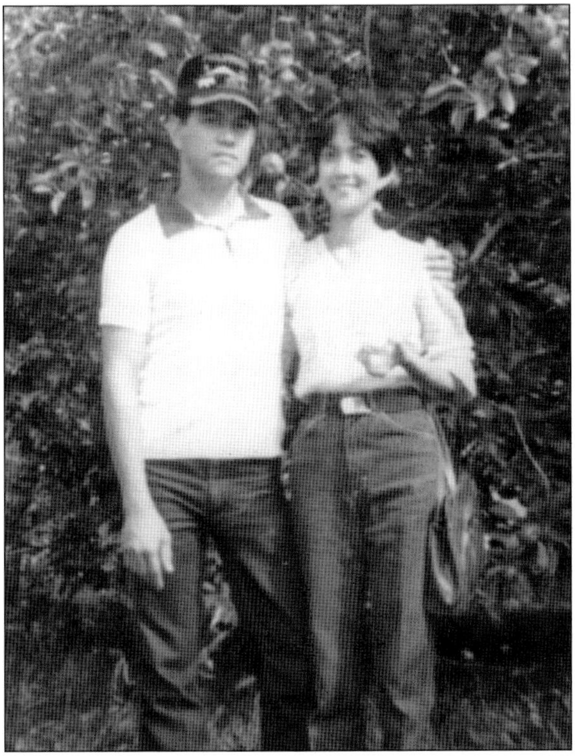

Bienvenido "Ben" Manzano and his wife, Tessie, were married in 1977. Ben was promoted to chief warrant officer 2 in the US Coast Guard in 1982. He worked as a supply officer on the USCGC *Bibb* (WHEC-31), which was homeported in New Bedford. Tessie worked as a medical technologist at the Veterans Affairs Healthcare System in Jamaica Plain. They have two children. (Courtesy of Ben Manzano.)

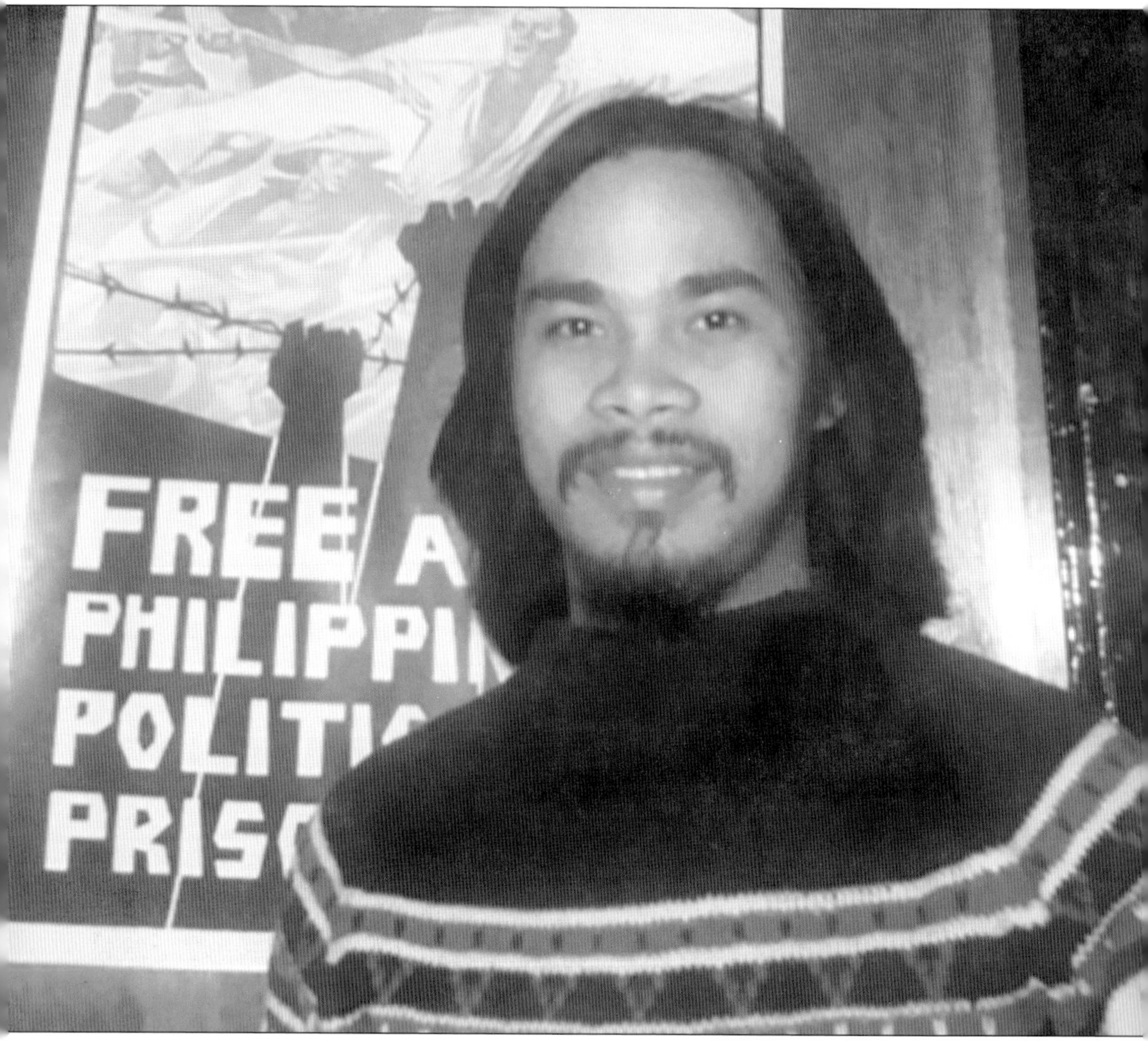

Filipino American students, mostly from the West Coast, including José Lalas, pictured here in 1976, came to Cambridge, Massachusetts, from 1974 to 1977 to pursue a master's degree in United States–Philippine relations offered by the Goddard-Cambridge Graduate School under instructor Dr. Daniel Boone Schirmer. Lalas went on to complete several advanced academic degrees in Washington State and has had a long academic career in California. Since the Goddard-Cambridge program began in the early years of martial law under Ferdinand Marcos in the Philippines, the class participated actively in the movement in the United States to oppose the regime. They participated in several Boston-based anti–martial law organizations, including the *Philippines Information Bulletin* and Friends of the Filipino People. (Courtesy of José Lalas.)

Four

THE AQUINO YEARS 1980–1983

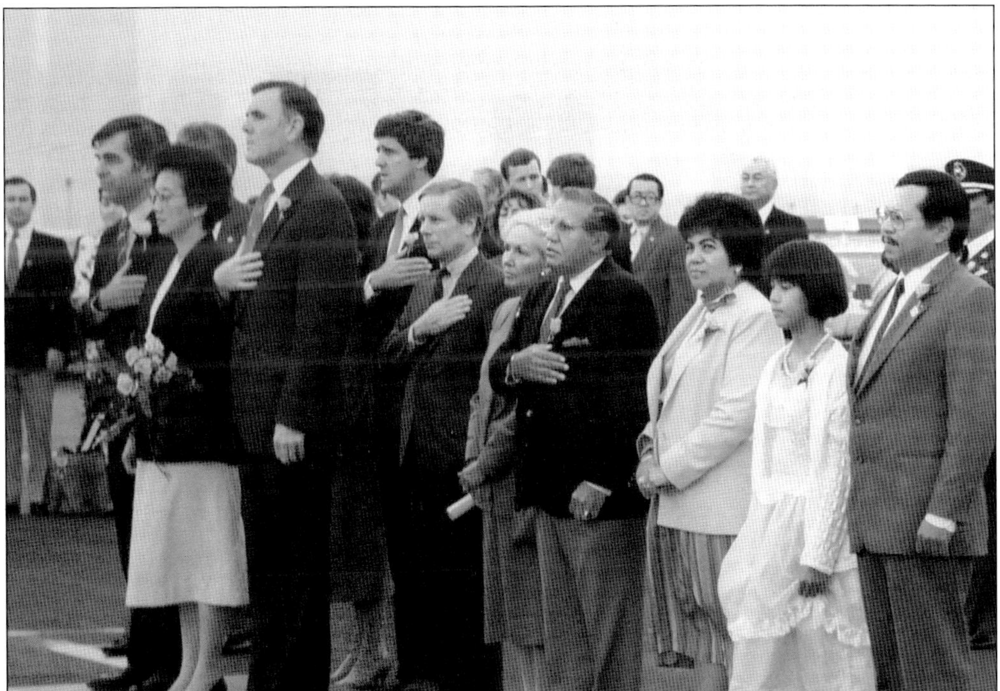

Benigno S. Aquino Jr. and his family came to Boston in 1980. He was assassinated upon his return to the Philippines on August 21, 1983. His wife, Corazon Aquino, led the People's Power Revolution and was elected president. Upon her return to Boston on September 20, 1986, President Aquino was greeted at Logan Airport by Gov. Michael Dukakis, Mayor Ray Flynn, Sen. John Kerry, and the Filipino community. (Courtesy of the Agular family.)

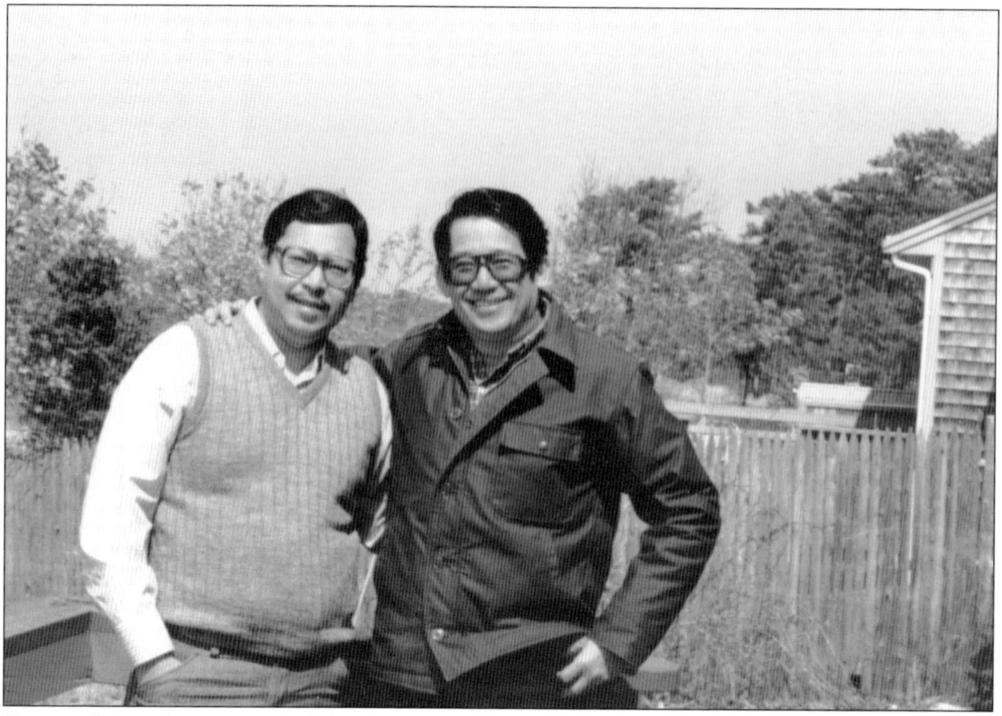

Benigno "Ninoy" Aquino Jr. (right) poses with Dr. Steve Agular in Cape Cod. Aquino was a Philippine senator who opposed the martial law regime of Pres. Ferdinand Marcos and was imprisoned for seven years. In 1980, he was allowed to go to the United States for bypass surgery following a heart attack. He and his family came to Boston in 1980 when he accepted a fellowship at Harvard and then MIT, leading study groups and seminars on Southeast Asia. Below, the Aquino family visits the Cape Cod vacation home of the Agular family. From left to right are Stephen and Stephanie Agular (children), Norma Bucal, Cyd Bucal, Dr. Almario Bucal, Maria Elena "Ballsy" Aquino, Ninoy Aquino, Dr. Rosario "Cher" Agular, Corazon Aquino, Victoria "Viel" Aquino, Aurora "Pinky" Aquino, and Kris Aquino. (Both, courtesy of the Agular family.)

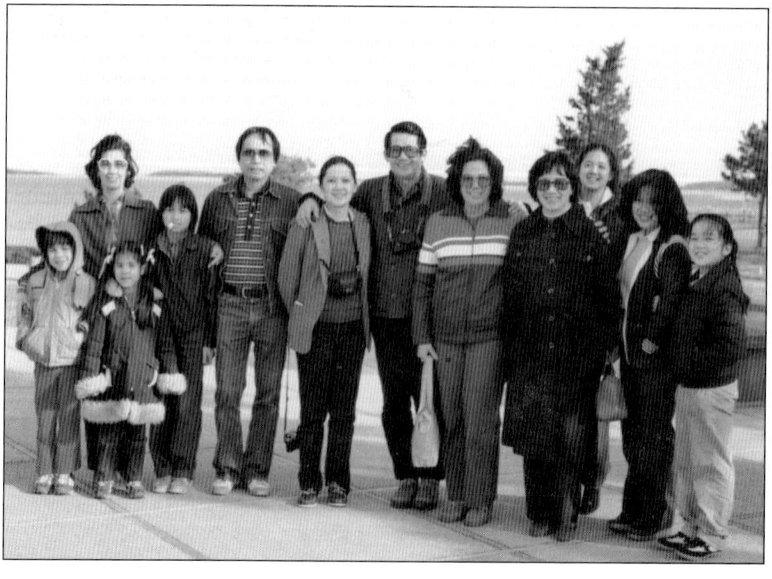

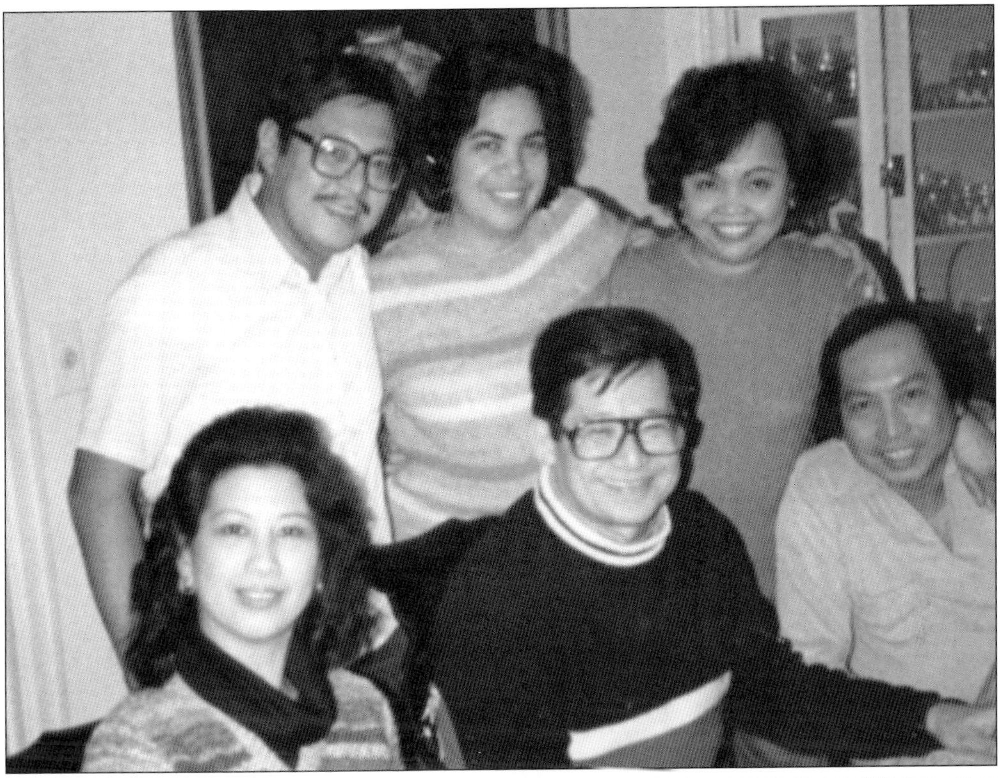

While in exile in Boston, Ninoy Aquino Jr. was embraced by a close-knit group of friends from the Filipino American community. Pictured from left to right are (first row, seated) Norma Bucal, Aquino Jr., and Dr. Almario "Mai" Bucal; (second row, standing) Drs. Steve and Rosario "Cher" Agular and Dr. Alice Layug. (Courtesy of the Agular family.)

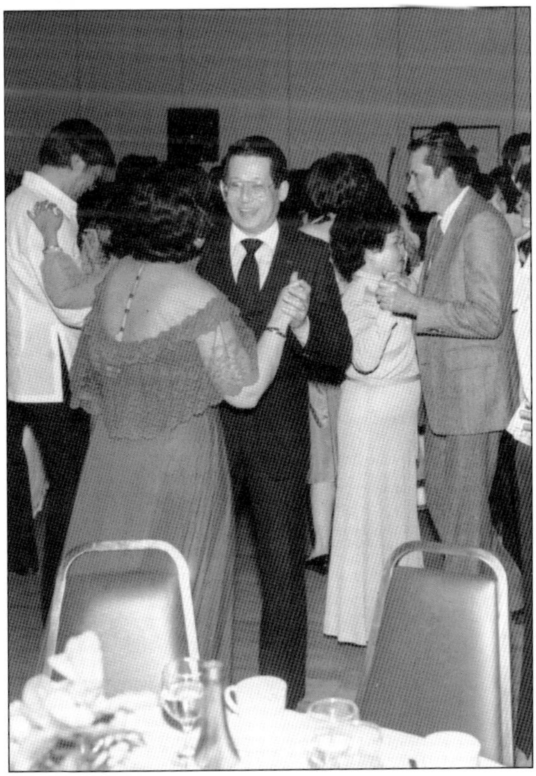

Ninoy Aquino Jr. and Dr. Cher Agular share a dance at a Philippine Medical Association of New England ball around 1982. Filipino Americans in Boston had the pleasure and privilege of meeting the Aquinos at community events such as this. (Courtesy of the Agular family.)

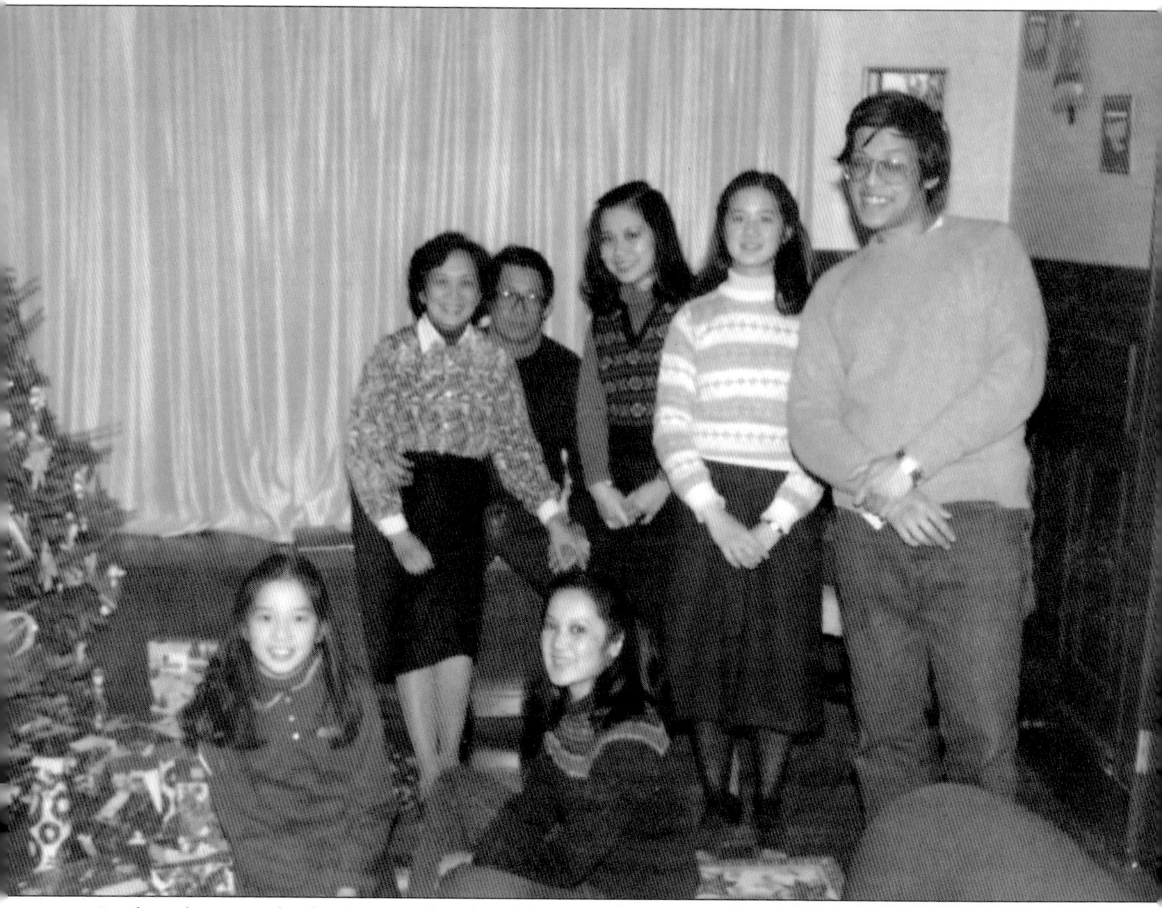

In this photograph, the Aquino family celebrates Christmas in Boston in 1982. According to Joju Bautista, cousin of Corazon Aquino, a professor of economics at Xavier University, and board member of the Benigno Aquino Jr. Memorial Foundation, this was one of the last photographs of the entire Aquino family. From left to right are (first row, seated) Kris and Ballsy Aquino; (second row, standing) future president Cory, Ninoy, Pinky, and Viel Aquino and future president Ninoy Aquino III. (Courtesy of José Juan Bautista.)

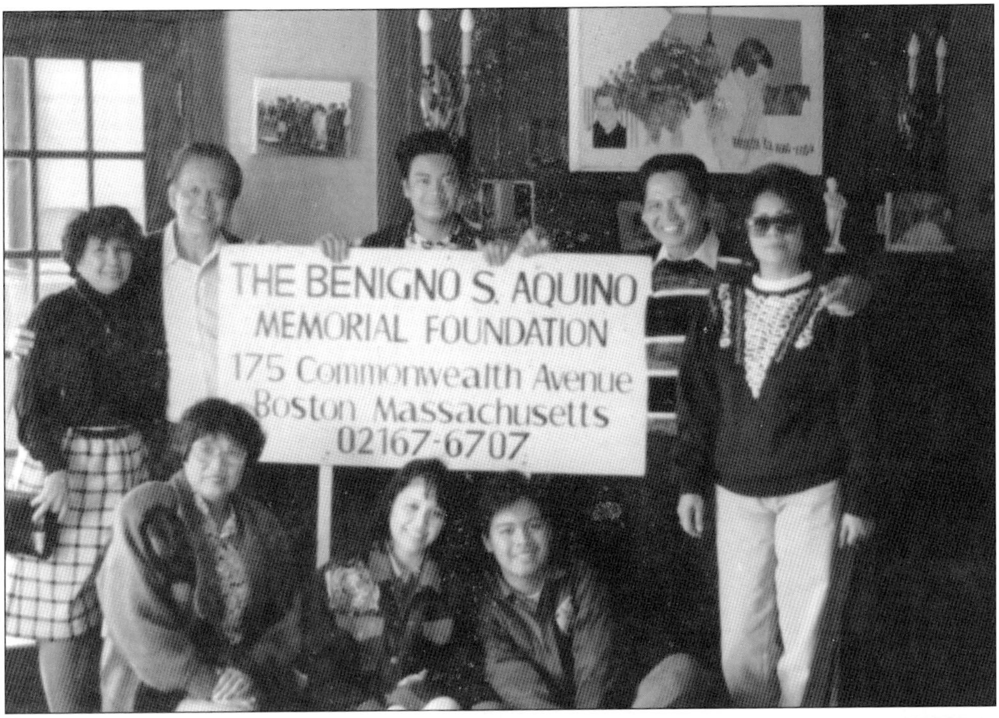

Filipinos in Greater Boston established the Benigno S. Aquino Jr. Memorial Foundation at the former home of the Aquinos on Commonwealth Avenue shortly after Aquino was assassinated on August 21, 1983, upon his return to the Philippines. According to the foundation's newsletter, a ribbon-cutting ceremony took place at the house on May 15, 1985. (Courtesy of the Bucal family.)

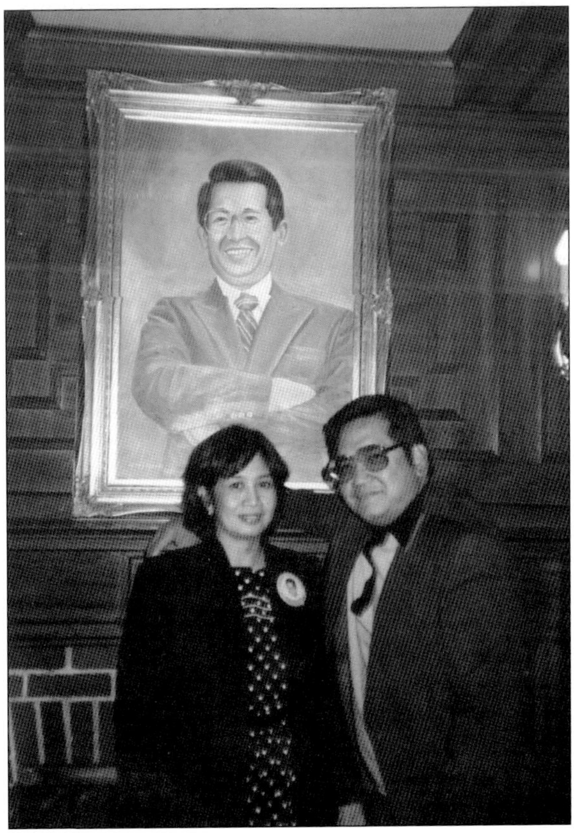

Drs. Ceferino and Marietta Bague pose in front of a portrait of Ninoy at the opening of the Benigno Aquino Jr. Memorial Foundation in 1985. (Courtesy of Bernadette M. Bague.)

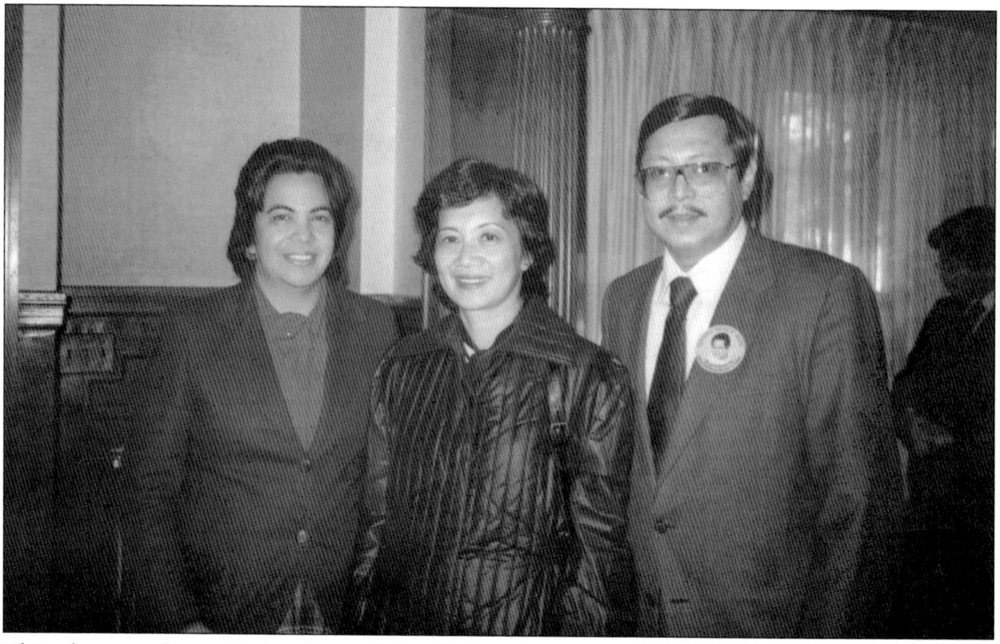

This photograph was likely taken in May 1984 at the Aquino house on Commonwealth Avenue during a brief visit by Cory Aquino (center) before she became president and when the Aquino Room at the Center for International Affairs at Harvard University was dedicated. Dr. Cher Agular is on the left, and Dr. Steve Agular (right) is wearing a pin that says, "Remember 'Ninoy' Aquino." (Courtesy of the Agular family.)

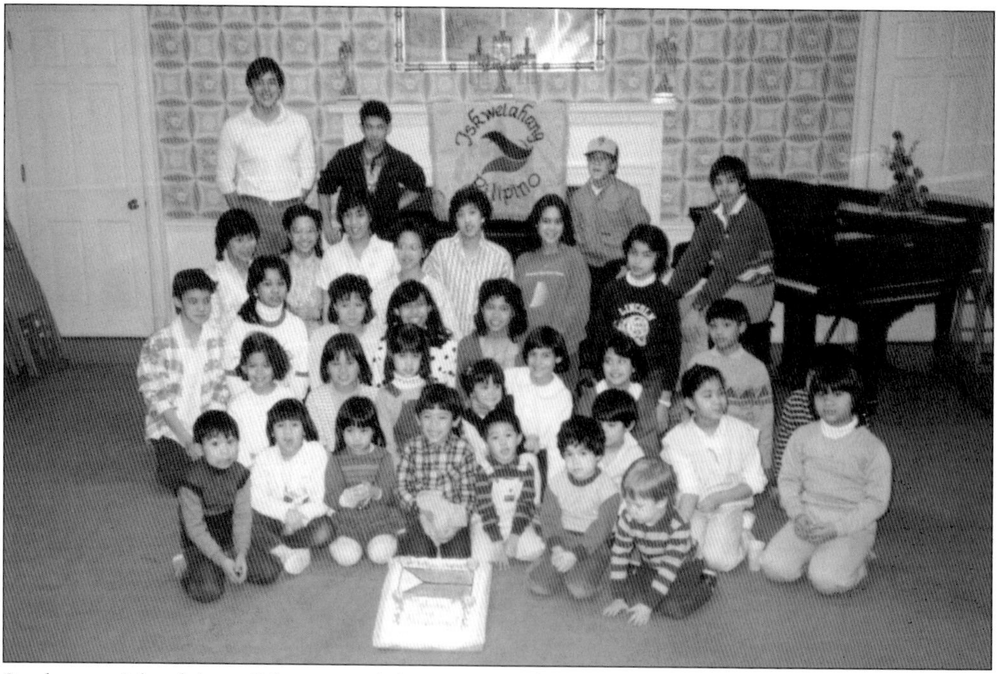

Students at Iskwelahang Pilipino send their congratulations to Cory Aquino when she was elected president of the Philippines in 1986 following the People's Power Revolution. (Courtesy of Rosalinda J. Ott.)

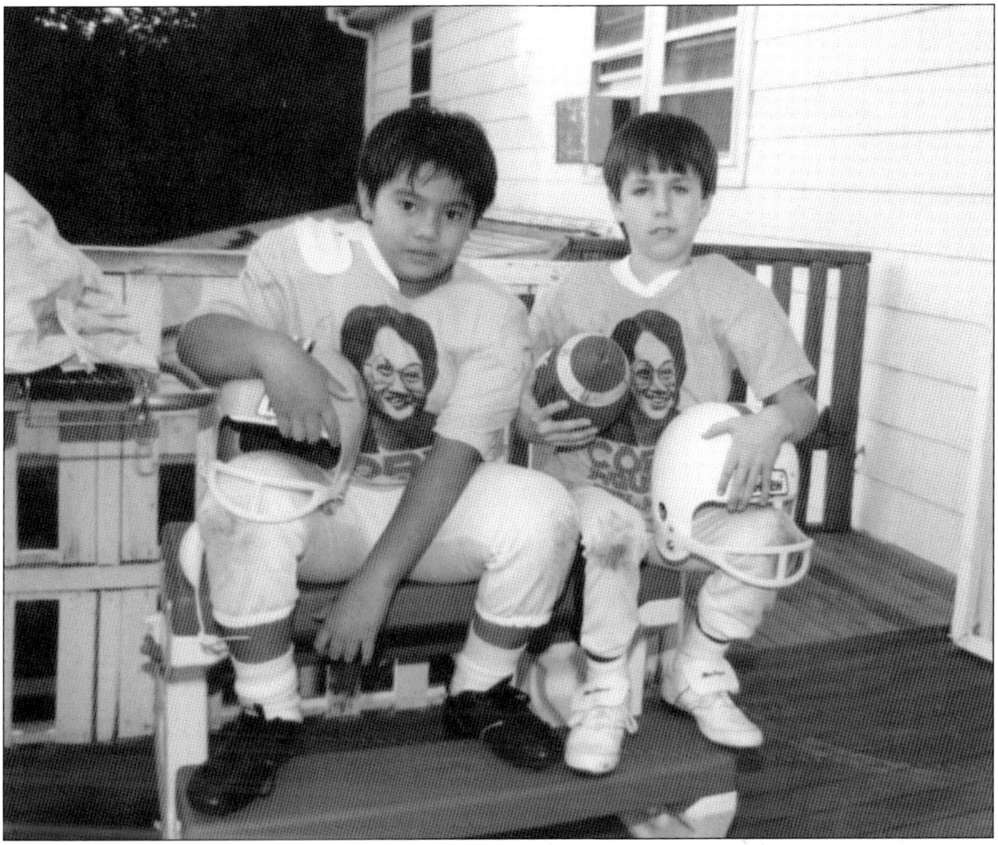

Paul Talusan (left) and classmate Mark pose wearing People's Power Revolution t-shirts in 1986.

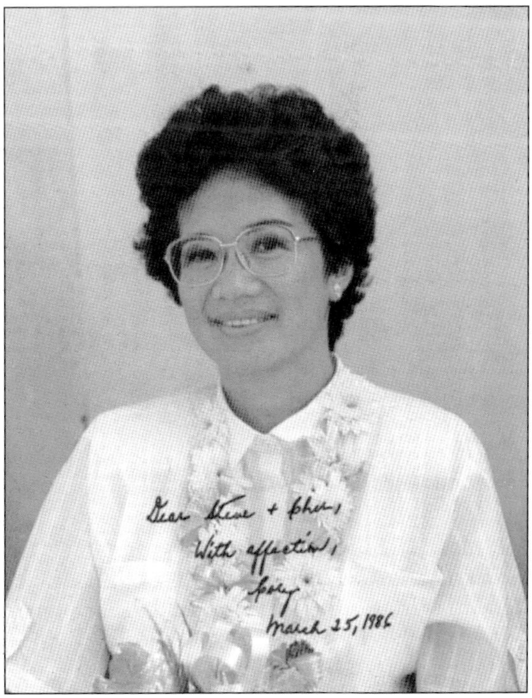

This photograph of Pres. Cory Aquino dated March 25, 1986, was sent to her friends in Boston, Drs. Steve and Cher Agular. (Courtesy of the Agular family.)

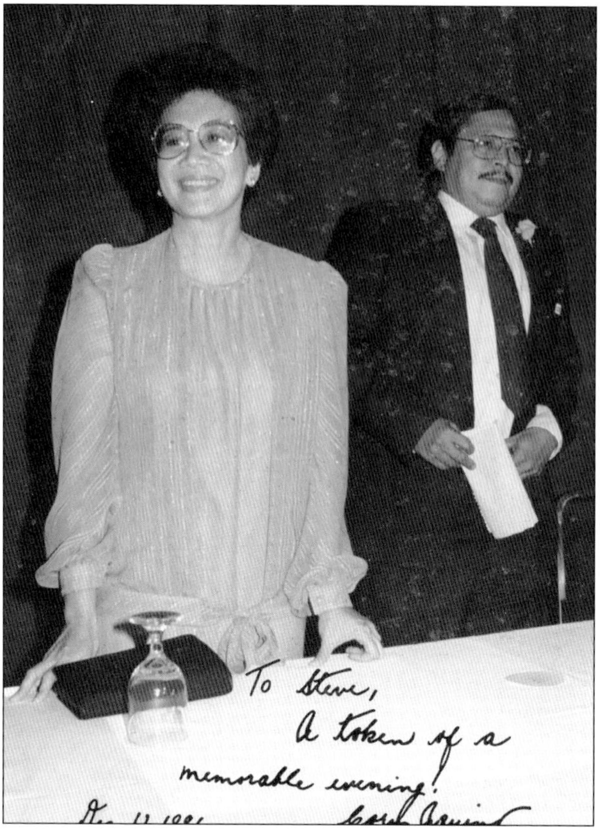

This photograph was taken in September 1986 during President Aquino's visit to Boston. A dinner in her honor was hosted by Mayor Raymond L. Flynn at Faneuil Hall. Members of the city council were also in attendance. Similar photographs of the event can be found in the City of Boston archives. (Courtesy of the Agular family.)

According to the *Official Gazette* of the Republic of the Philippines, President Aquino gave a speech at Mayor Flynn's reception in which she referred to Boston as "the cradle of freedom." She also stated that her late husband called Boston "the Athens of America" and that she and her family had "happy memories" of the city. In this image, Sen. John Kerry gives Aquino a plaque.

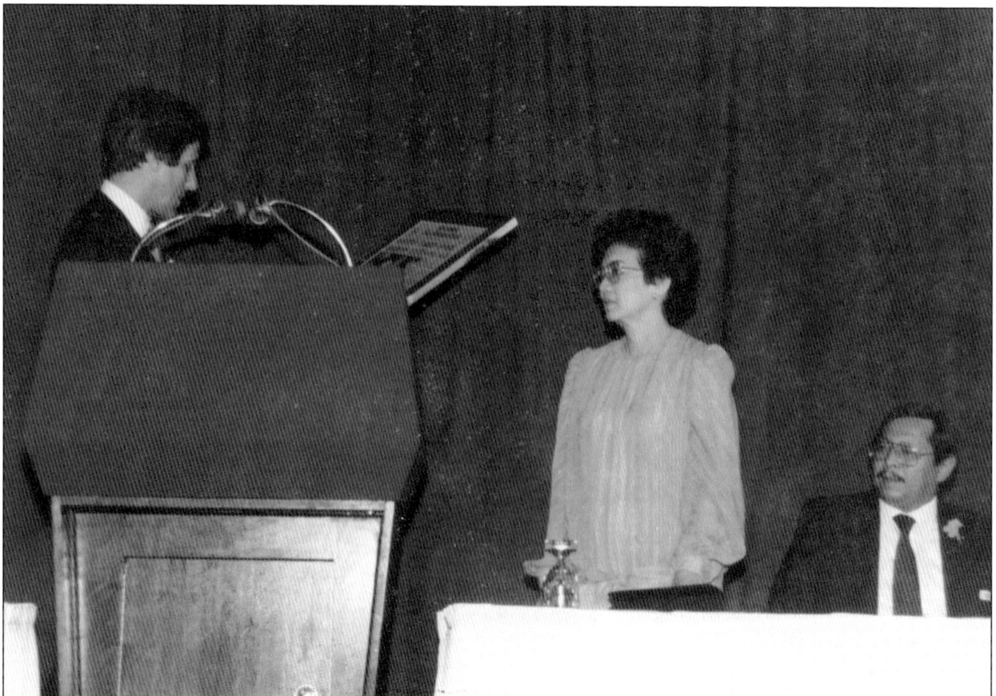

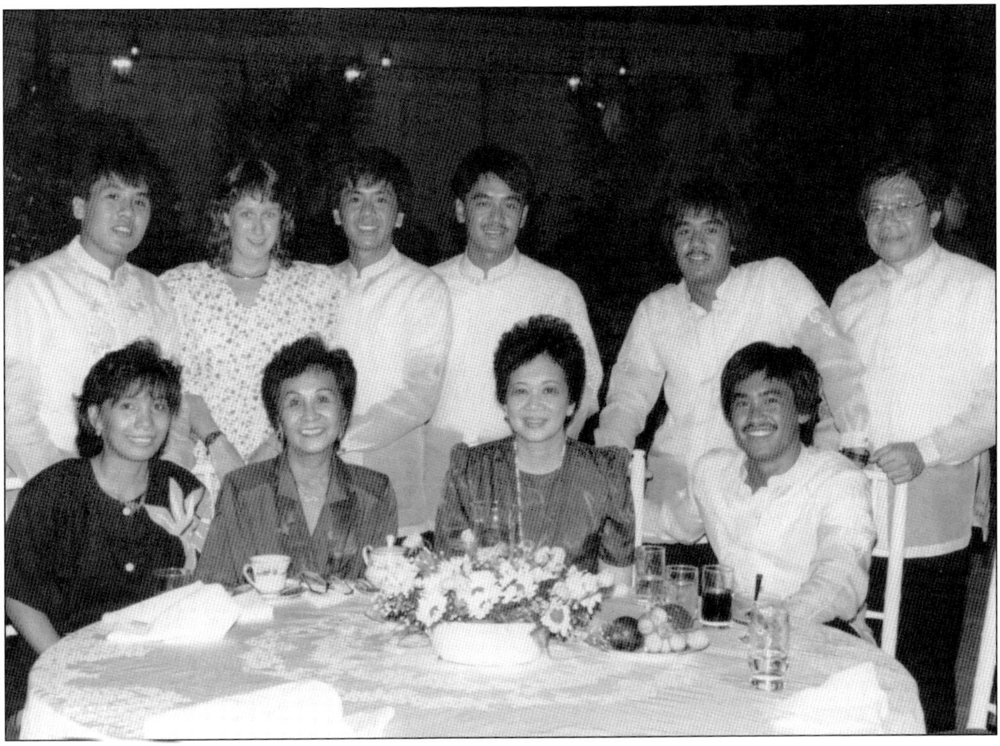

President Aquino returned to Boston in 1992 to give a speech at Harvard University on September 28. A video of the speech is available on Harvard's website. Here, she is pictured at a dinner hosted by the Filipino community with members of the Hipona family and their friends. (Courtesy of the Hipona family.)

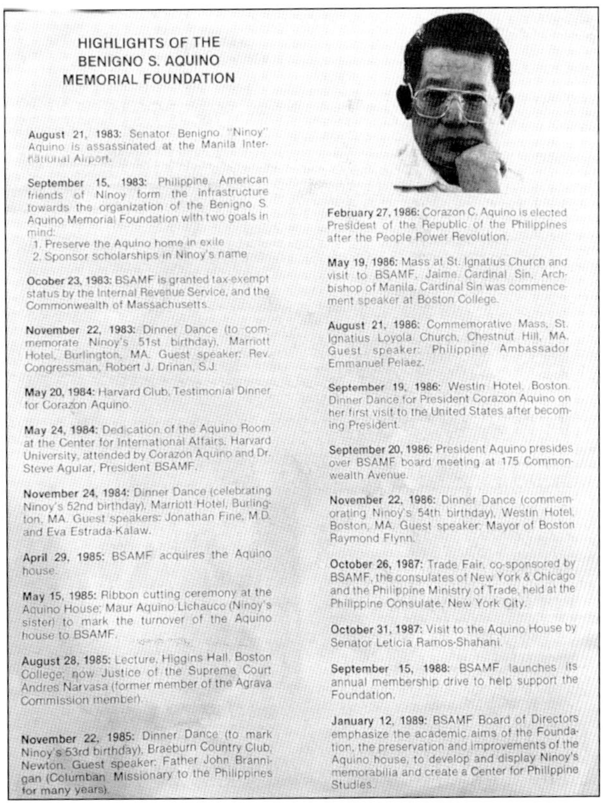

HIGHLIGHTS OF THE BENIGNO S. AQUINO MEMORIAL FOUNDATION

August 21, 1983: Senator Benigno "Ninoy" Aquino is assassinated at the Manila International Airport.

September 15, 1983: Philippine American friends of Ninoy form the infrastructure towards the organization of the Benigno S. Aquino Memorial Foundation with two goals in mind:
1. Preserve the Aquino home in exile
2. Sponsor scholarships in Ninoy's name

Ocober 23, 1983: BSAMF is granted tax-exempt status by the Internal Revenue Service, and the Commonwealth of Massachusetts.

November 22, 1983: Dinner Dance (to commemorate Ninoy's 51st birthday), Marriott Hotel, Burlington, MA. Guest speaker: Rev. Congressman, Robert J. Drinan, S.J.

May 20, 1984: Harvard Club, Testimonial Dinner for Corazon Aquino.

May 24, 1984: Dedication of the Aquino Room at the Center for International Affairs, Harvard University, attended by Corazon Aquino and Dr. Steve Agular, President BSAMF.

November 24, 1984: Dinner Dance (celebrating Ninoy's 52nd birthday), Marriott Hotel, Burlington, MA. Guest speakers: Jonathan Fine, M.D. and Eva Estrada-Kalaw.

April 29, 1985: BSAMF acquires the Aquino house.

May 15, 1985: Ribbon cutting ceremony at the Aquino House; Maur Aquino Lichauco (Ninoy's sister) to mark the turnover of the Aquino house to BSAMF.

August 28, 1985: Lecture, Higgins Hall, Boston College; now Justice of the Supreme Court Andres Narvasa (former member of the Agrava Commission member).

November 22, 1985: Dinner Dance (to mark Ninoy's 53rd birthday), Braeburn Country Club, Newton. Guest speaker: Father John Brannigan (Columban Missionary to the Philippines for many years).

February 27, 1986: Corazon C. Aquino is elected President of the Republic of the Philippines after the People Power Revolution.

May 19, 1986: Mass at St. Ignatius Church and visit to BSAMF, Jaime Cardinal Sin, Archbishop of Manila. Cardinal Sin was commencement speaker at Boston College.

August 21, 1986: Commemorative Mass, St. Ignatius Loyola Church, Chestnut Hill, MA. Guest speaker: Philippine Ambassador Emmanuel Pelaez.

September 19, 1986: Westin Hotel, Boston. Dinner Dance for President Corazon Aquino on her first visit to the United States after becoming President.

September 20, 1986: President Aquino presides over BSAMF board meeting at 175 Commonwealth Avenue.

November 22, 1986: Dinner Dance (commemorating Ninoy's 54th birthday), Westin Hotel, Boston, MA. Guest speaker: Mayor of Boston Raymond Flynn.

October 26, 1987: Trade Fair, co-sponsored by BSAMF, the consulates of New York & Chicago and the Philippine Ministry of Trade, held at the Philippine Consulate, New York City.

October 31, 1987: Visit to the Aquino House by Senator Leticia Ramos-Shahani.

September 15, 1988: BSAMF launches its annual membership drive to help support the Foundation.

January 12, 1989: BSAMF Board of Directors emphasize the academic aims of the Foundation, the preservation and improvements of the Aquino house, to develop and display Ninoy's memorabilia and create a Center for Philippine Studies.

This is a page from the *Benigno S. Aquino Memorial Foundation Newsletter*, Vol. 6 Special Edition, 1989. It highlights the important activities of the foundation to honor the life and work of Ninoy Aquino. Dr. Steven G. Agular wrote in his "President's Appeal" that "we believe that in honoring one's heroes, we give honor to ourselves and our heritage." (Courtesy of Bernadette M. Bague.)

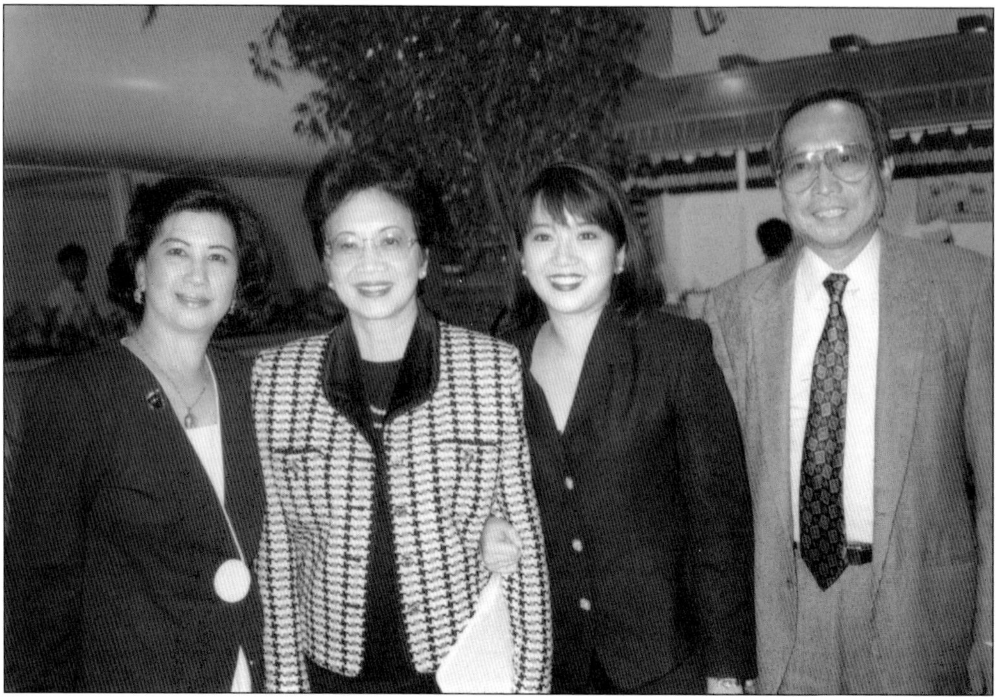

In this photograph, President Aquino poses with Norma Bucal (left), Sasa Lichauco, and Dr. Mai Bucal after her speech at Harvard University on September 28, 1992. (Courtesy of the Bucal family.)

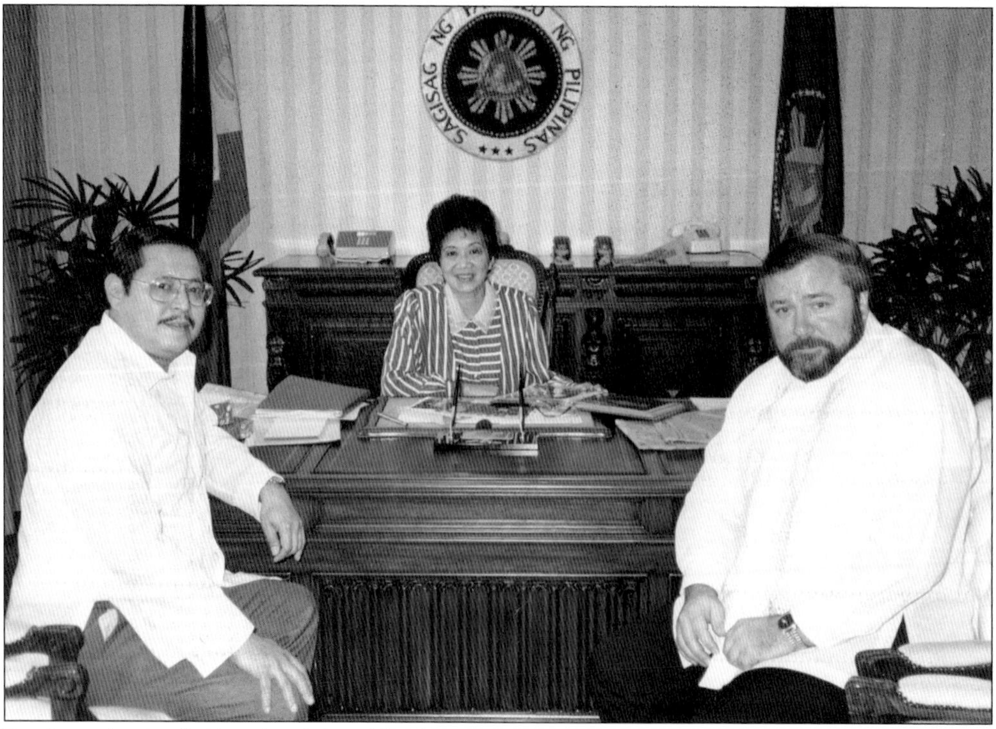

Dr. Steve Agular (left) and Bob Strickland visit the office of Philippine president Cory Aquino on a trip to the Philippines in the early 1990s. (Courtesy of the Agular family.)

Five

Passing on Traditions to Filipino American Youth 1980s

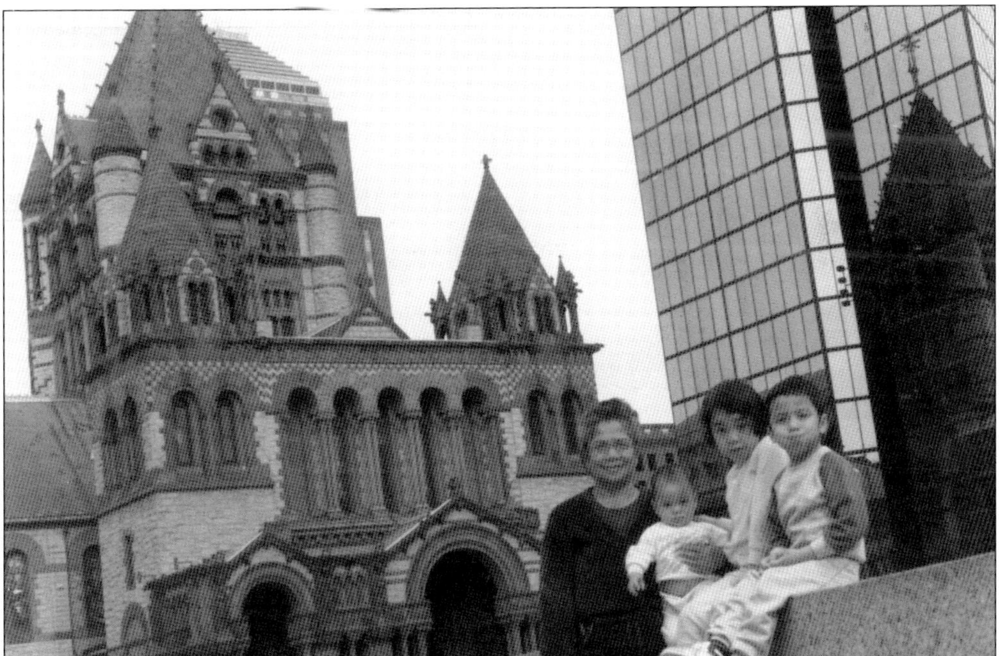

Seen here at Copley Square in 1984, the children of Ofelia and Rudy Villanueva pose with their grandmother, who was visiting from the Philippines. Visits by grandparents and other relatives were precious opportunities for the American-born generation to reconnect with their Filipino heritage. (Courtesy of Ofelia Villanueva and family.)

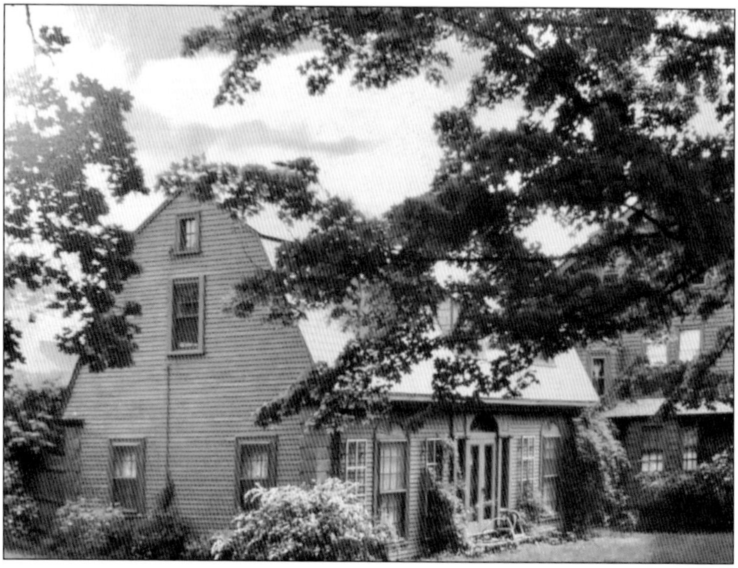

Students from the Philippines are still welcome at the Lichauco home near Cambridge. Members of the Lichauco family planted roots in Boston in the early 1900s and sent two daughters to the Academy of the Sacred Heart in Newton. Marcial Lichauco was the first Filipino to graduate from Harvard College in 1923. (Courtesy of Nelly Lichauco.)

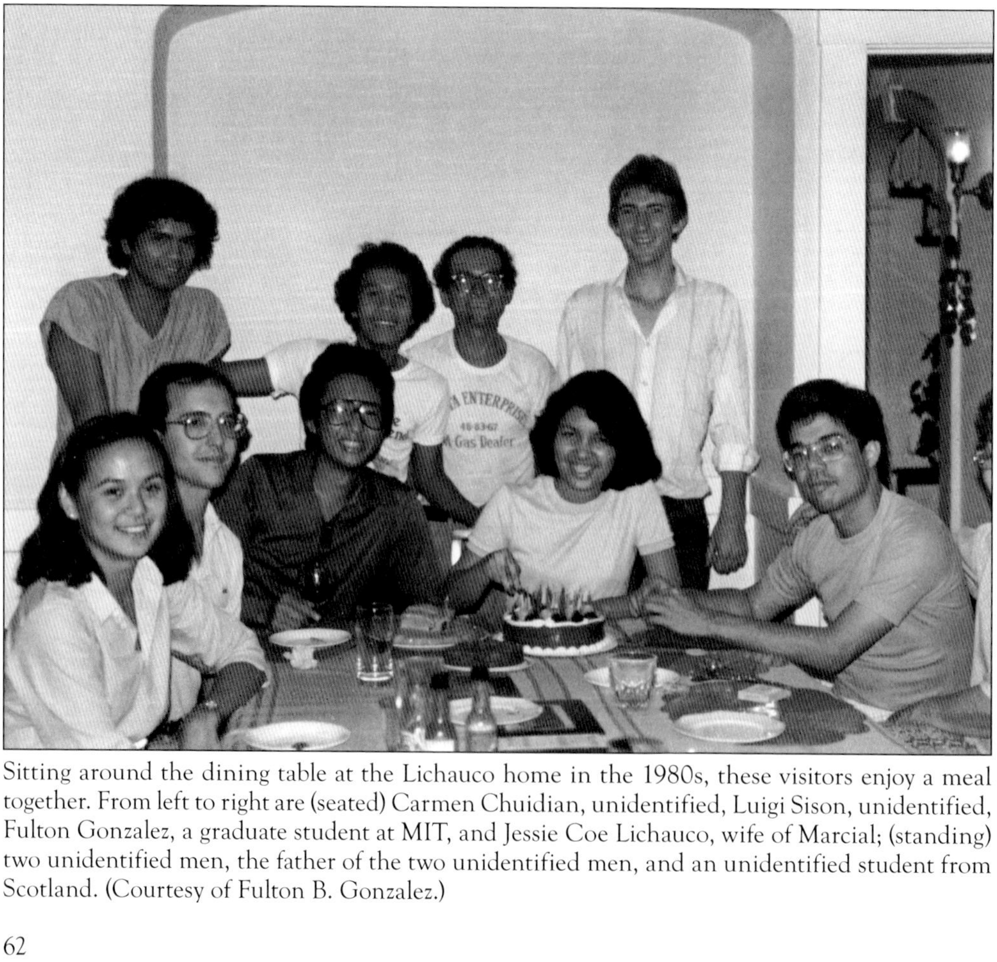

Sitting around the dining table at the Lichauco home in the 1980s, these visitors enjoy a meal together. From left to right are (seated) Carmen Chuidian, unidentified, Luigi Sison, unidentified, Fulton Gonzalez, a graduate student at MIT, and Jessie Coe Lichauco, wife of Marcial; (standing) two unidentified men, the father of the two unidentified men, and an unidentified student from Scotland. (Courtesy of Fulton B. Gonzalez.)

Two students from the Philippines were welcomed into the homes of Boston Filipinos for the holidays. Composer Louie Ocampo, who attended Berklee College of Music from 1981 to 1982, and pianist Carolyn Kleiner-Cheng, who attend the New England Conservatory of Music, both became famous musicians in the Philippines. (Courtesy of Rosalinda J. Ott.)

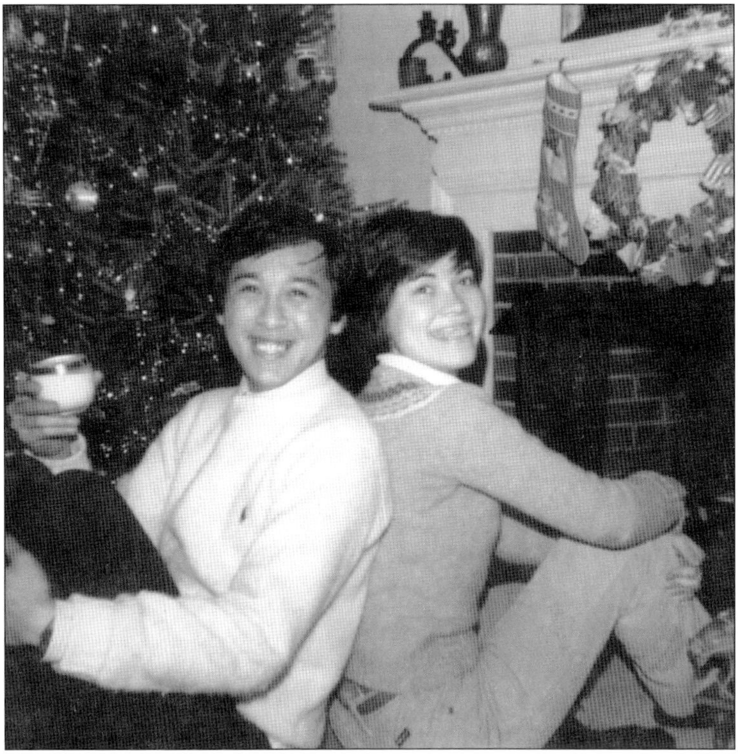

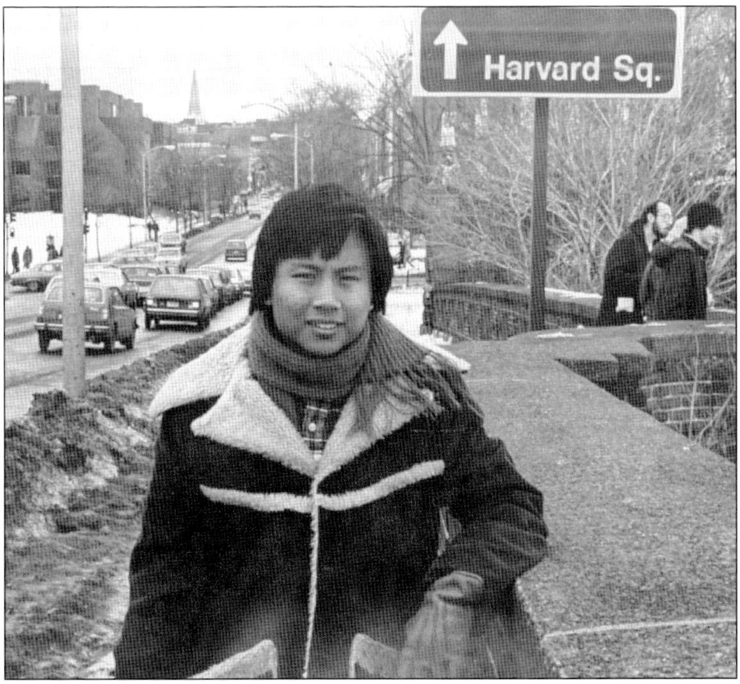

Horacio "Howie" Gorospe Severino was a campus journalist at Tufts University for four years before graduating in 1983. While in Boston, he got to know Ninoy Aquino. Today, he is a Filipino broadcast journalist best known for his work with the Philippine Center for Investigative Journalism, the Probe Team, and GMA Network. (Courtesy of Howie Severino.)

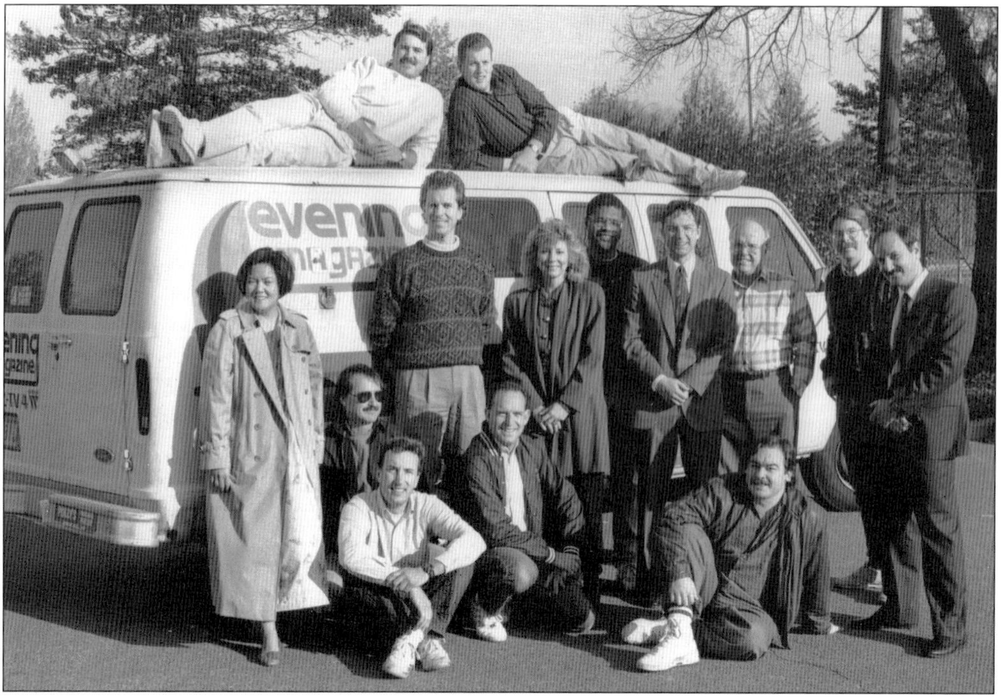

Patricia "Patty" Yusah (left) is pictured here with the crew of WBZ's *Evening Magazine*. Her broadcasting career in Boston spanned from 1986 to 2011. She also worked for WCVB's *Chronicle* and WGBH's *American Experience*. (Courtesy of Patricia Lim Yusah.)

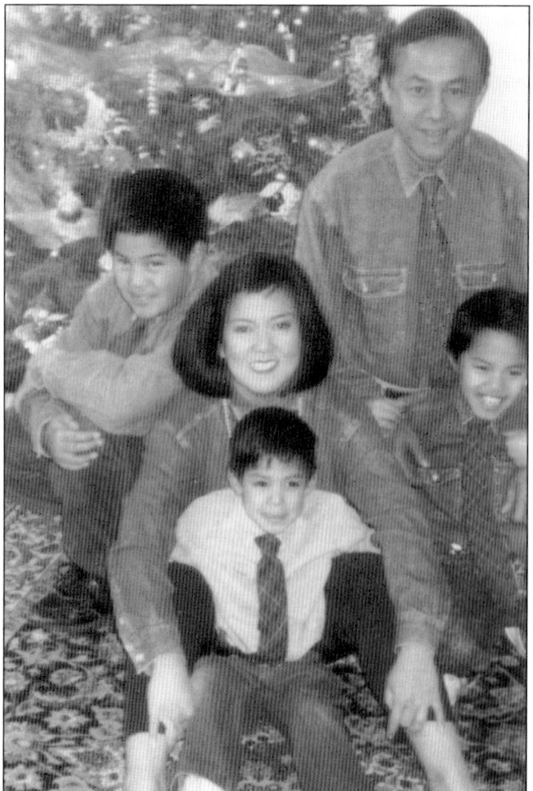

Patty and Winnie Yusah are pictured in this c. 1980s family photograph. Their sons, Zeke (left), Michael (right), and Willi (center), all went to public schools in Lexington, Massachusetts. They still reside in this community. (Courtesy of Patricia Lim Yusah.)

This photograph was taken in 1982, when Alfreda "Nida" Prado and her daughter, Pia, first immigrated to the United States and moved to Brockton, Massachusetts. Nida worked in a nursing home as a nurse's aide. She met other Filipinos through the church and was active in the Santo Nino tradition with Lucy Lauron, wife of Boston Pop's flutist Ildephonso Lauron. (Courtesy of Pia McCusker.)

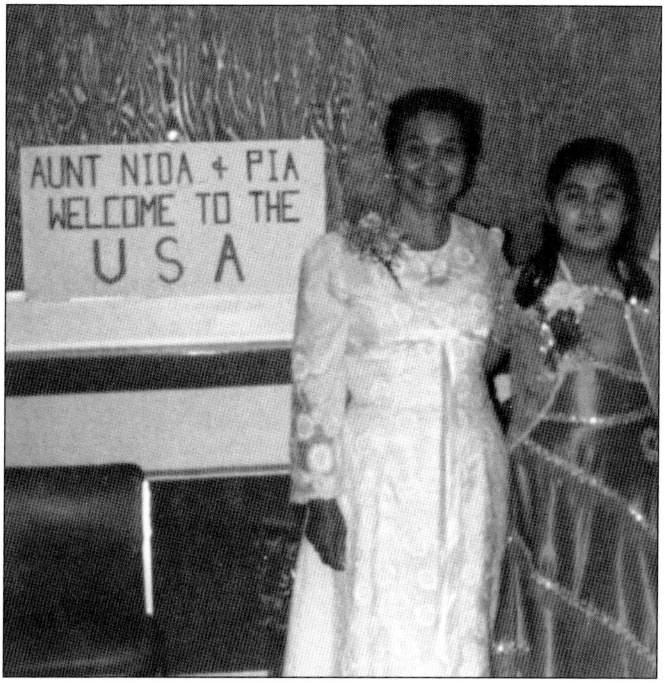

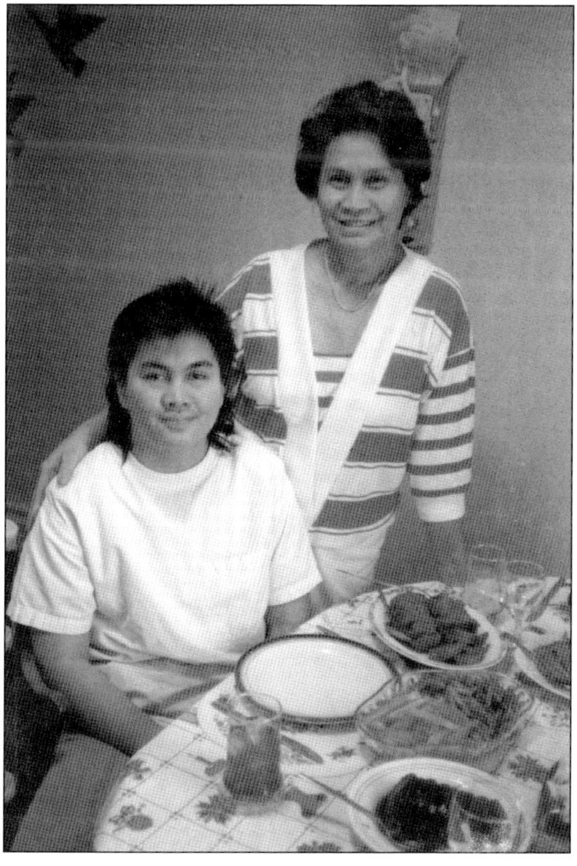

Nida and Pia pose in 1987, five years after they arrived in Massachusetts. Pia made the honor roll consistently throughout high school at Brockton High and won many awards for athletics, including a scholarship to Brandeis University. (Courtesy of Pia McCusker.)

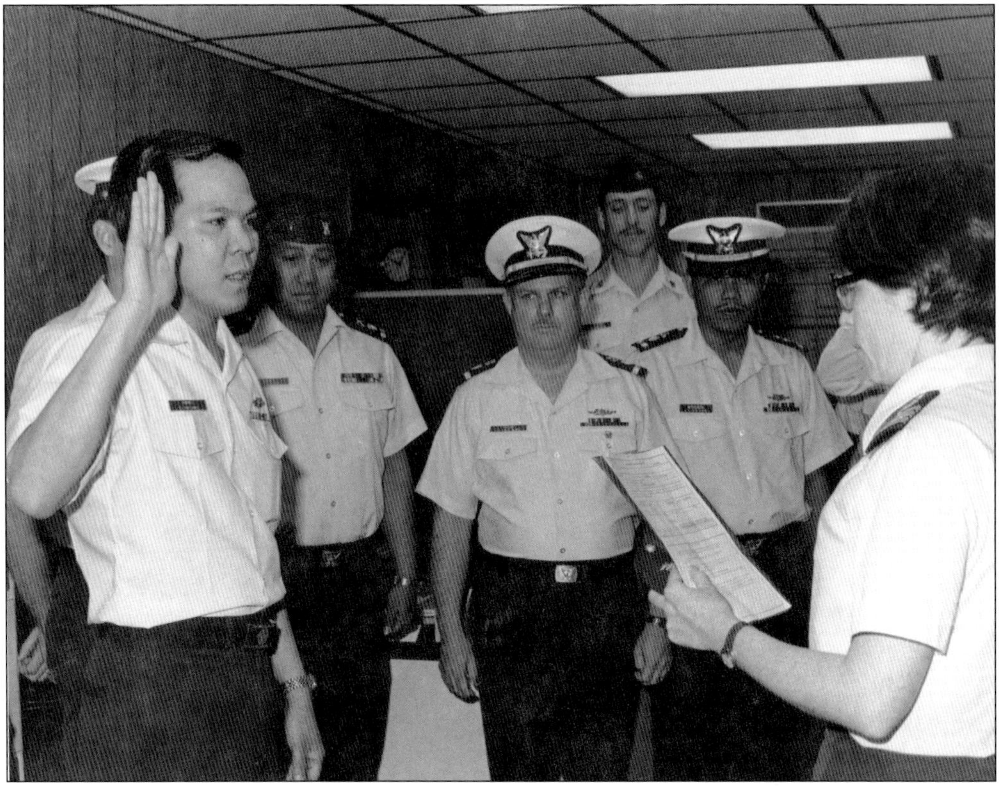

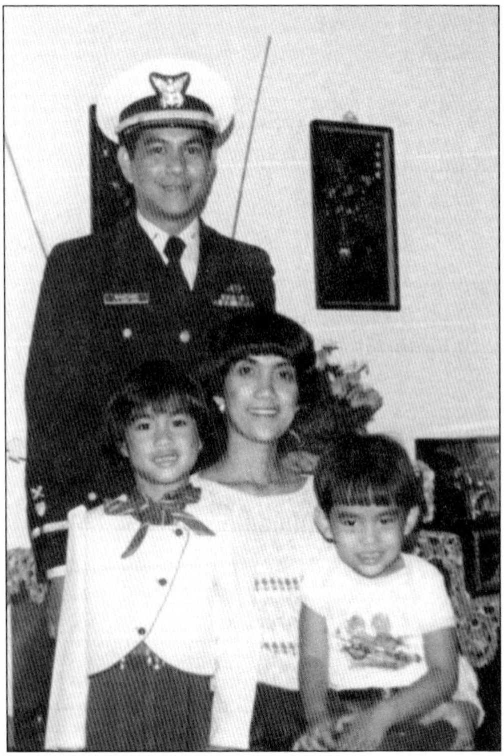

In 1982, José Jacin "Jesse" Marmol was sworn in as chief medical administrator. He was the first Filipino in the Coast Guard chosen for warrant officer in the medical field. He retired in September 1988 as a commissioned chief warrant officer and worked with Governor Dukakis. (Courtesy of the Marmol family.)

Ben Manzano was chief warrant officer 3 onboard the USCGC *Bibb* (WHEC-31), homeported in New Bedford. He is pictured with his wife Tessie, daughter Venessa Grace, six years ol '., and Benedict Glenn, four years old. This photograph was taken in 1985 at their home in Randolph, where they still live. (Courtesy of the Manzano family.)

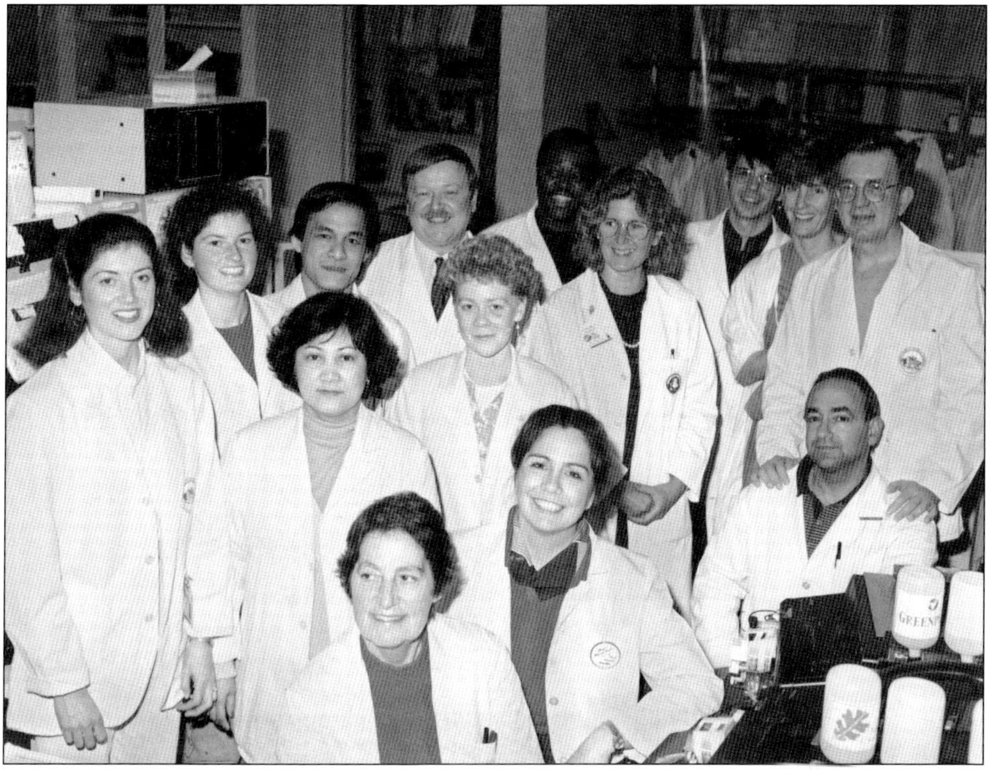

Taken in the 1980s, this photograph shows Epifania "Fanny" Valencia (left, middle row) with coworkers at the Massachusetts General Hospital lab where she worked for 40 years. She is married to José "Peping" Valencia. To the right are their children Joseph and Christine visiting the Boston Children's Museum in 1989. (Both, courtesy of the Valencia family.)

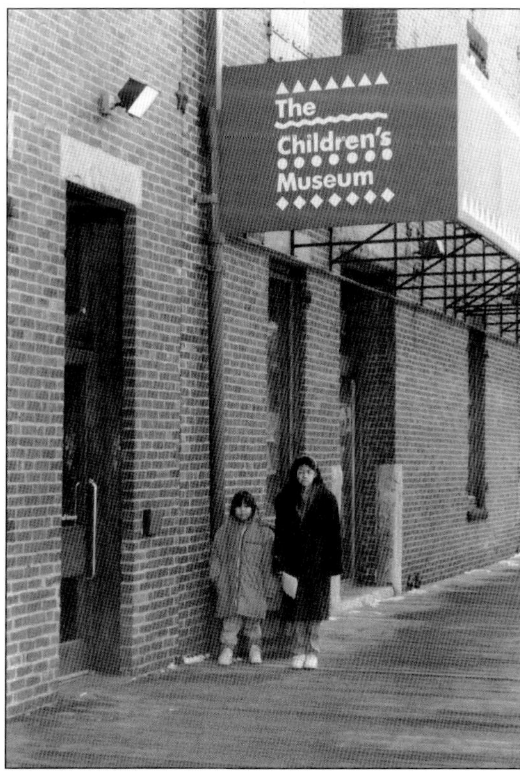

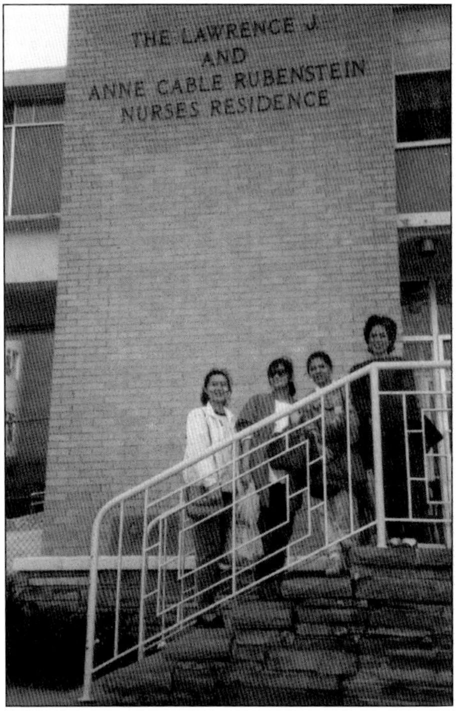

Due to staff shortages during the 1980s, nurses from the Philippines immigrated to work in Boston-area hospitals. From left to right, Beth Mangilog, Lorna Caranto, Eden Gianan, and unidentified pose outside their dorm at the Jewish Memorial Hospital and Rehabilitation Center. (Courtesy of the Mangilog family.)

Socorro Talamera poses in 1985 in front of her dorm at the Jewish Memorial Hospital, where she worked as a nurse. She and her former coworkers are still close friends. (Courtesy of Socorro Talamera.)

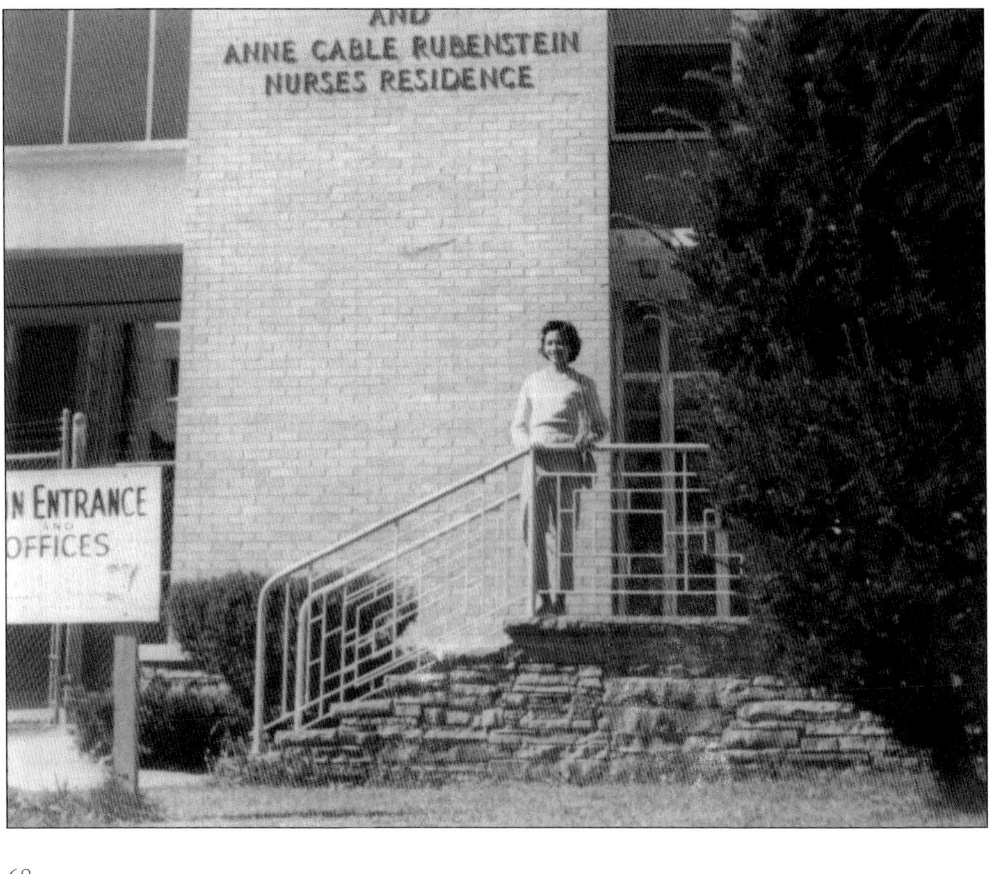

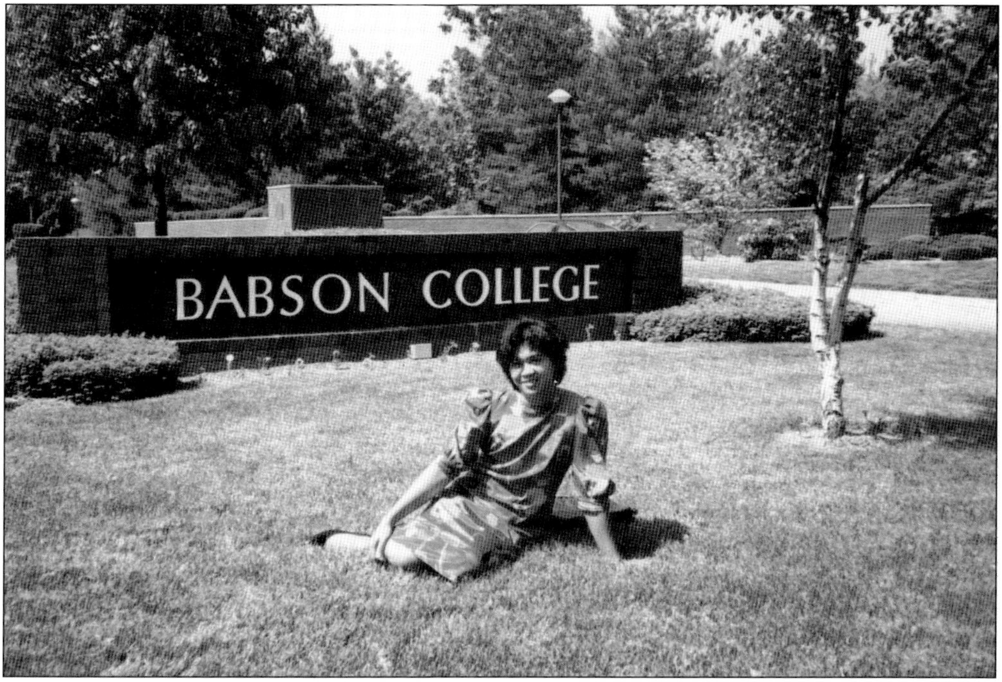

Nurses enjoyed sightseeing around Boston on their days off. In this photograph, Loida Dinglasa poses in front of Babson College in 1988. (Courtesy of Loida Dinglasa.)

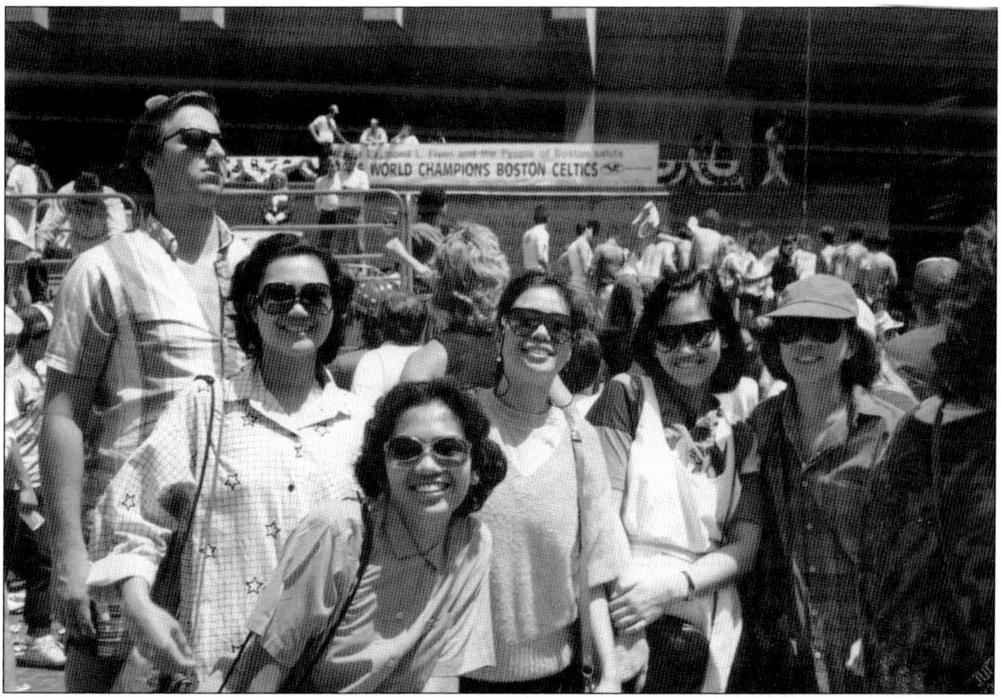

Filipinos are big fans of Boston sports teams. Immediately after their night shift, these nurses went directly to the celebration taking place at Government Center for the Celtics' NBA championship win in 1986. (Courtesy of Socorro Talamera.)

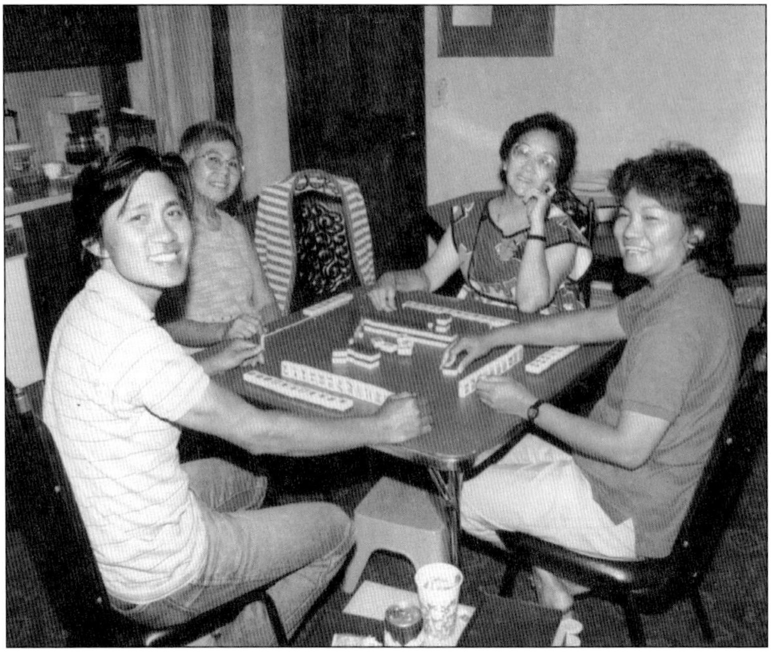

Mahjong is a favorite game among Filipinos. Taken in the 1980s, this photograph shows, from left to right, Roger Bayug, Rose Soqui, an unidentified friend, and Arcel Talusan playing for hours at the Bucal family vacation home in Cape Cod.

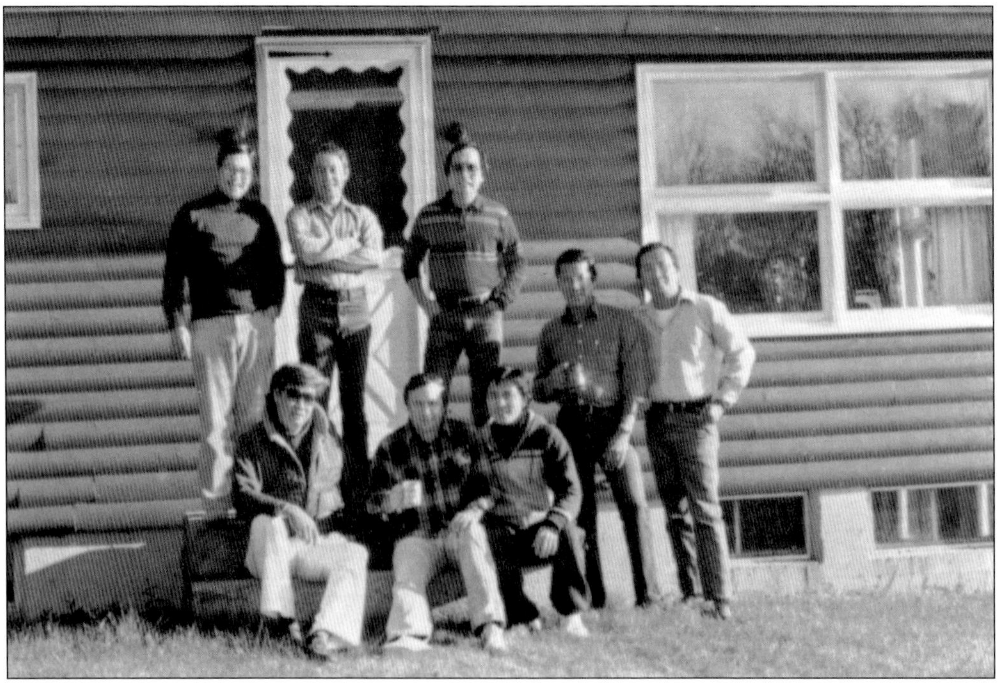

A *barkada*, or group of close friends, poses outside the Bucal vacation home in Cape Cod during a get-together. From left to right are (first row, seated) Tony Layug, Bob Strickland, and Roger Bayug; (second row, standing) Steve Agular, Winnie Yusah, Mai Bucal, Ben Lagman, and José "Pong" Angeles. (Courtesy of Dr. Mimi Strickland.)

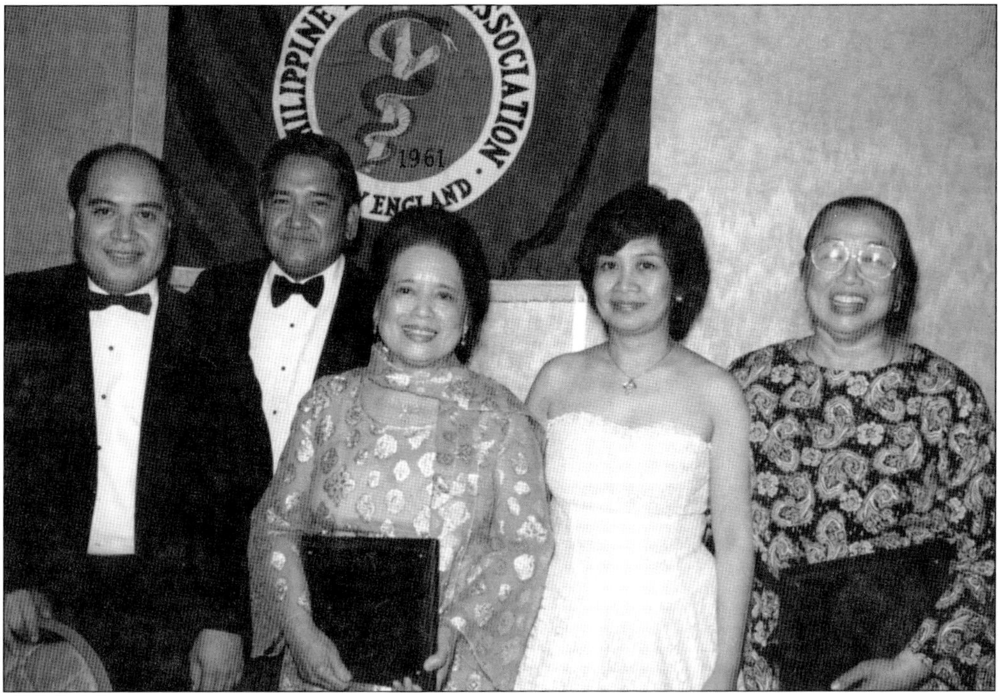

These photographs were taken at the Philippine Medical Association of New England ball in 1987. Above, from left to right are Aaron Friedman, Dr. Ceferino F. Bague, Catalina Cornista Friedman, Dr. Marietta Bague, and Dr. Lucy Lee. Below are the officers of PMANE. (Both, courtesy of Bernadette M. Bague.)

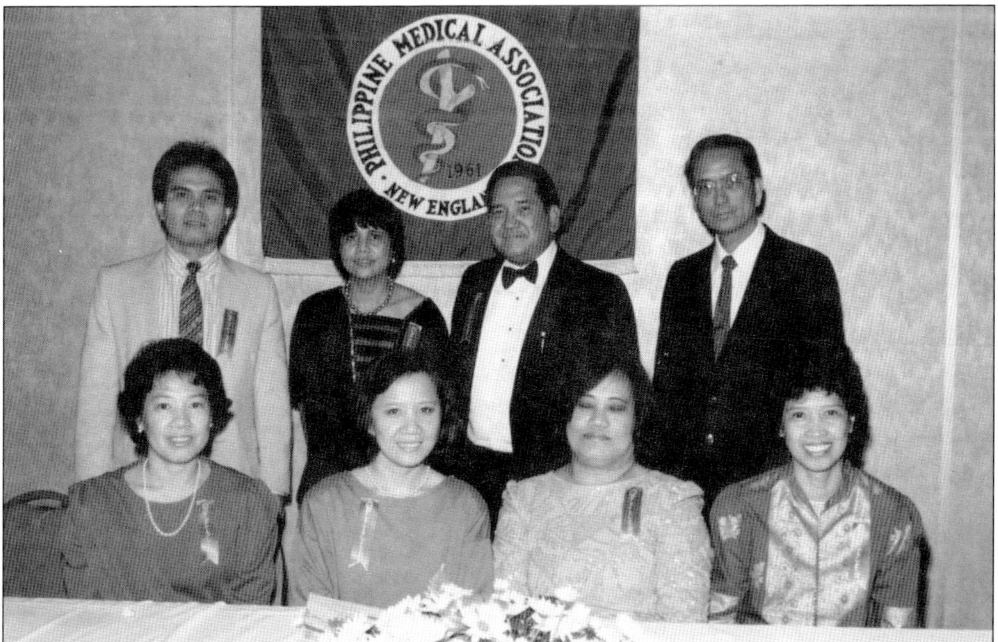

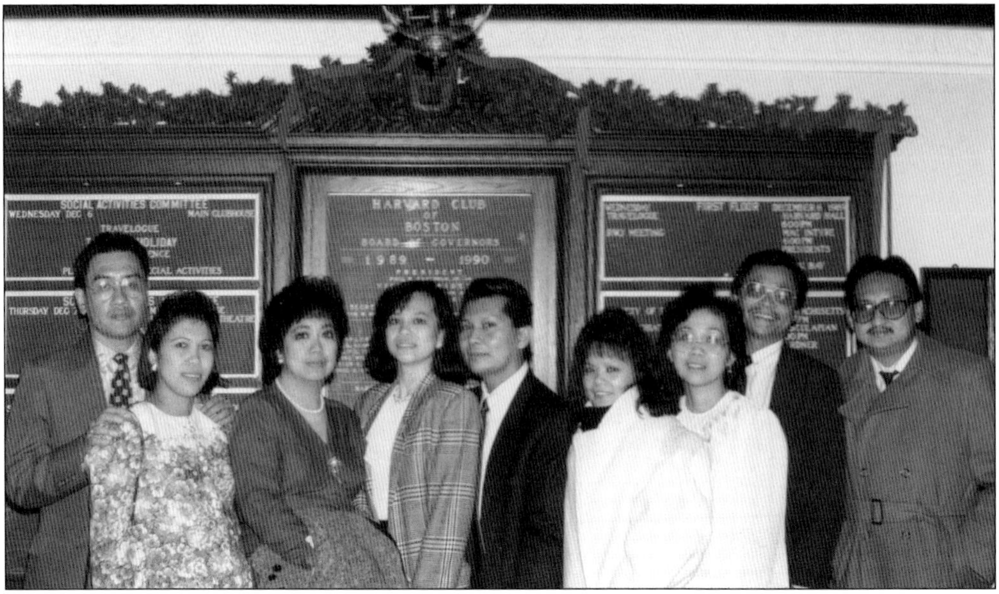

These psychiatrists came to Massachusetts from the Philippines to train at the Veterans Affairs Boston Harvard South Shore psychiatry residency program. This photograph with their spouses was taken in 1989 at a Christmas party at the Harvard Club in Boston. From left to right are Nestor and Dr. Fe Festin, Dr. Luz Dizon, Carisa and Dr. Danny Mendoza, Dr. Susan Yason, Dr. Jocelyn and Noel Ulanday, and Dr. Leo Yason. (Courtesy of Dr. Fe Festin.)

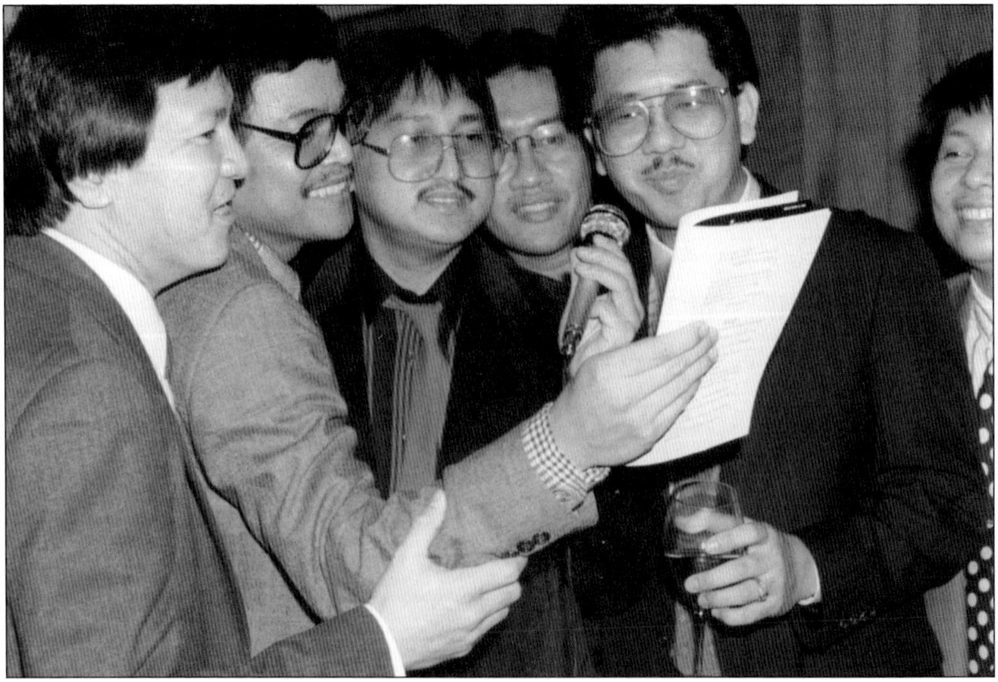

During a Christmas party in 1988, these psychiatrists treated the crowd with a favorite pastime: karaoke. From left to right are Alex Ziga, Noel Ulanday, Leo Yason, Nestor Festin, Alfredo Chan, and Danny Mendoza. (Courtesy of Dr. Fe Festin.)

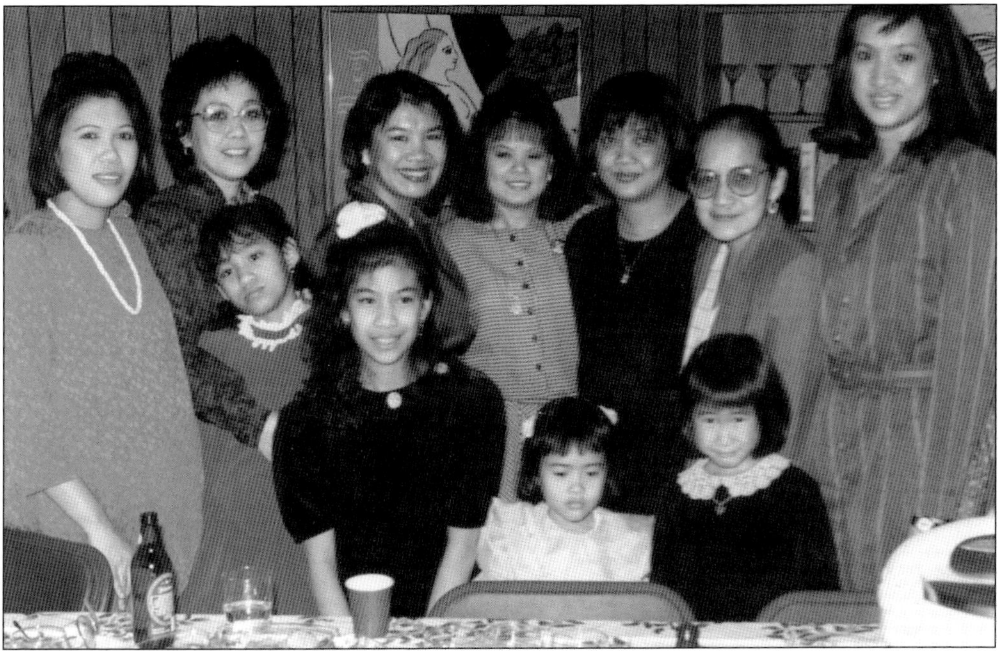

Christmas was an important time for the families of Filipino psychiatrists who arrived in the 1980s to get together and let their children get to know one another. Often, traditional Filipino food was served. Below, the Festin and Ulanday families pose together in 1988. (Both, courtesy of Dr. Fe Festin.)

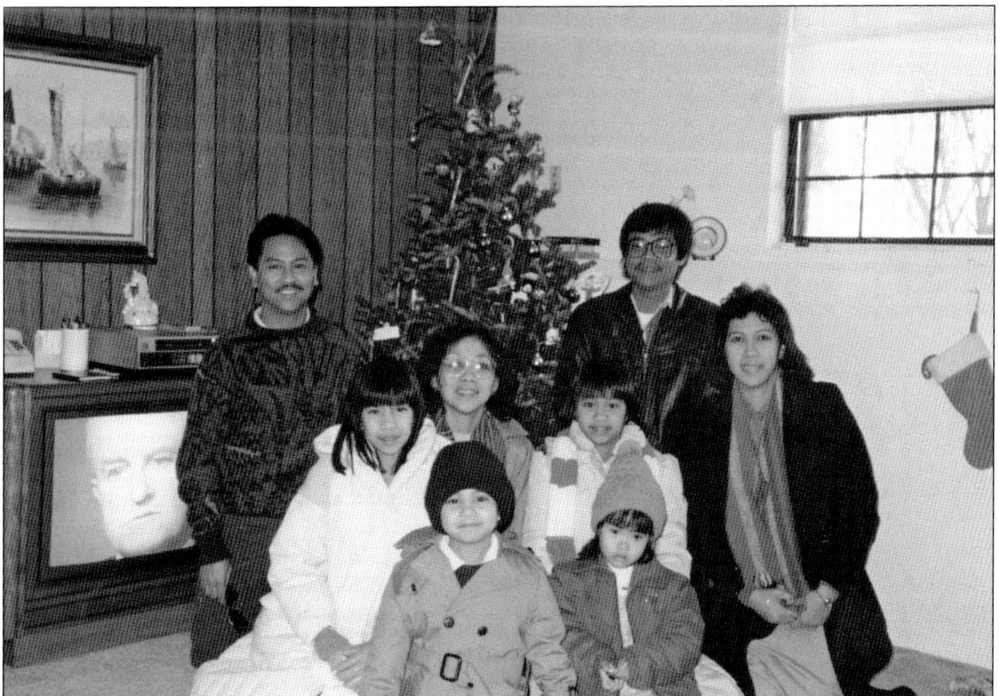

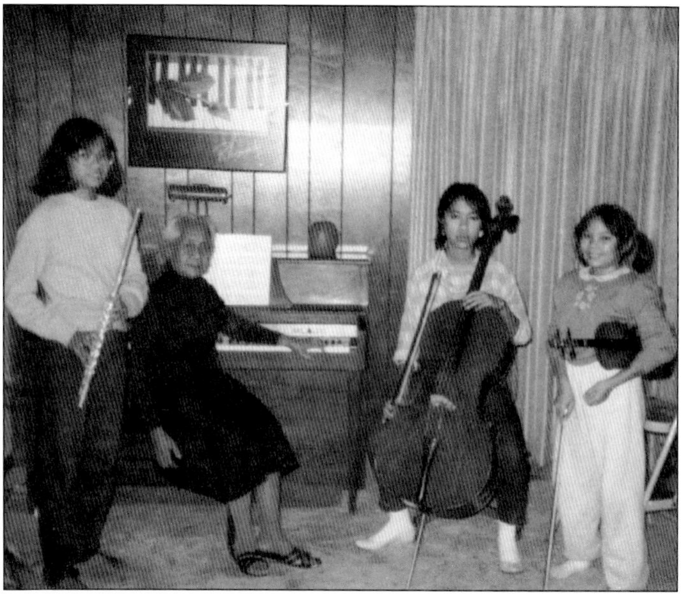

Irene Navarro Gamalinda (piano) visited her grandchildren Grace (flute), Mary (cello), and Liza (viola) in Easton. Her father, Capt. Pedro B. Navarro, was part of the famed Philippine Constabulary Band when they played at Boston's Symphony Hall in 1909. Her stories about Navarro and the band inspired Mary Talusan to write the book *Instruments of Empire: Filipino Musicians, Black Soldiers, and Military Band Music during US Colonization of the Philippines.*

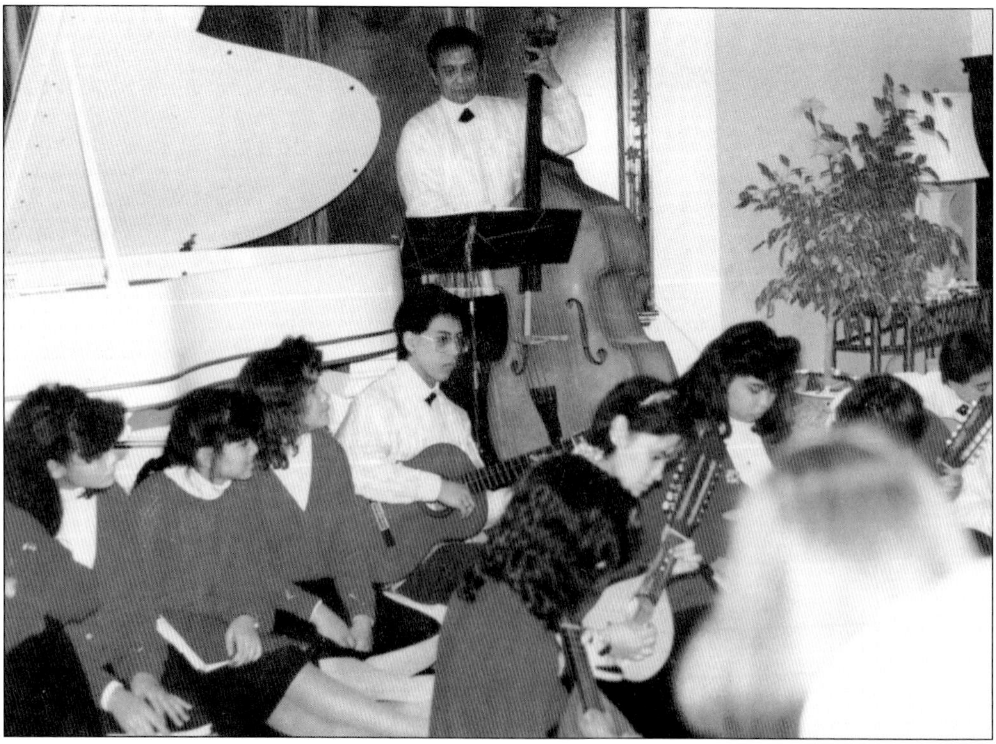

A *rondalla* ensemble and chorus from Iskwelahang Pilipino (Filipino school) perform Filipino Christmas songs at a holiday party in 1988 hosted by Dr. Almario and Norma Bucal in Sudbury. Mabini Castro is playing the contrabass (stand-up bass). IP is the first and only Filipino school in New England and has brought together many families in the Filipino community to learn about their heritage. (Courtesy of the Bucal family.)

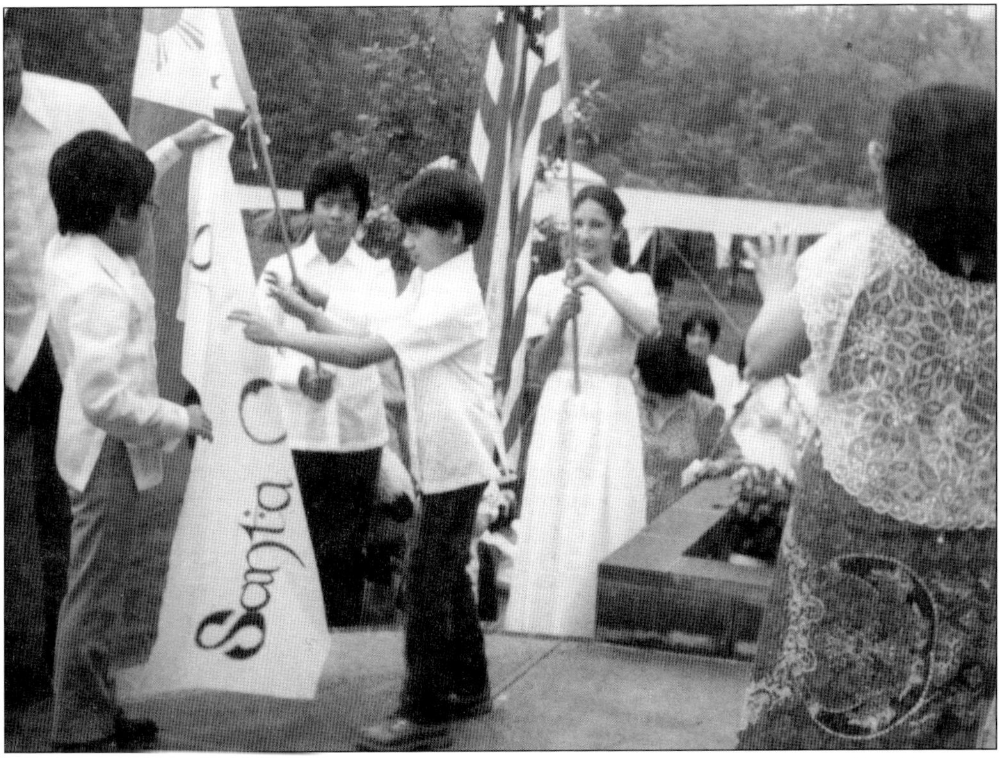

The Santacruzan is a ritual pageant held at the end of the Flores de Mayo ("flowers of May") festival celebrated throughout the Philippines, which was introduced by the Spanish to honor the Virgin Mary. This one was held in 1983 by Iskwelahang Pilipino at the Sons of Mary Missionary Society in Framingham. Tina Casper and Christian Castro hold the flags while Antonio Endriga and an unidentified person unfurl a banner. Rosalinda Morales Goulet, the founder of IP, stands at left. Below, another Santacruzan in 1984 was held at the Perkins School of the Blind in Watertown, where Cristina Castro worked. Tina Casper (center) represents Reyna Elena, mother of Constantine the Great, who is honored for finding the True Cross in the fourth century. From left to right are Len Casper, Maria Garcia, Eddie Endriga, Cindy Marmol, and Julie Ott. (Both, courtesy of Linda Ty-Casper.)

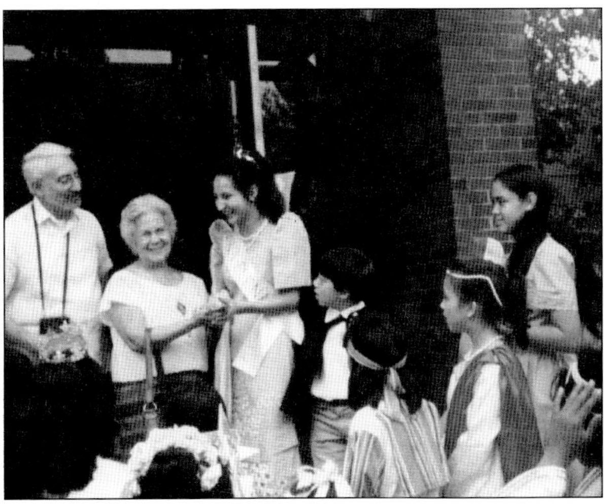

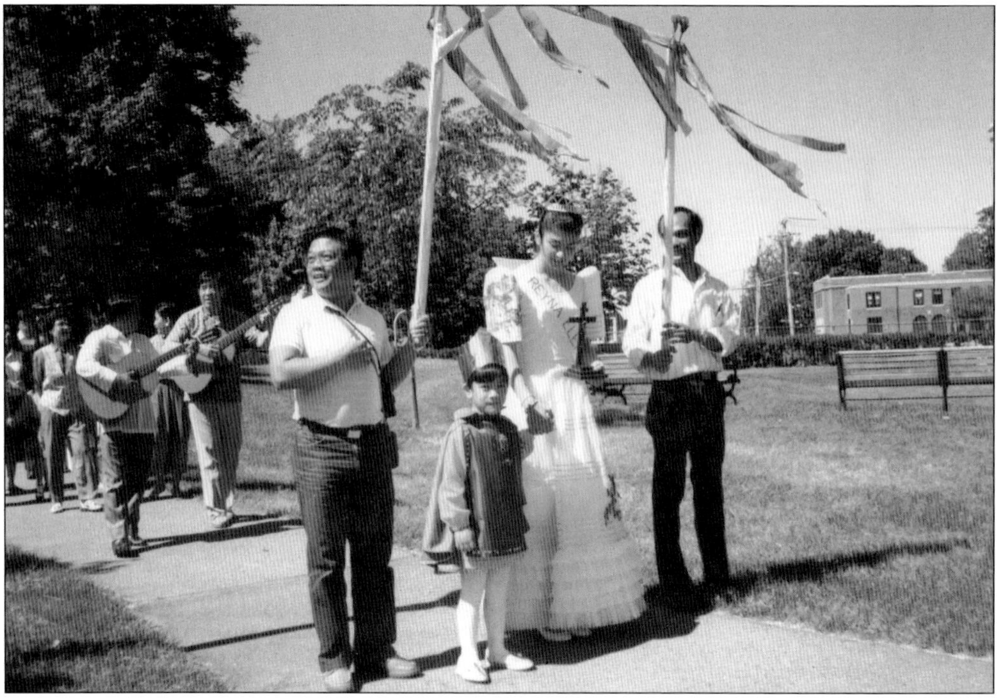

This Santacruzan procession took place at Eliot Church and Farlow Park in Newton during the late 1980s by Iskwelahang Pilipino. Reyna Elena is represented by Elsa Christiansen Janairo, and a boy, ? Pring, plays Constantine, who became the great Roman emperor. Holding the arch are Phil Pring on the left and Arnold Barayuga on the right. On the guitars are Romy Galiguis and Dr. Raul Endriga. (Courtesy of Rosalinda J. Ott.)

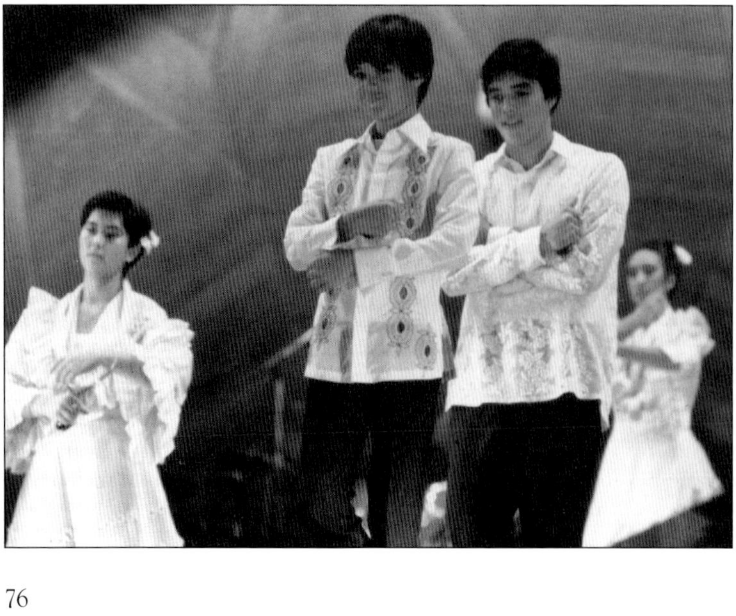

Students of Iskwelahang Pilipino learn traditional folk dances from the Philippines. In this photograph, from left to right, Martina Todd, Dino Korten, Scott Yusah, and Patricia Endriga dance the Maria Clara dressed in traditional Spanish-influenced attire during the 1980s. (Courtesy of Rosalinda J. Ott.)

Iskwelahang Pilipino students learn about the diverse cultures of the Philippines. They perform a dance that hails from the Kalinga, people of the Cordillera highlands. The Banga-Salidsid is a choreographic suite influenced by the Bayanihan Philippine Dance Company to demonstrate the grace of young women who balance *banga*, or tall pots, on their heads combined with a courtship dance *salidsid* using traditional woven cloth. (Courtesy of Rosalinda J. Ott.)

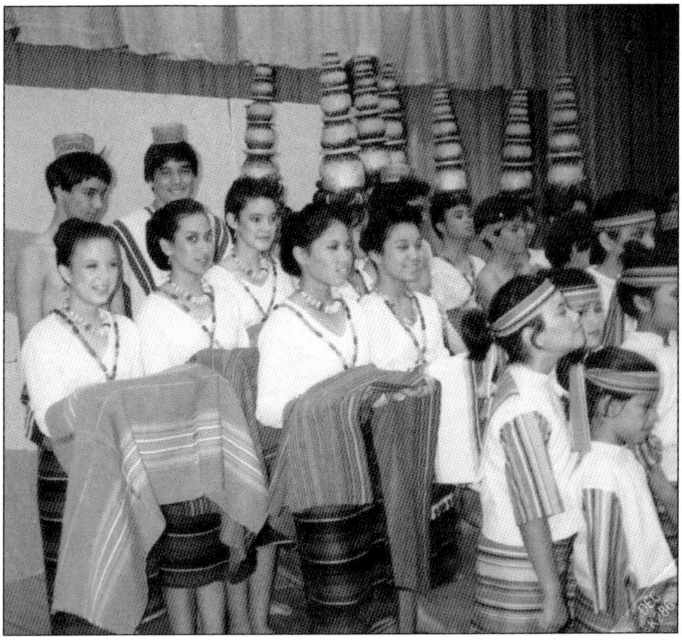

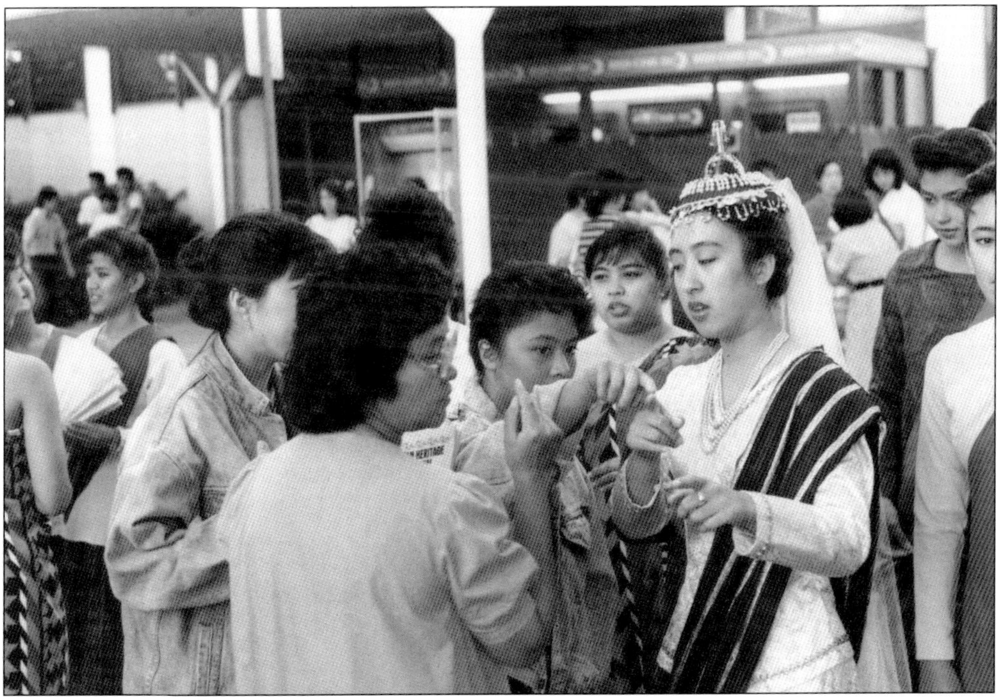

Iskwelahang Pilipino dancers get ready to perform for an Asian heritage cultural show in Boston in 1989. Trish Endriga (center) is dressed as a princess for the dance Singkil, traditionally from Maranao (Muslim Filipino) culture. The modern choreography emulated by folk dance groups was made popular by the Philippine Bayanihan Dance Company. She is assisted by Linda Ott (back to camera), Christ-Anne Castro (center), and Cynthia Endriga (standing behind Trish, facing camera). (Courtesy of Dr. Rosalinda J. Ott.)

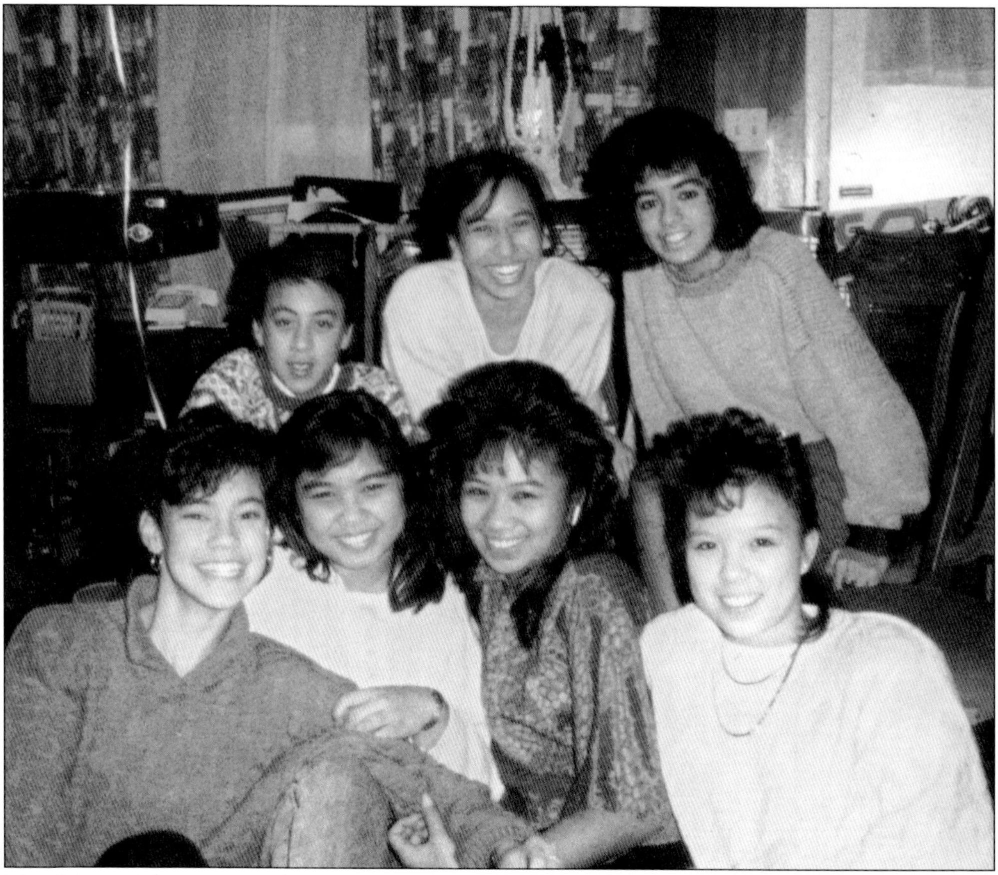

Iskwelahang Pilipino created a space for children of Filipino immigrants to form lifelong friendships. In this 1987 photograph are, from left to right, (first row) Michelle Ott, Marie Endriga, Arlene Amo, and Cindy Marmol; (second row) Eddie Endriga, Krishna Butani, and Melo-Rissa Abriam. (Courtesy of Dr. Rosalinda J. Ott.)

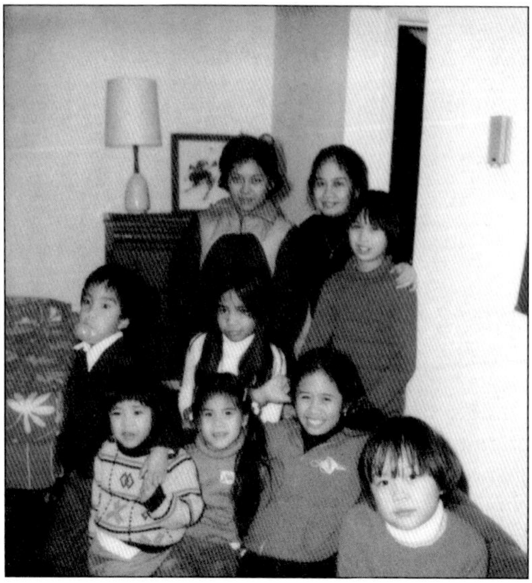

This group of friends, children of post-1965 Filipino immigrants, thought of each other as cousins. They are pictured visiting Loon Mountain in New Hampshire in 1982. From left to right are (first row) Ruby Bayog, Stephanie Bucal, Berni Bague, and Larissa Layug; (second row) Franz Bayog and Emi Bague; (third row) unidentified, Dr. Marietta Bague, and Cyd Bucal. (Courtesy of Bernadette M. Bague.)

Six

Expressing Community Pride 1990s

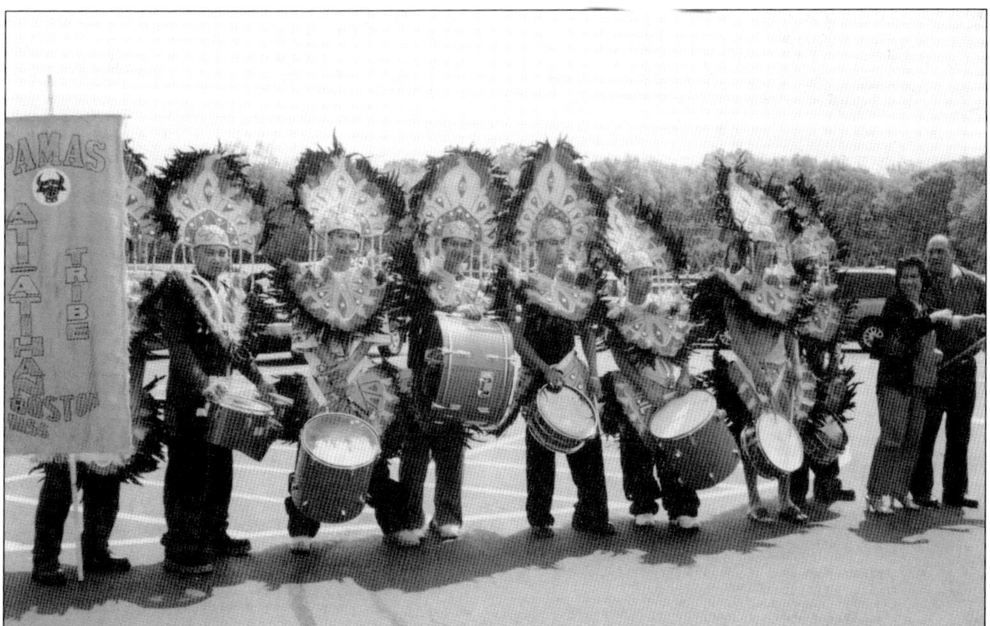

This is a photograph of the first Ati-Atihan celebration held in Massachusetts in 1998, organized by the Pilipino-American Association of New England. The Ati-Atihan is a Philippine festival that takes place every January to celebrate the Santo Niño or Infant Jesus. It originates in the province of Aklan on the island of Panay and features street parades with colorful costumes and marching bands to accompany stylized dancing. (Courtesy of Aida Kalb.)

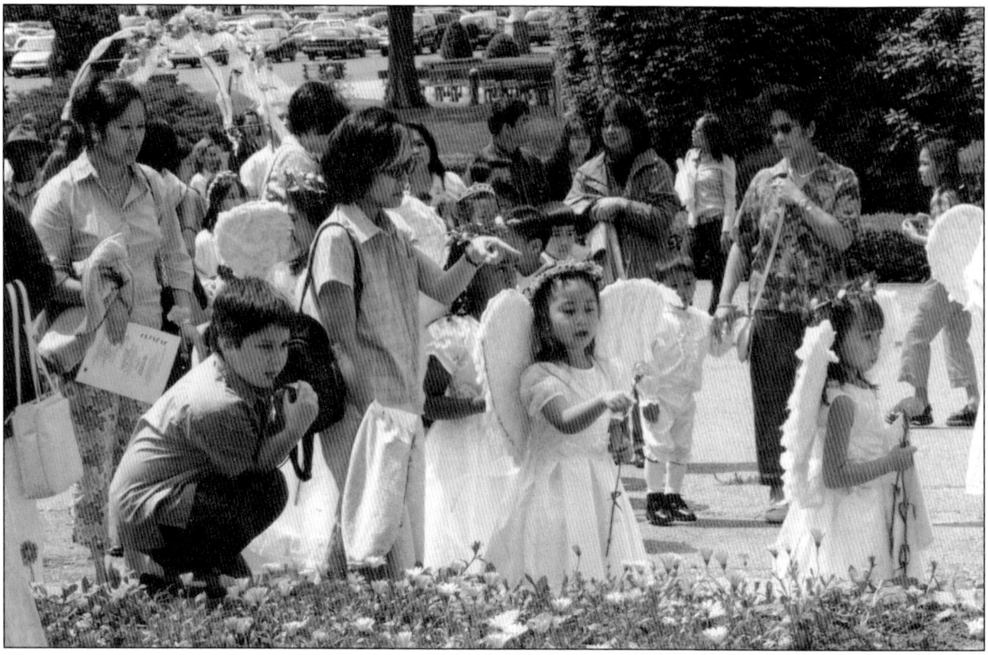

These photographs of the Santacruzan parade held at the National Shrine of Our Lady of La Salette in Attleboro were taken in 1993. The celebration was made possible through the efforts of Gloria Platon and the Santo Niño Prayer Group. Preceding the procession, a novena, or prayer lasting nine days, was held. Below, Greia Lyn Amarra (Marlow) is holding the cross, while Leia Amarra (Balmforth) carries a statue of the Blessed Virgin Mary. (Both, courtesy of Leila C. and Gregorio A. Amarra.)

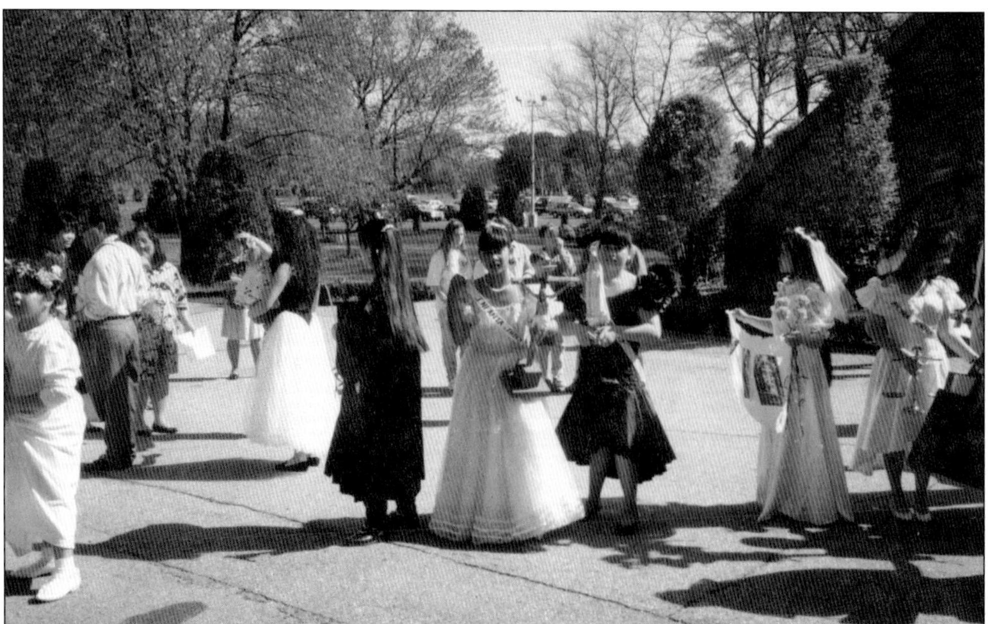

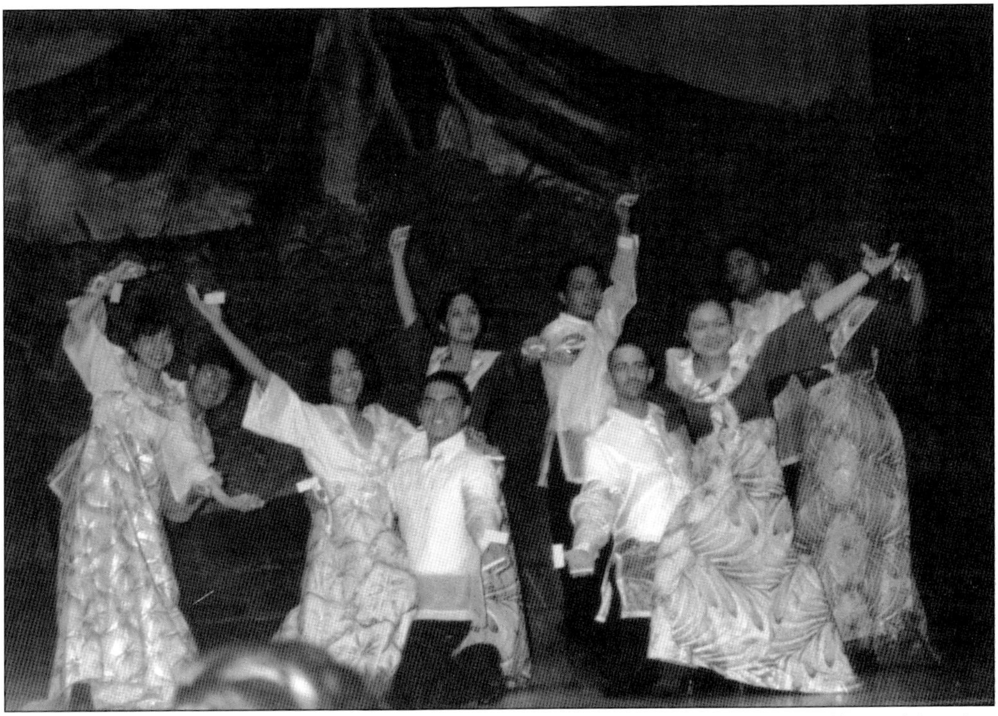

These photographs were taken in 1998 during a cultural show held at Mass College of Art that featured a cast from the Philippines. The performance was directed by James Bertram Reuter SJ, who was an American Jesuit Catholic priest living in the Philippines. He taught at Ateneo de Manila University and was a well-known writer, director, and producer in theater, radio, and film. Below, the visiting group recruited youngsters from Pilipino-American Association of New England to join their performance including Jessamyn Celoza (left) and Greg Lorenz (right). (Both, courtesy of Leila C. and Gregorio A. Amarra.)

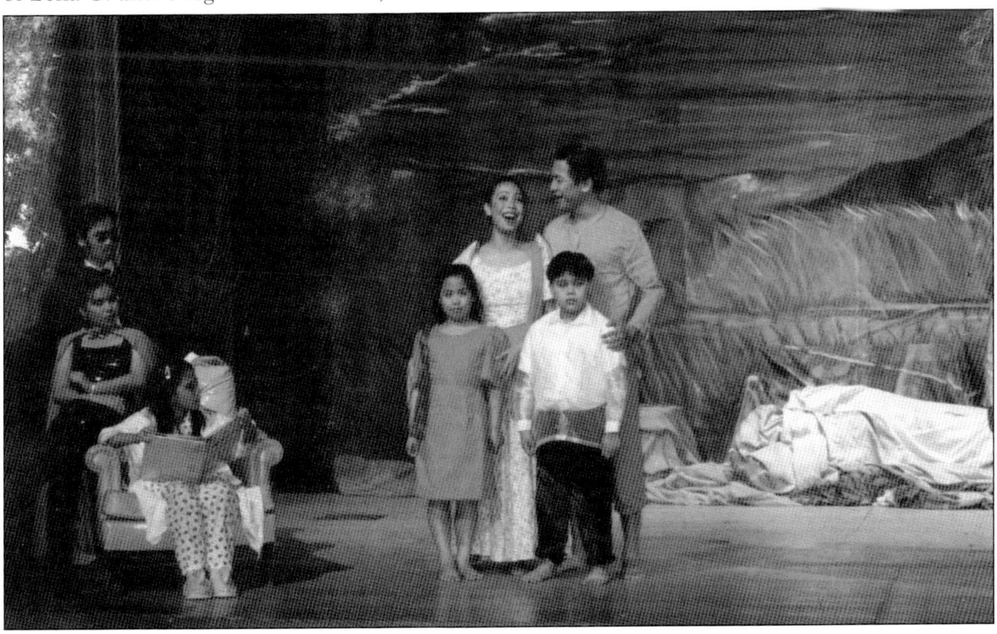

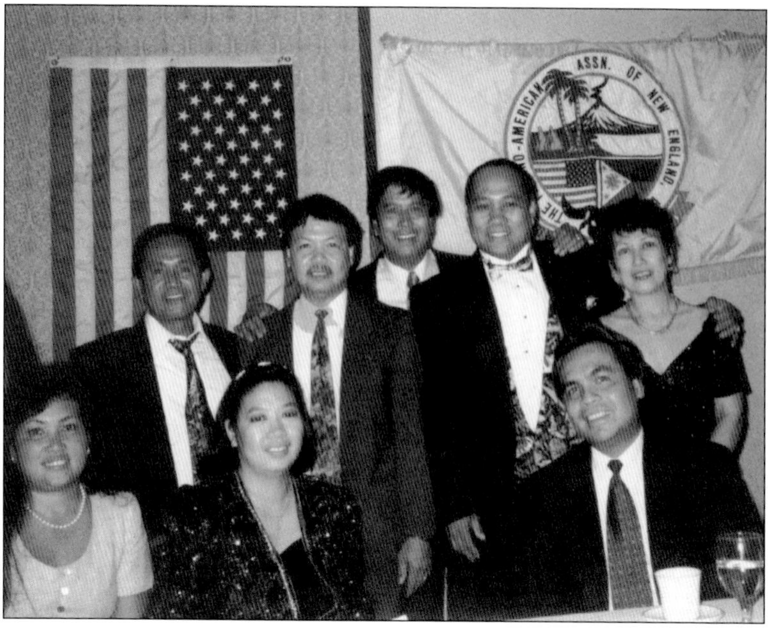

This photograph was taken during the induction of Pilipino-American Association of New England officers in 1991. Francisco "Frank" Celazo, standing second from the left, was a founding member in 1978 along with Antonio "Tony" Mateo, standing second from the right. Both served in the US Coast Guard. (Courtesy of Francisco Celazo.)

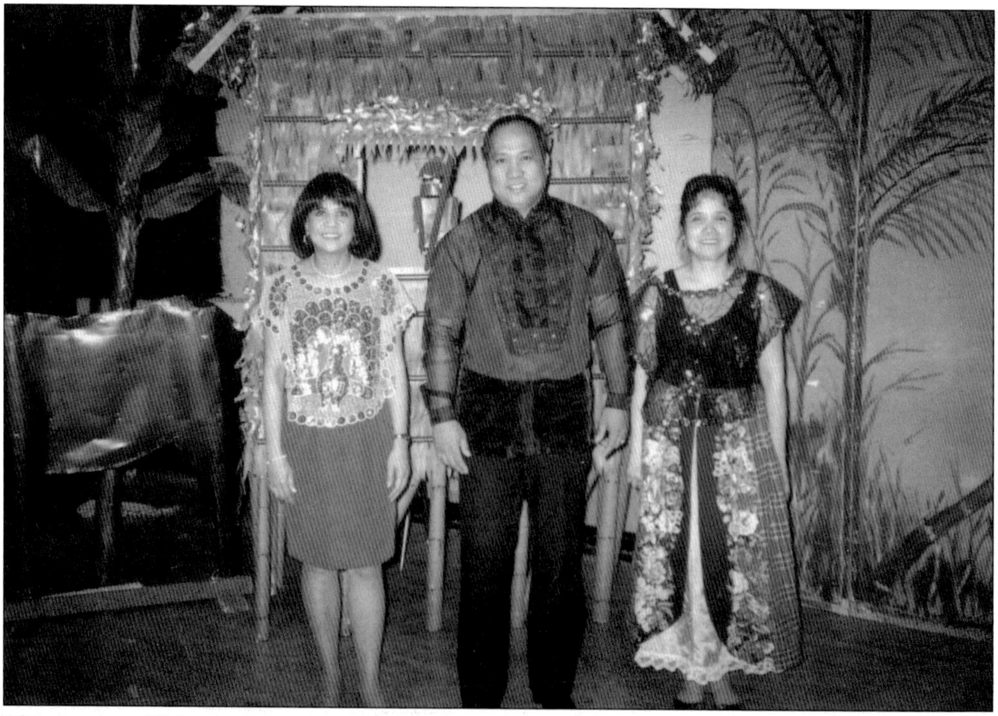

This image of Pilipino-American Association of New England members was taken in 1995 at Randolph High School. From left to right are Flor Escobar, Tony Mateo, and Aida Kalb. (Courtesy of Aida Kalb.)

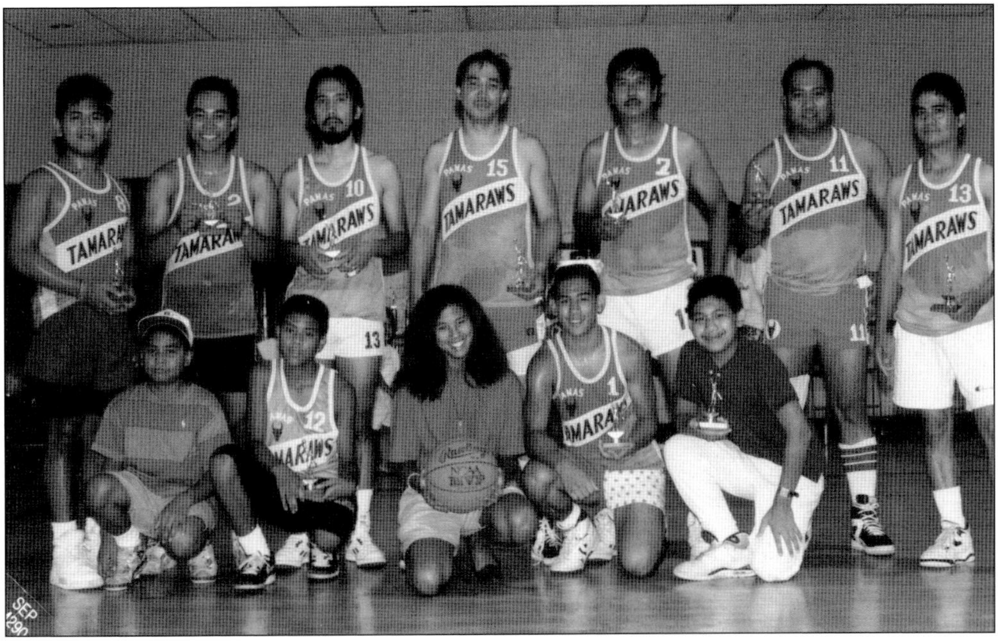

The Pilipino-American Association of New England sponsored basketball games for Filipino American youth. The photograph, taken during the 1990s, is of team Tamaraws, named after a buffalo found on the island of Mindoro. Standing second from the right is Tony Mateo, cofounder of PAMAS. Ligaya Lauron, daughter of Boston Pops flautist Ildefonso Lauron, is seated at the center. (Courtesy of Angelito Santos.)

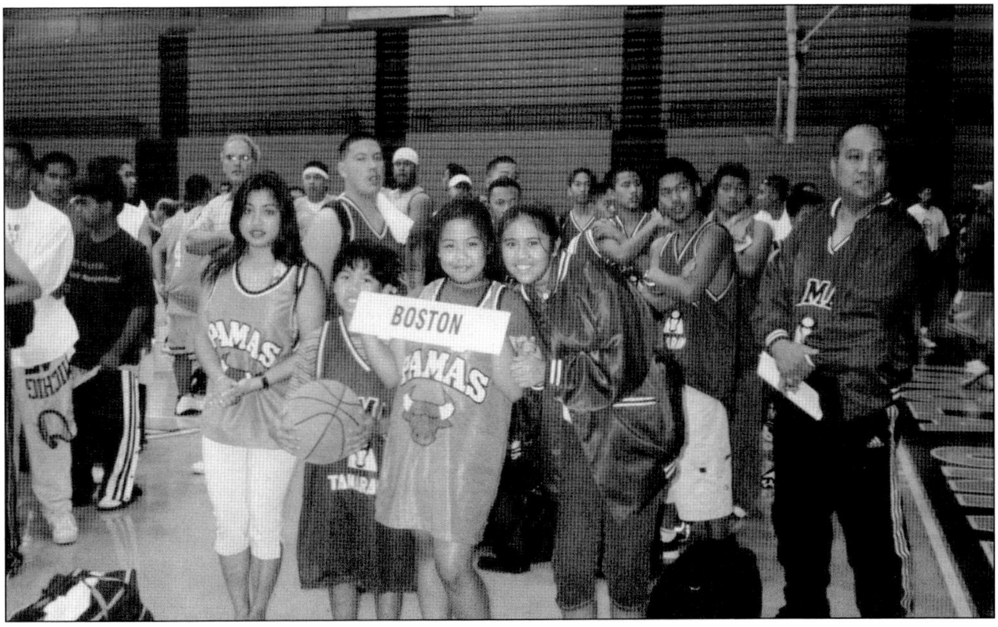

The PAMAS basketball team Tamaraws traveled to Detroit in 1997 to play other Filipino American teams. They held up a "Boston" sign to represent their hometown. (Courtesy of Francisco Celazo.)

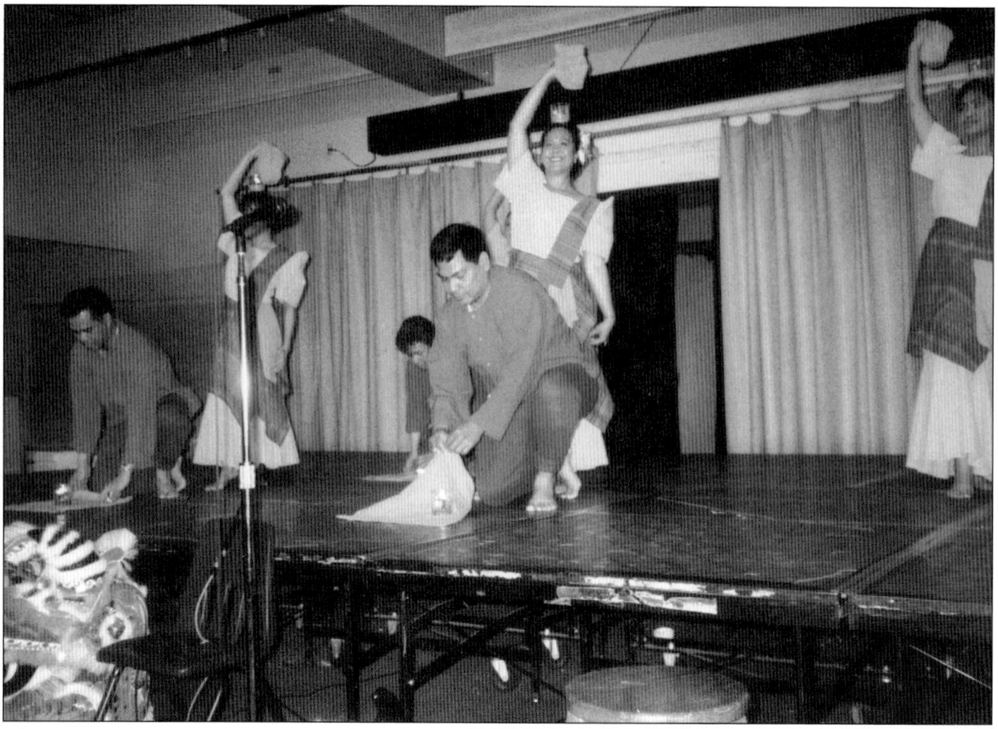

These two photographs show a cultural performance in 1987 by the Philippine Dance Company of Boston, now Philippine Dance and Culture Organization. The group was invited by schools, other organizations, and private parties to showcase Filipino folk dances. Above, they dance Pandanggo sa Ilaw ("fandango with lights"), gracefully balancing lighted candles. Below, they perform Pasigin, a flirtatious dance in which fishermen "catch" young ladies in their nets. (Both, courtesy of Ben Manzano.)

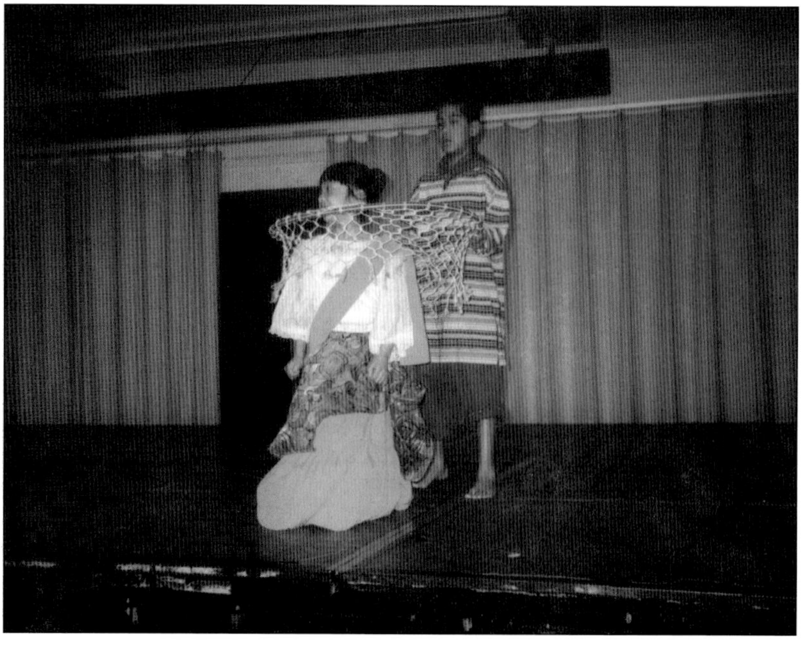

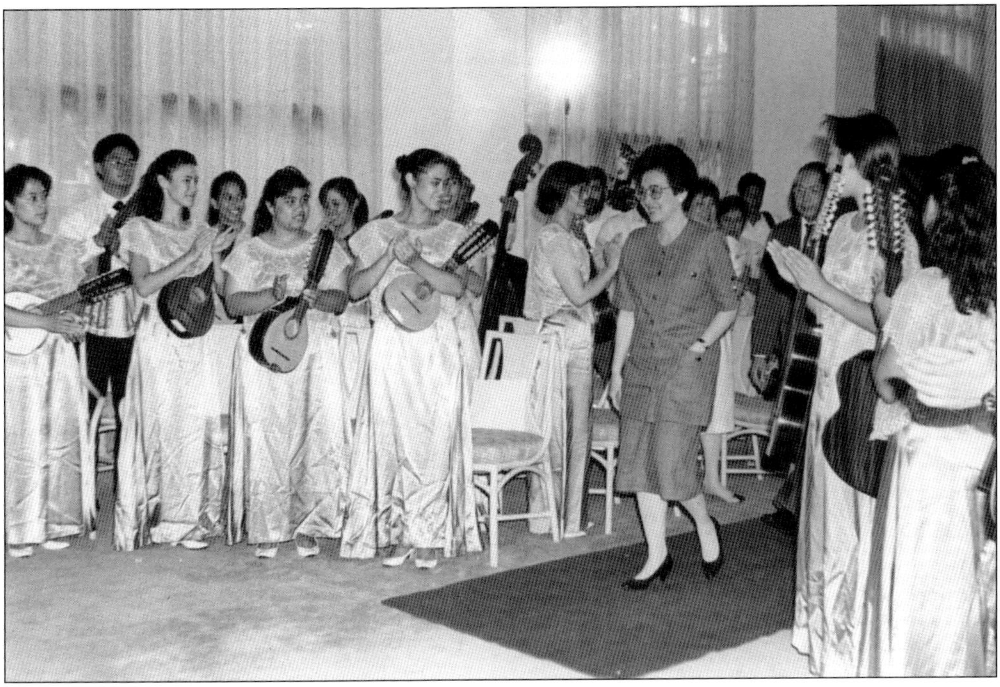

The Iskwelahang Pilipino Rondalla Ensemble of Boston toured the Philippines in 1990. At its performance at Malacañang Palace, the members clap for the entrance of Pres. Corazon Aquino, who lived in Boston while in exile with her family. Below, the group poses on the staircase inside Malacañang Palace with President Aquino (center). Michael Dadap, second from the left, was the founding music director of the ensemble. He studied composition and conducting at Mannes College of Music in New York and is married to the sister of world-renowned cellist Yo-Yo Ma. Rondalla is a traditional Philippine musical ensemble of various-sized plucked stringed instruments. (Both, courtesy of Iskwelahang Pilipino.)

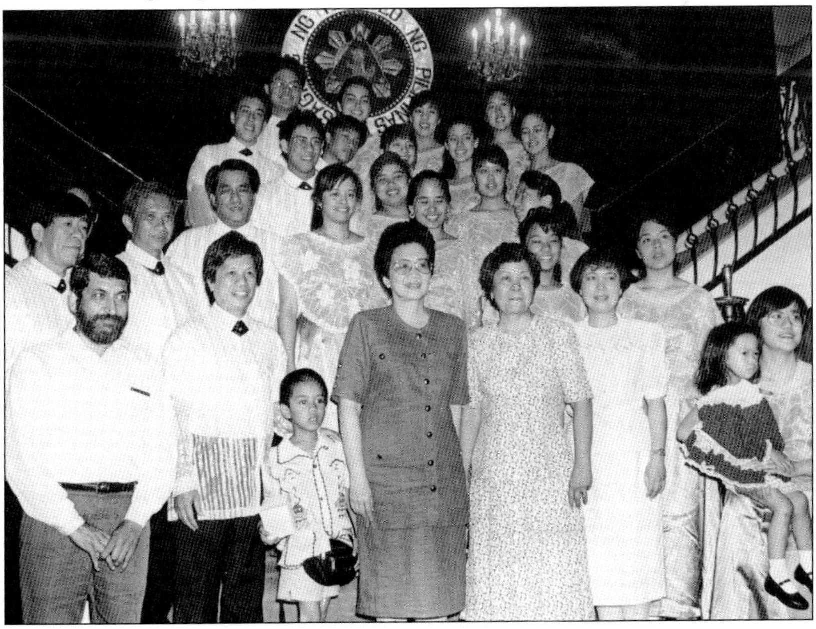

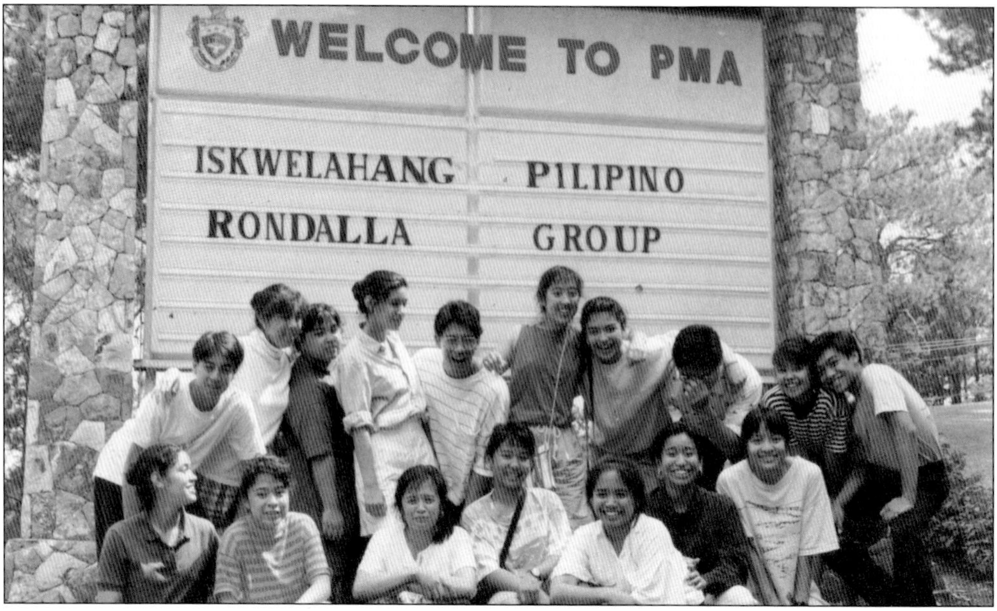

Members of the Iskwelahang Pilipino Rondalla Ensemble of Boston traveled to Baguio, a vacation town in the Cordillera highlands of the Philippines, to perform at the Philippine Military Academy. This photograph was taken during their tour of the Philippines in 1990. (Courtesy of Bernadette M. Bague.)

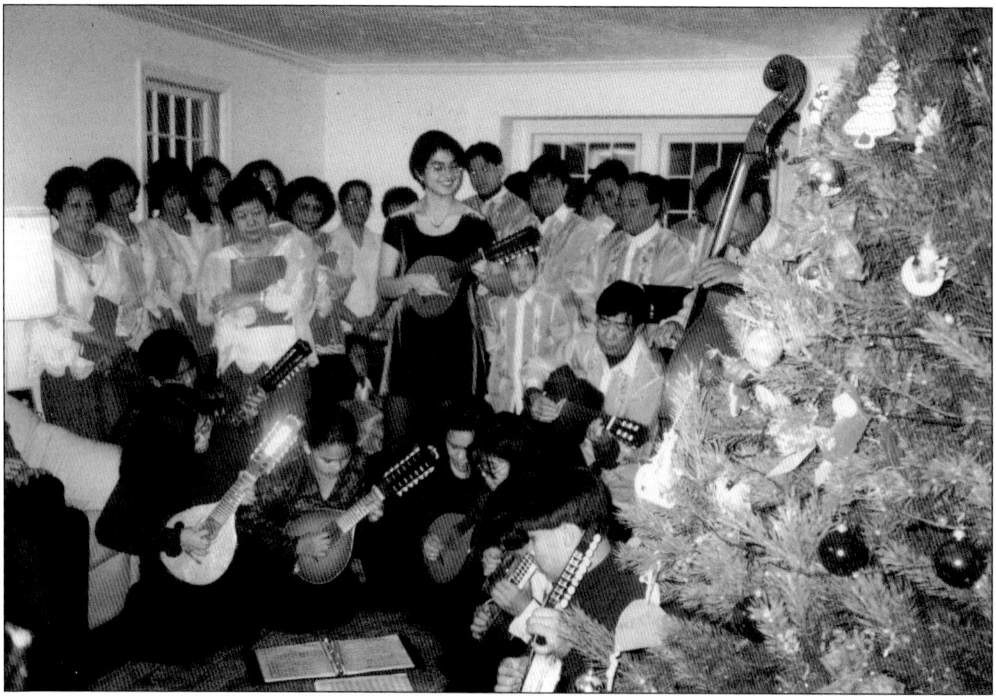

Iskwelahang Pilipino Christmas carolers accompanied by the rondalla ensemble perform at the home of Drs. José "Pepito" and Mariam Villanueva in Lexington on December 6, 1997. Social gatherings during the holidays such as this strengthened the ties between Filipino immigrants and gave their American-born children a chance to experience Filipino traditions. (Courtesy of the Bucal family.)

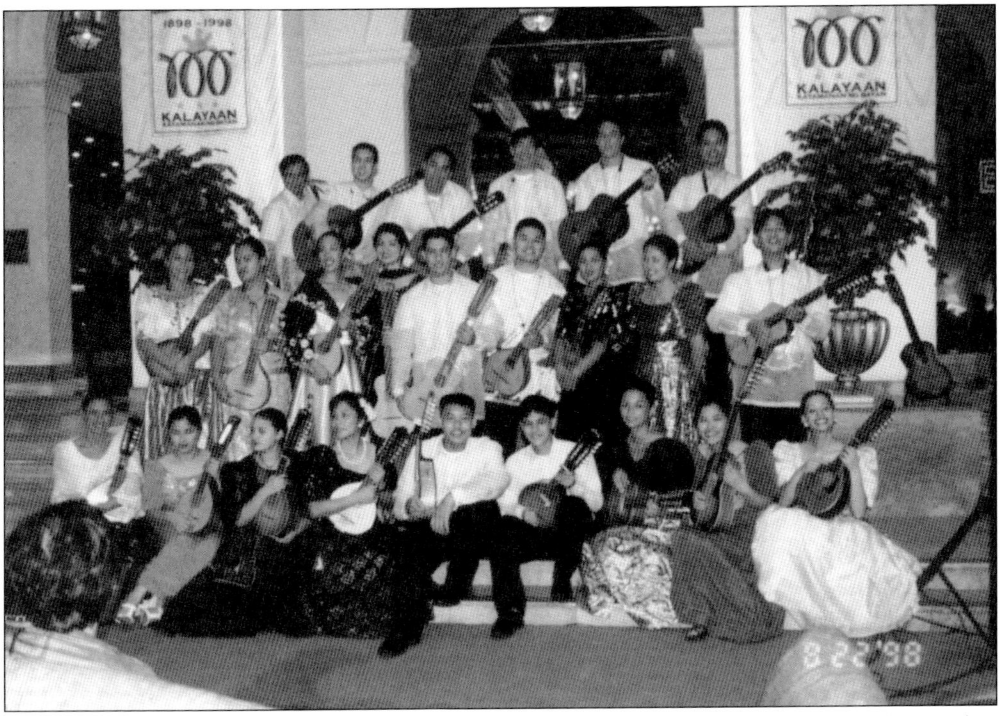

In 1998, the Iskwelahang Pilipino Rondalla Ensemble returned to the Philippines for another tour during the Philippine Centennial, celebrating Philippine independence from Spain in 1898. Above, the members prepare for their performance at Manila Hotel dressed in traditional Filipino attire. Below, they pose amid the scenic hills of the vacation town of Baguio. These photographs were provided by Myra Liwanag, who is the current executive director of Iskwelahang Pilipino. (Both, courtesy of Myra O. Liwanag.)

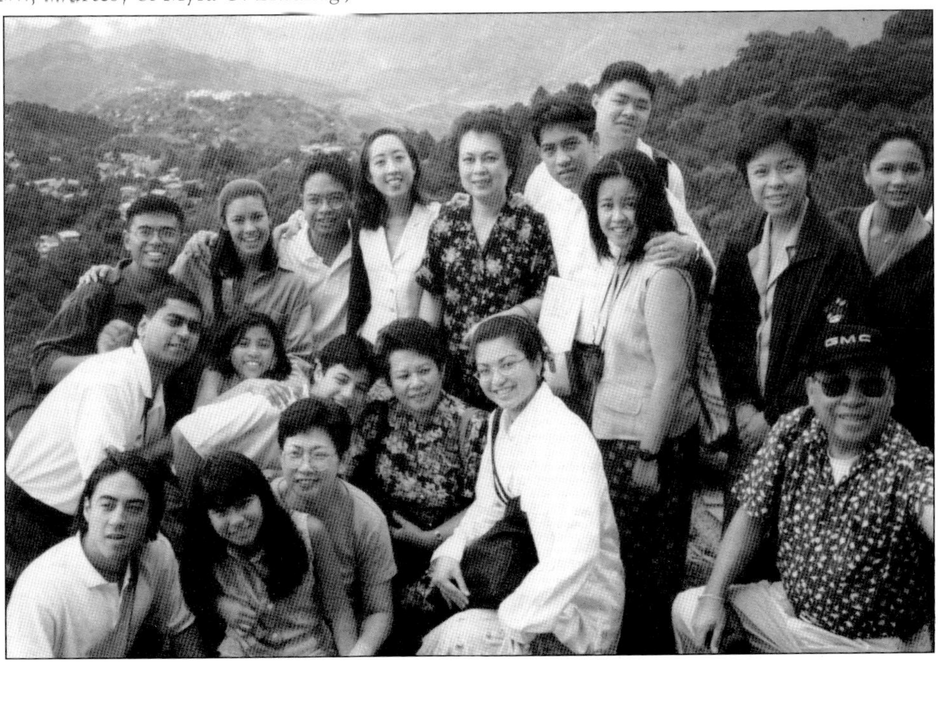

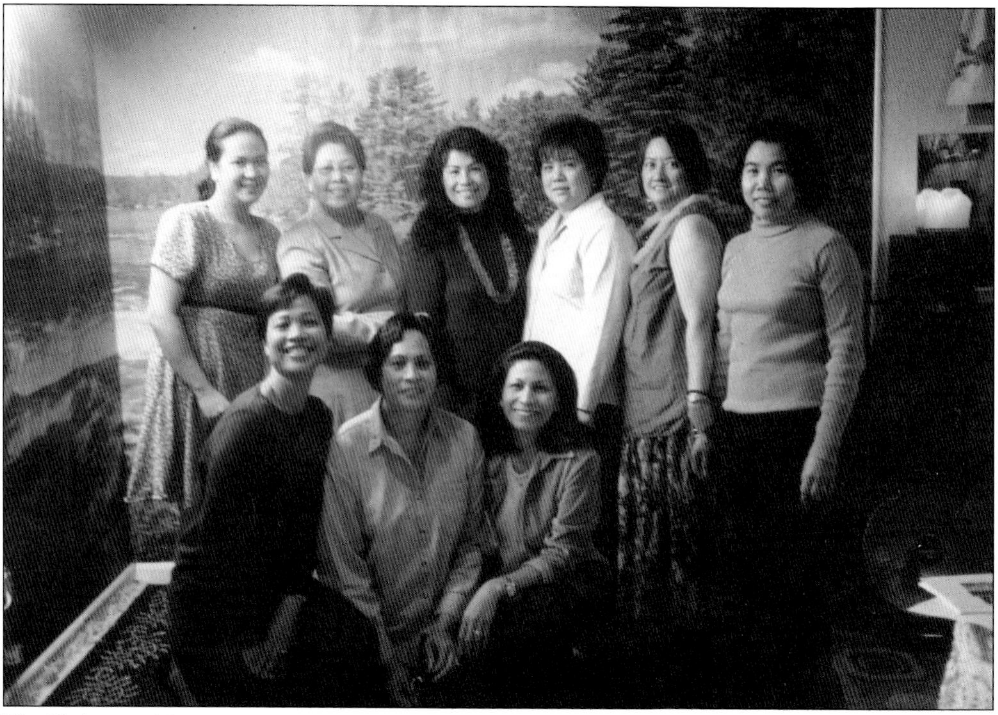

The Philippine Nurses Association of New England, an affiliate of the Philippine Nurses Association of America, was incorporated as a nonprofit in 1990. The organization sponsors education programs, provides networking opportunities, and creates visibility for its members. Above is a photograph of the 1998 officers, all nurses from the Philippines who immigrated to Boston to work in hospitals and settled in various towns to raise their families. Below is a photograph of their annual ball, held in Boston. (Both, courtesy of Rosario "Chit" Abriam.)

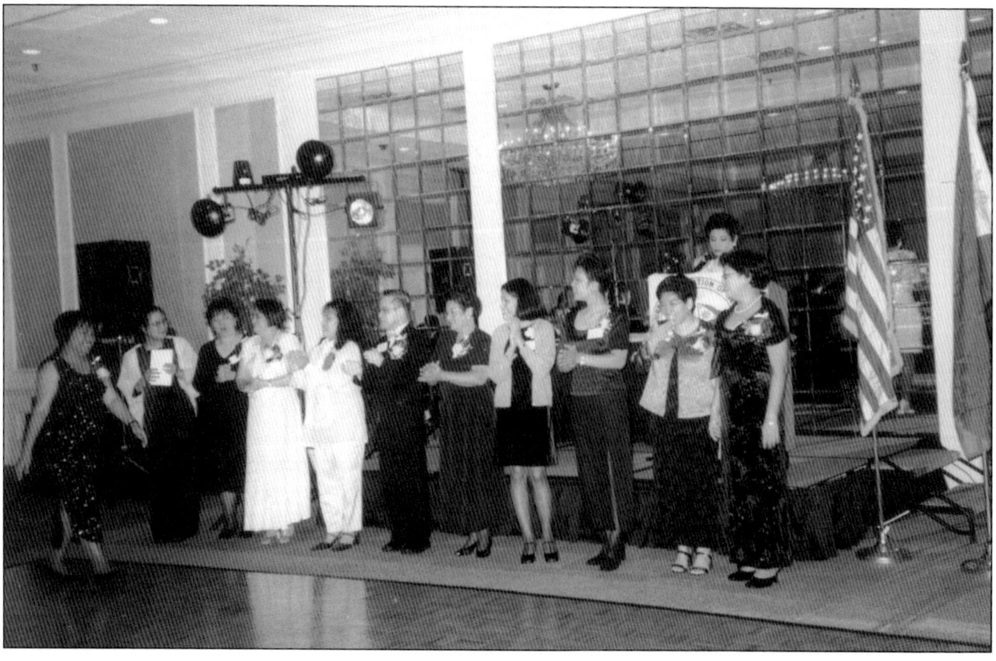

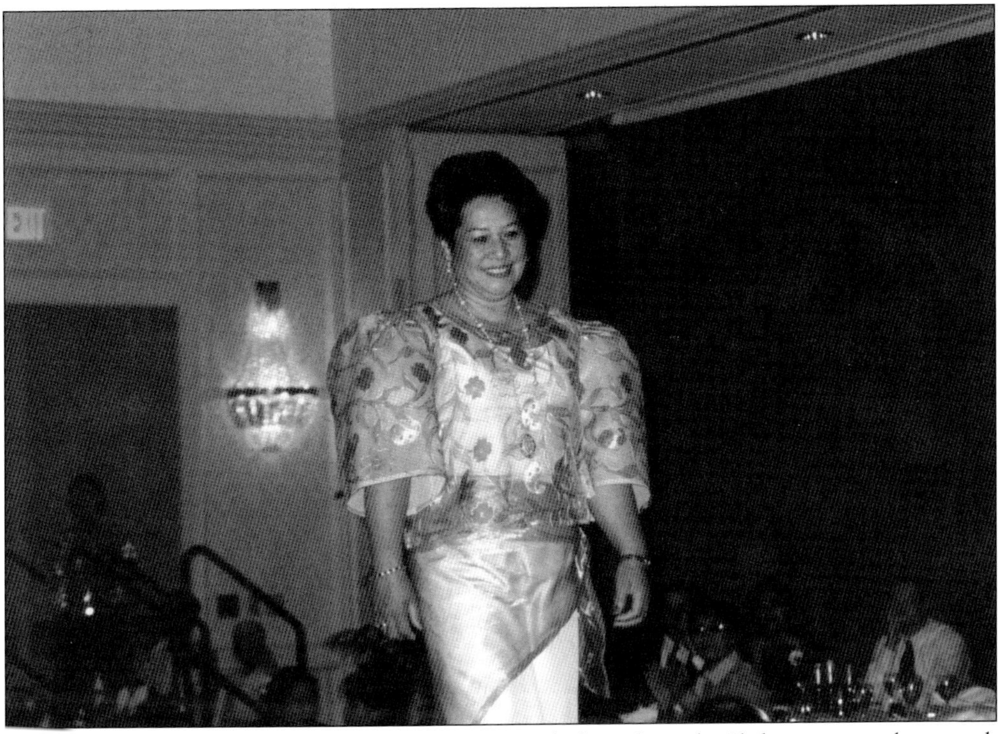

As part of the PNANE annual ball, a fashion show of clothing from the Philippines was showcased. In this photograph, Chit Abriam wears an elegant Filipiniana gown with traditional butterfly sleeves. Below, Chit poses with her husband, Liberato, a civil engineer, and their two children, Glenn and Rissa, who grew up in Natick. She was a registered nurse at the MetroWest Medical Center in Framingham from 1971 until she retired in 2013. (Both, courtesy of Rosario "Chit" Abriam.)

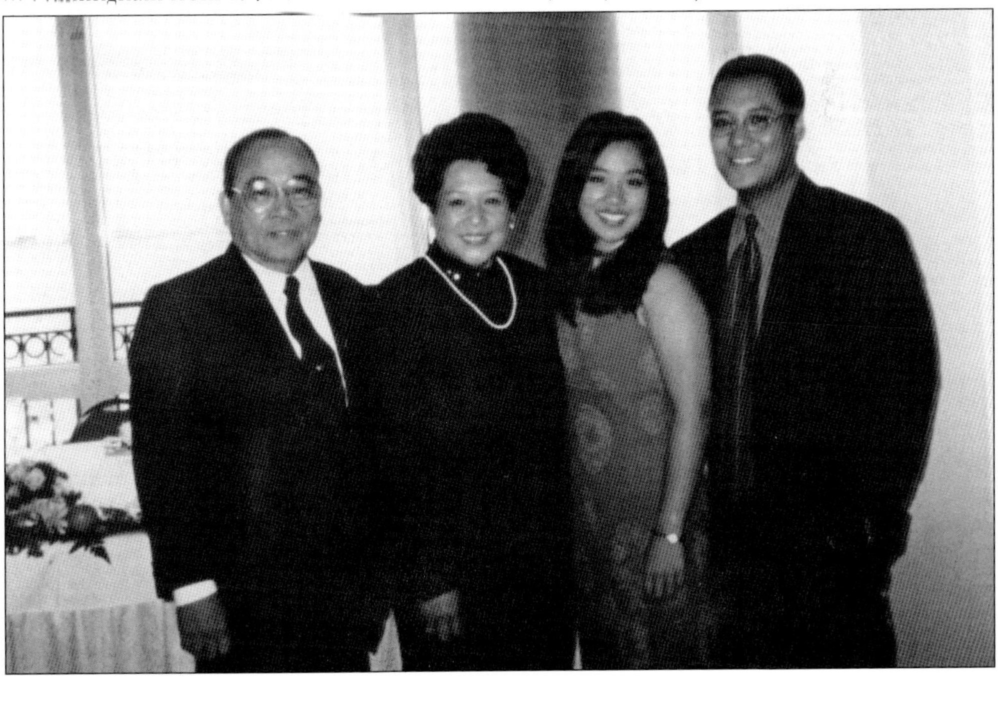

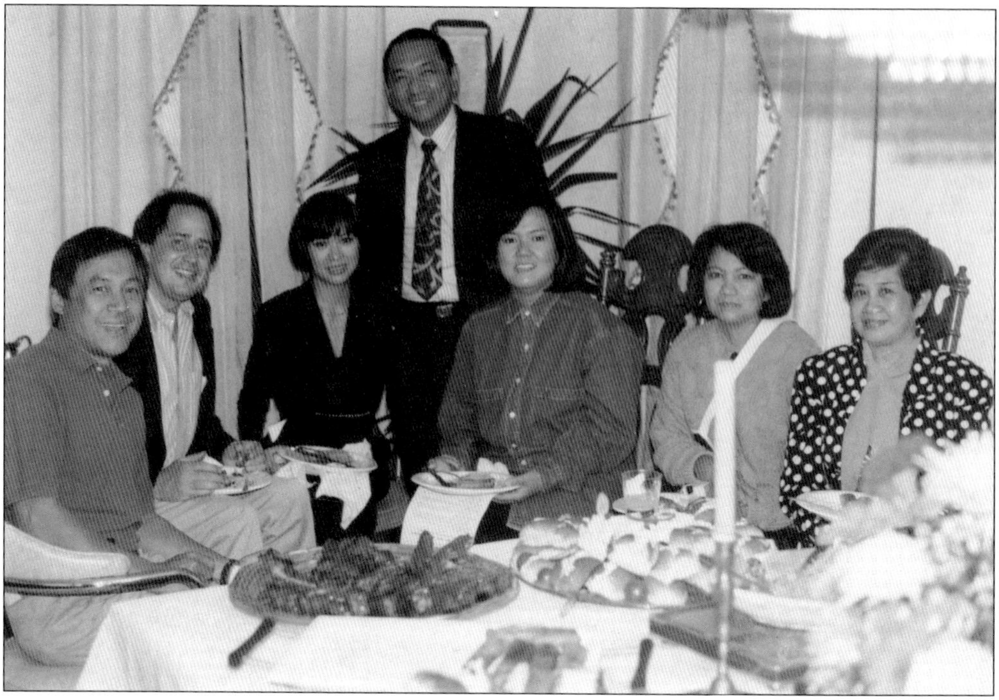

In both photographs, Gen. Eduardo R. Ermita, former executive secretary of the Philippines and spokesperson for Pres. Gloria Arroyo, visited the home of Dr. Almario and Norma Bucal in Sudbury on October 4, 1991. Above, Ermita (standing center) poses with, from left to right, Dr. Winnie Yusah, Stuart Bloom, Maritess Salientes Bloom, Patty Yusah, Dr. Arcel Talusan, and Dr. Marietta Bague. Below, he poses with other members of the Filipino community. (Both, courtesy of the Bucal family.)

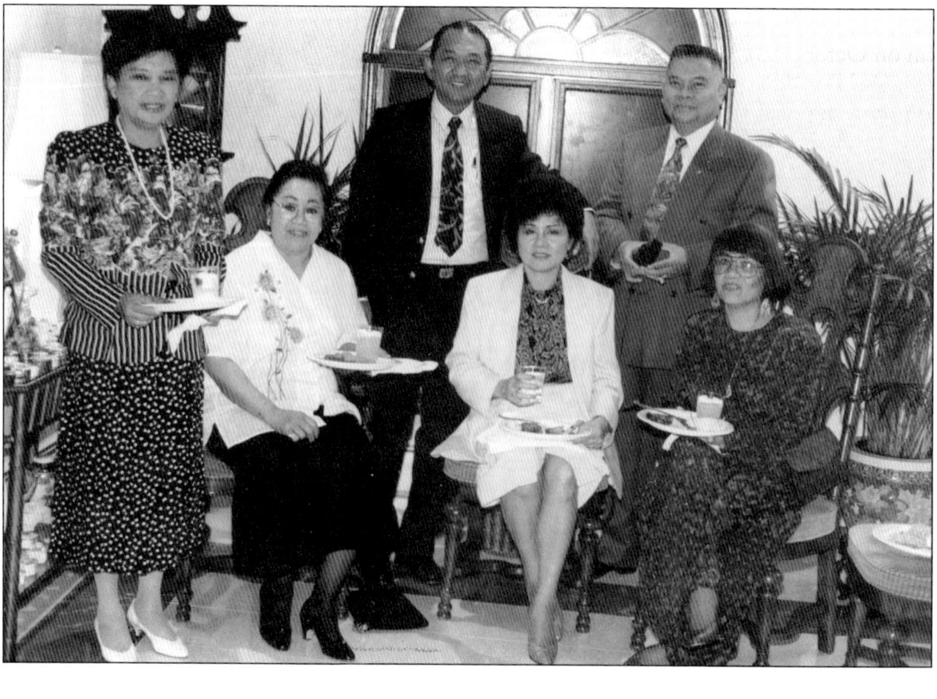

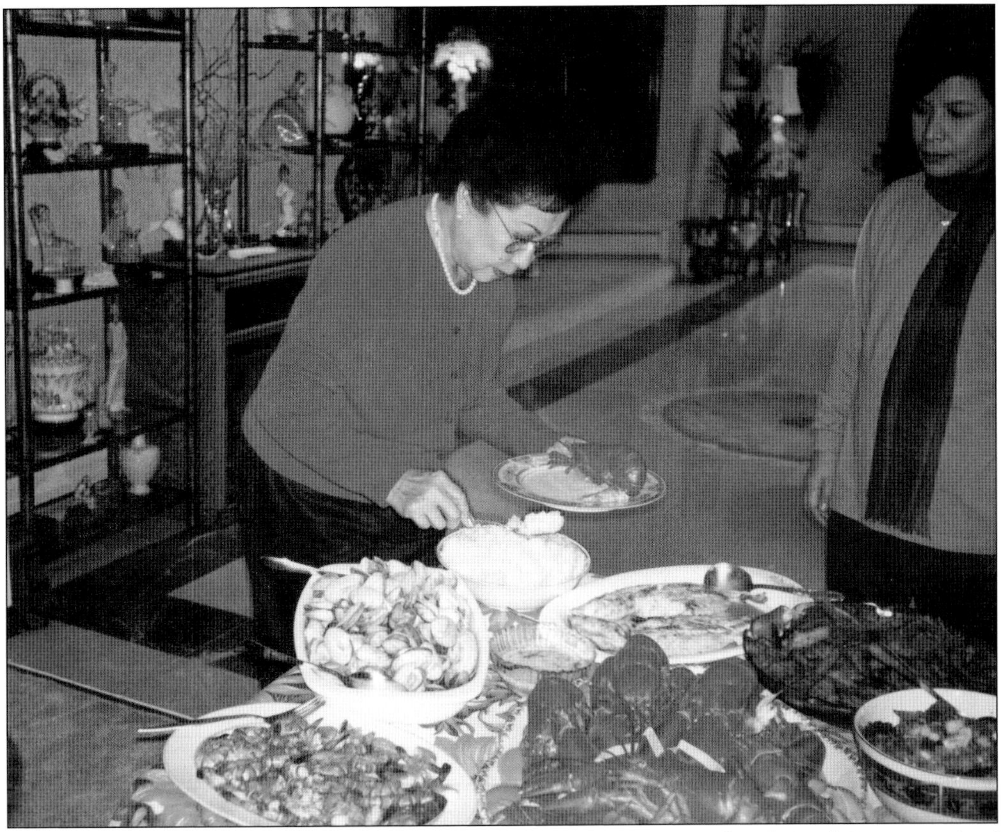

These photographs were taken during a dinner held in honor of Amelita "Ming" Ramos, wife of Pres. Fidel Ramos and first lady of the Philippines from 1992 to 1998. She is treated to Maine lobster and clam chowder along with Filipino dishes at the home of Dr. Almario and Norma Bucal on October 20, 1996. Below, Ming (third from left) poses with, from left to right, Dr. Alice Layug, Cyd Bucal, Norma Bucal, unidentified, Dr. Arcel Talusan, and unidentified. This visit was a homecoming of sorts since Ming studied at Boston University, earning a bachelor of science degree in physical education. (Both, courtesy of the Bucal family.)

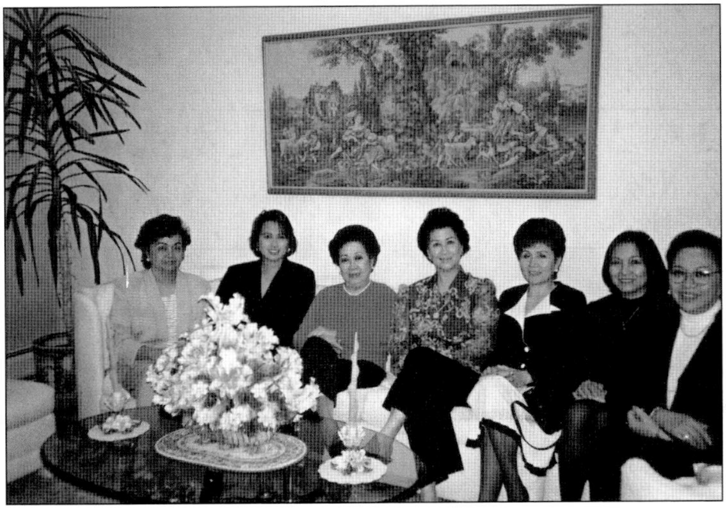

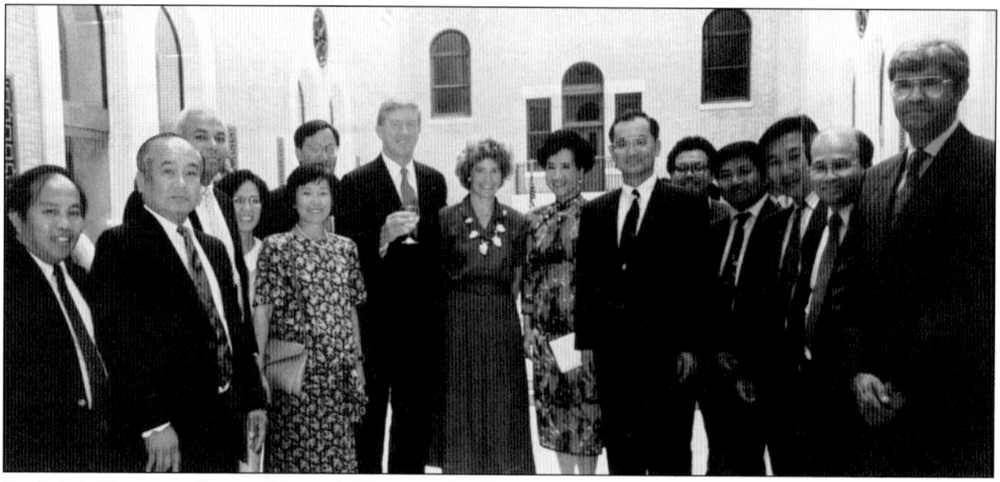

Rudolph Hermosa (second from left) was asked by Gov. William Weld (center) to create an Asian American commission in 1990, the first such commission in Massachusetts. Hermosa was recruited by the US Department of Labor, Occupational Safety and Health Administration, as a compliance officer in 1985. He was the first Filipino and only the second person of Asian heritage to be elected to public office in Massachusetts. (Courtesy of Rudolph Hermosa.)

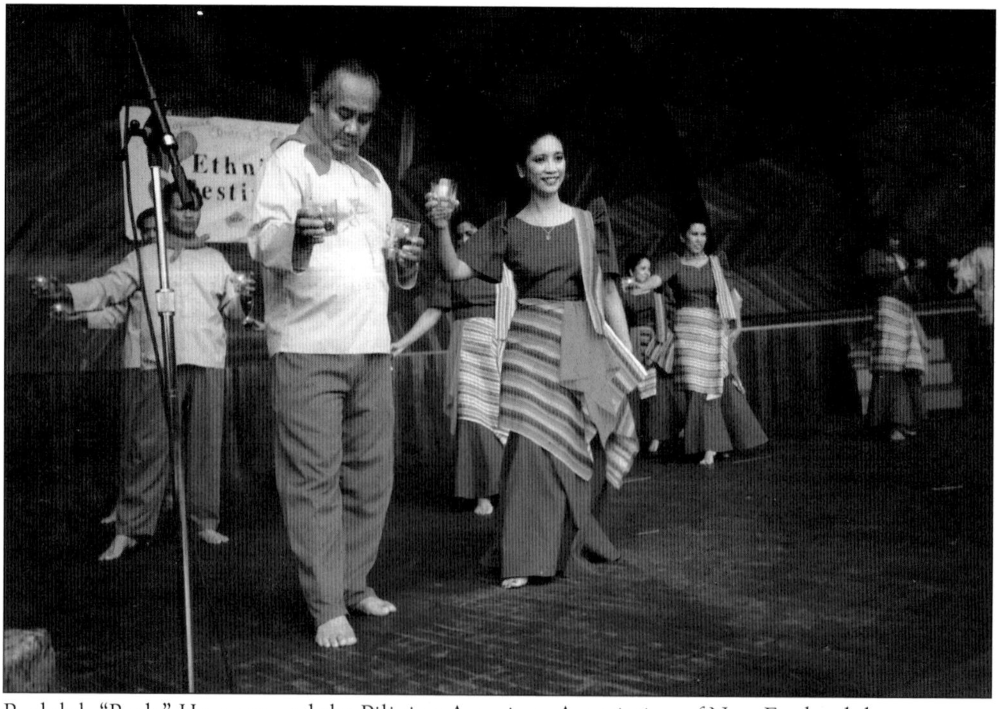

Rudolph "Rudy" Hermosa and the Pilipino-American Association of New England dance troupe performed at the Esplanade Hatch Shell as a part of an Asian Pacific Heritage Month celebration during the early 1990s. Hermosa, along with Susan Roosevelt Weld and others on the Massachusetts Asian-American Commission, organized this and other events to create visibility for Asian Americans in Massachusetts. (Courtesy of Rudolph Hermosa.)

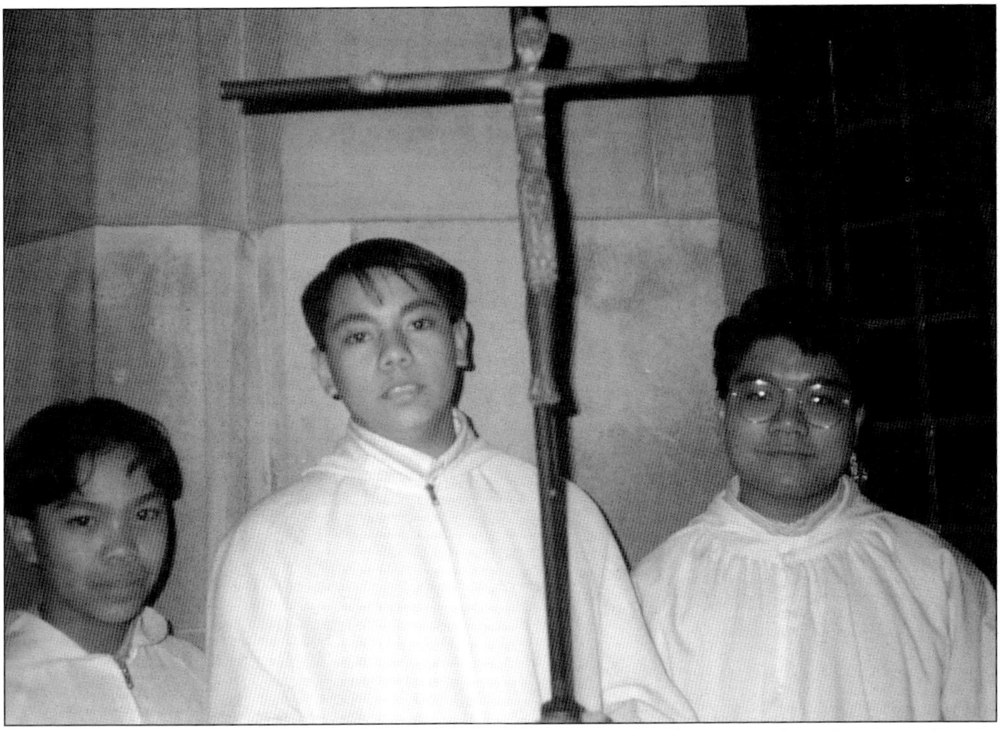

From left to right, Jon Talusan, Paul Talusan, and Emmanuel Felina served as altar boys for the Filipino Apostolate, Archdiocese of Boston, in 1992. The Archdiocese of Boston formed the Filipino Apostolate in 1977. Activities include masses, retreats, Christmas celebrations, and picnics. Churches listed on the apostolate's flyers include St. Joseph's Catholic Church in Malden and Holy Name Parish in West Roxbury. During the COVID-19 pandemic, they held many services online.

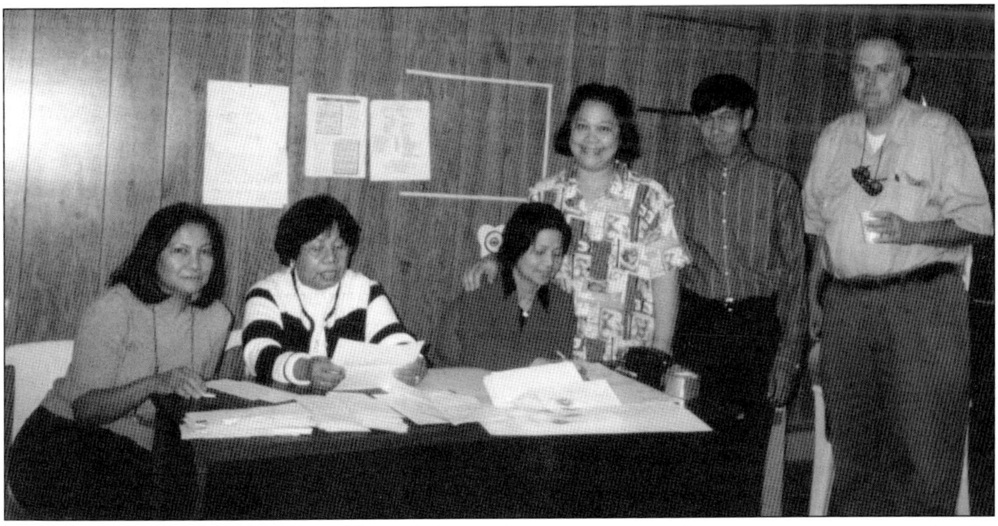

Members of organizations worked hard behind the scenes to coordinate important events for the Filipino American community. These affairs sustained connections, continued traditions, developed pride in heritage and identity, and formed a bridge with the larger society. The volunteers are opening mail and keeping track of tickets for a performance by the Philippine Dance Company of Boston in the 1990s.

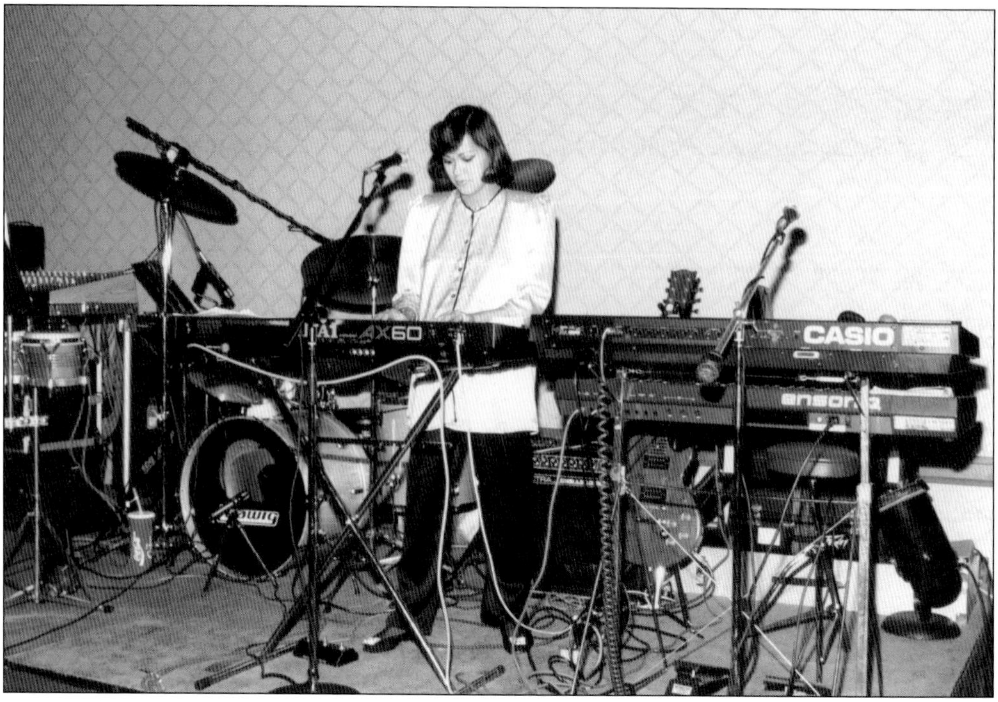

Maritess "Tess" Salientes Bloom performed for the Philippine Medical Association of New England ball in 1990. She graduated from the Berklee College of Music with a degree in composition. She lived in Boston for 25 years and raised two children before moving back to the Philippines in 2005 to embark on a successful career in jazz performance.

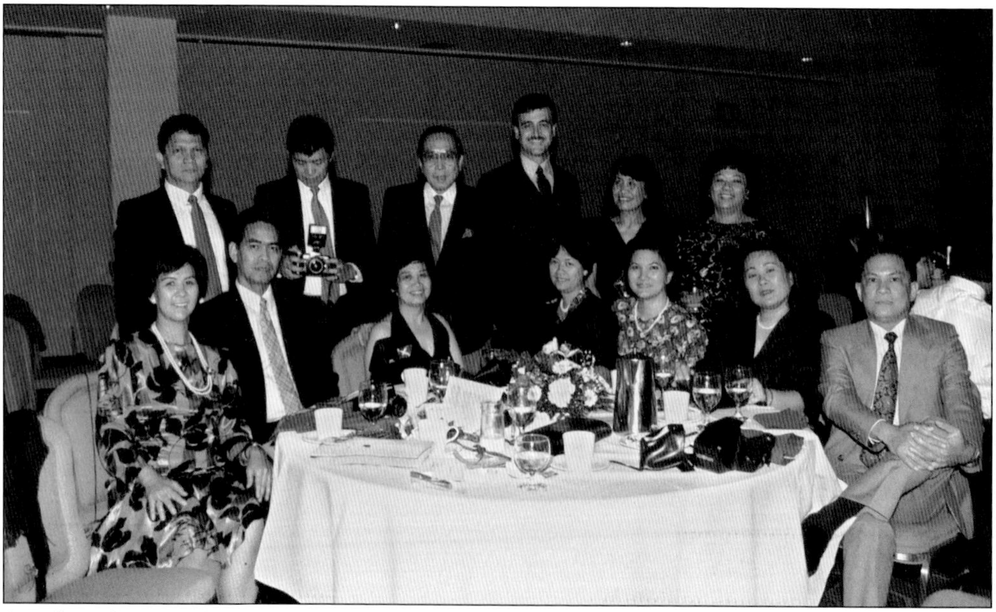

Another photograph of the 29th annual Philippine Medical Association of New England ball shows members of the organization just after dinner. It was held at the Sheraton Boston Hotel in the Back Bay area of Boston on May 12. Dr. Eduardo Talusan, the author's father, served as president from 1988 to 1990.

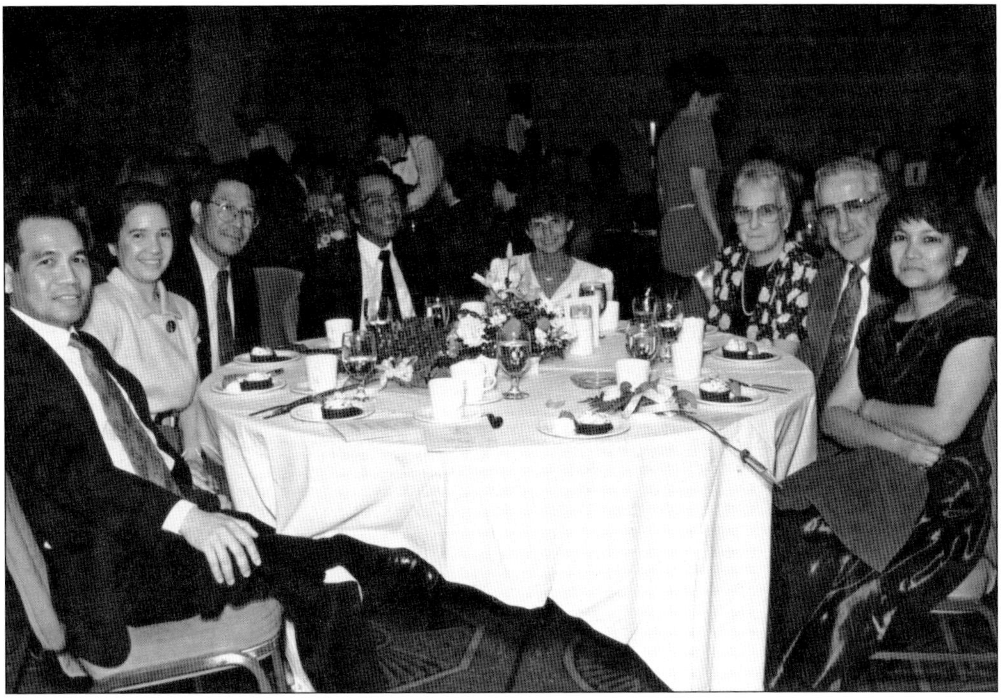

These are more photographs of the 29th annual Philippine Medical Association of New England ball on May 12, 1990. Dr. Arcel G. Talusan (right) organized an elegant affair with dinner and entertainment by the band the Manila Connection. The mistress of ceremonies was Mercy Songcayauon-Chan. Officers for the next term were announced at the ball. The medical ball provided opportunities to reconnect with old friends and network with new members.

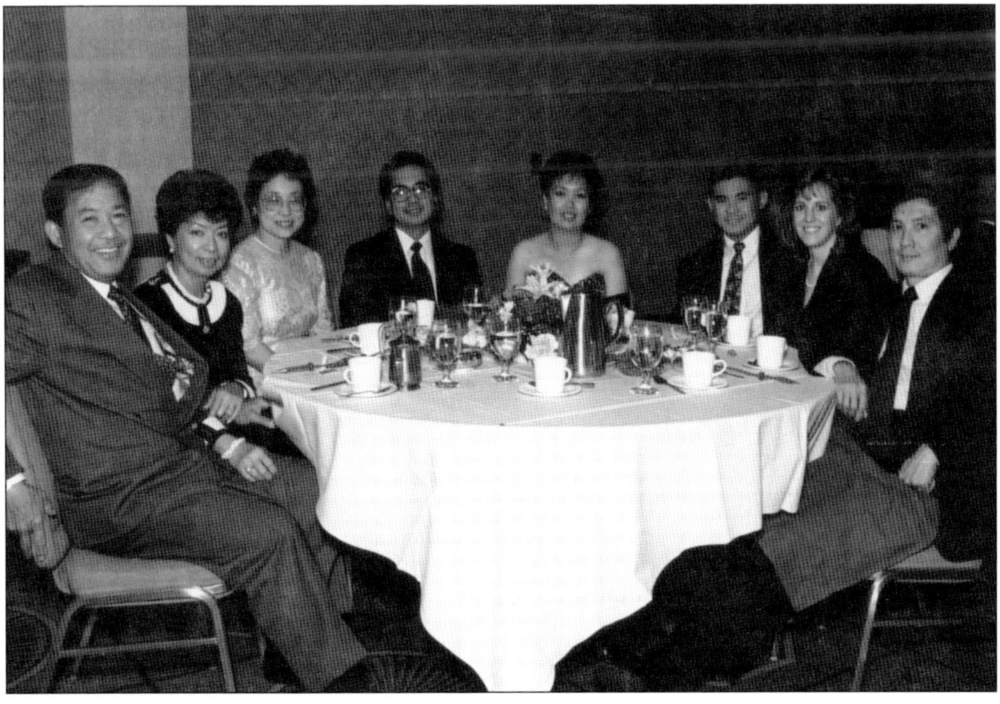

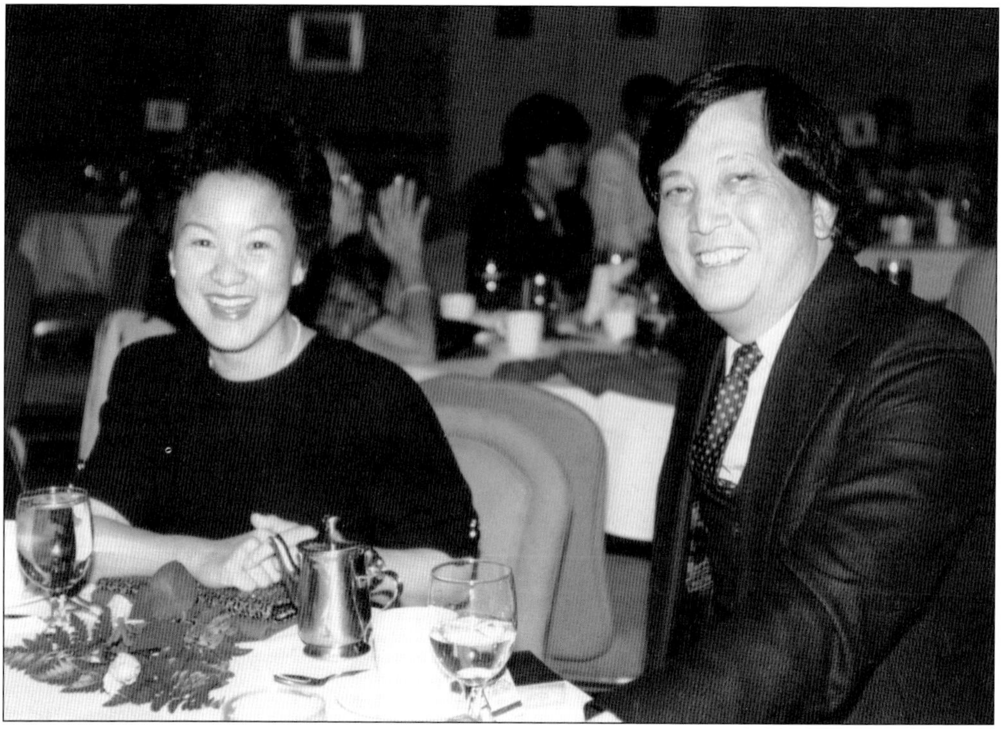

Drs. Miriam and José "Pepito" Villanueva pose during the Philippine Medical Association of New England ball in 1990. They raised four sons in Lexington: Alexander, Jeffrey, Jonathan, and Andrew. Miriam is a psychiatrist for Veterans Affairs, and Pepito has a private practice as a urologist.

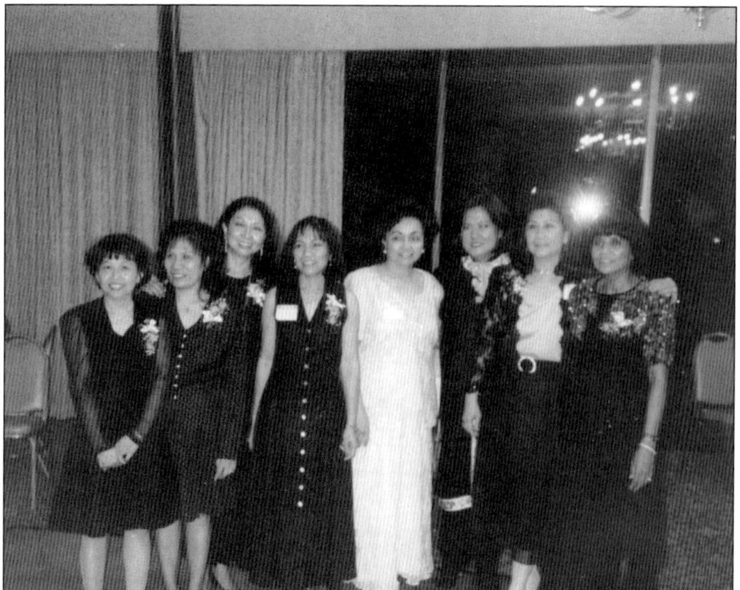

This photograph was taken at the 1996 Philippine Medical Association of New England ball. From left to right are Zenaida Castro, Margie Mateo, Mary Rose Jacinto Ezpeleta, Arcel Talusan, Alicia Layug, Patty Yusah, Norma Bucal, and Flor Escobar. (Courtesy of Margie Mateo.)

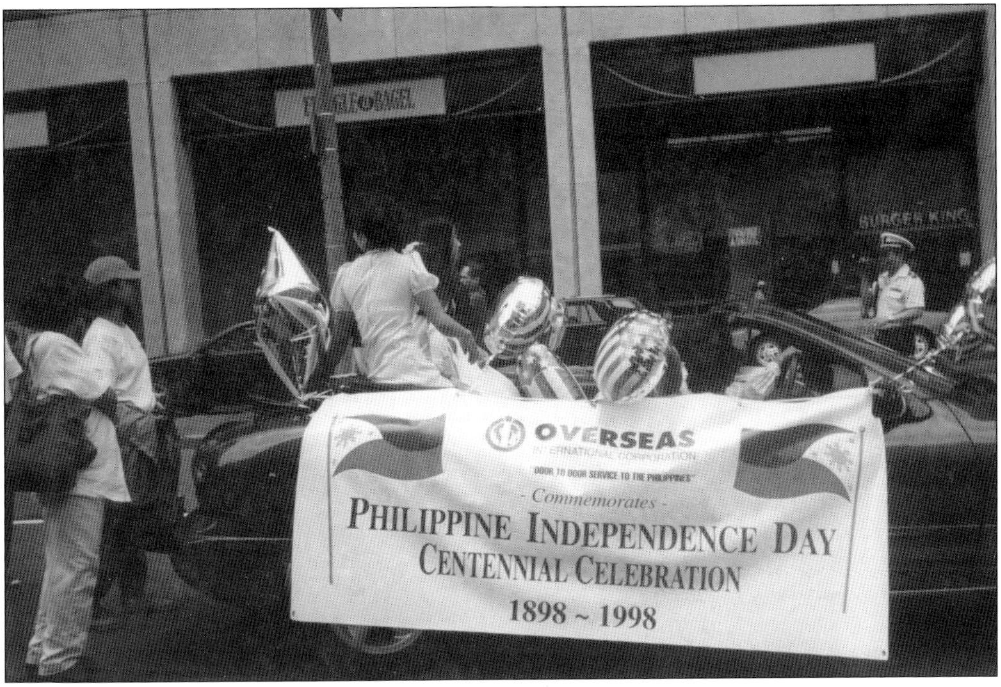

In 1998, Filipino organizations in Greater Boston collaborated to hold several events to commemorate the 100th anniversary of Philippine independence from Spain, declared on June 12, 1898. These photographs are of the parade in downtown Boston near City Hall Plaza, Government Center. As part of this effort, Philippine-American Mainstream Advocacy for Nonpartisan Associations, Inc., was established. Its mission is to "foster cooperation among Filipino American organizations in New England and hold Philippine Independence Day celebrations." (Both, courtesy of the Solar family.)

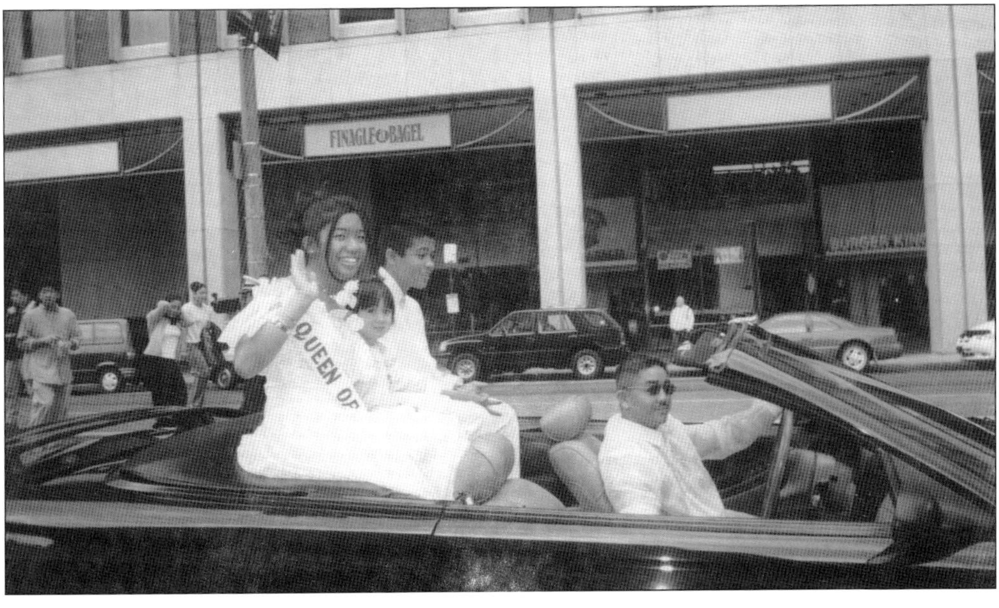

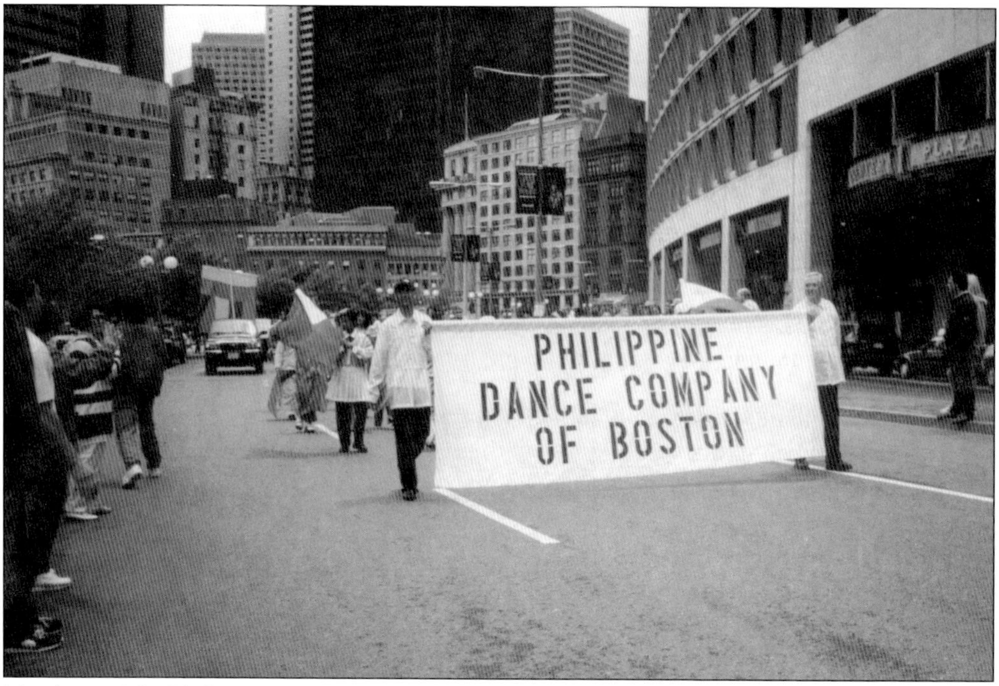

Members of the Philippine Dance Company of Boston march with their banner during the 1998 Philippine Centennial Celebration parade in downtown Boston. Many marched proudly wearing traditional Filipino attire such as barong tagalog and elegant Filipiniana gowns with butterfly sleeves. (Courtesy of the Solar family.)

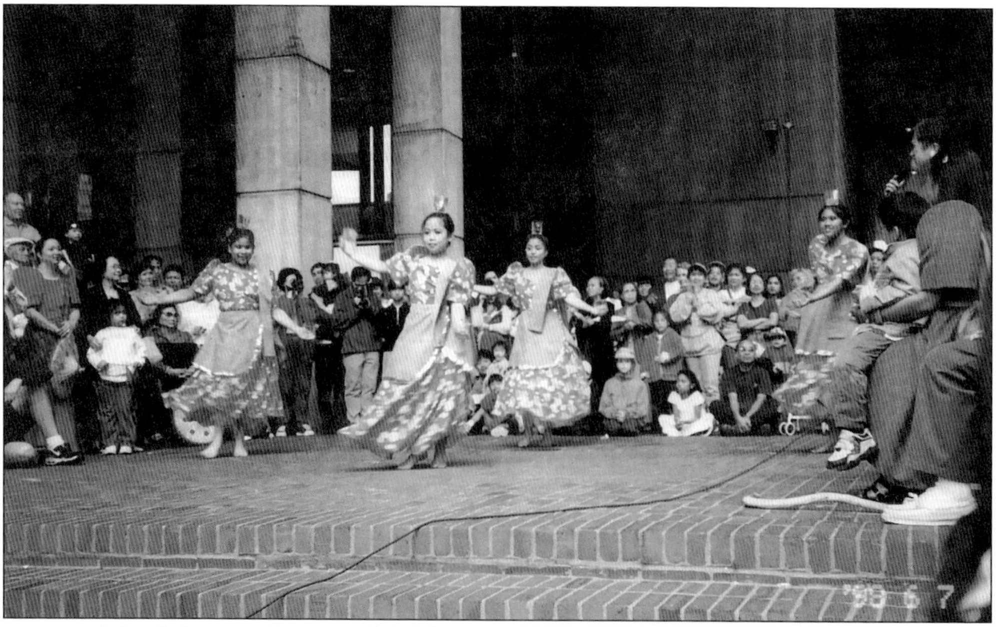

As part of the Philippine Centennial Celebration in Boston, cultural dance was presented to the crowds at Boston City Hall Plaza. Dressed in traditional attire with butterfly sleeves, these dancers balanced drinking glasses in their hands and on their heads in a dance called Binasuan. (Courtesy of Francisco Celazo.)

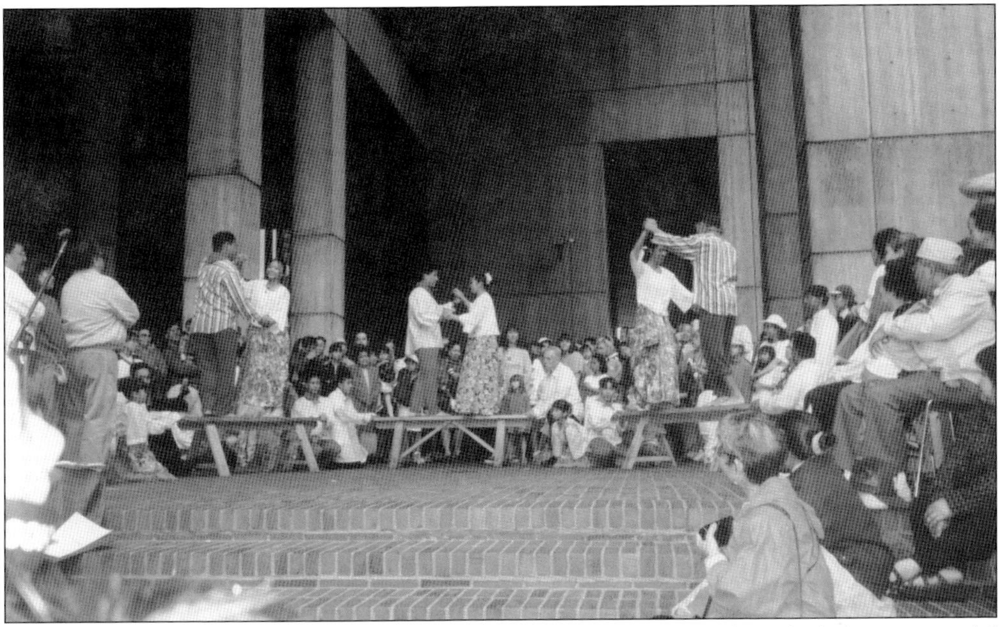

These dancers are performing a rural folk dance called Sayaw sa Bangko, which features careful balancing on benches while dancing. Cultural dances such as this were presented to crowds celebrating the Philippine Centennial Celebration at Boston City Hall Plaza in 1998. (Courtesy of the Solar family.)

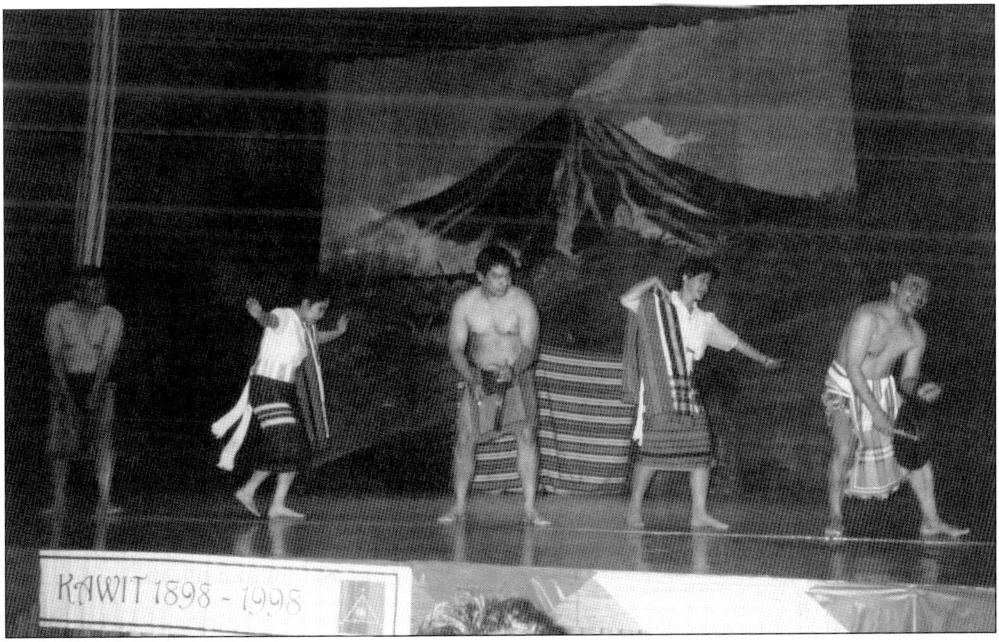

Several events were held to commemorate the Philippine Centennial of 1998. This one took place at the Massachusetts College of Art and Design in Boston. The dancers perform Tadek, a courtship dance from the Cordillera mountains, a region from which some of the dancers proudly hail. From left to right are Manny Felina, unidentified, Fr. Tim Nocho, unidentified, and Gras Awatin. The men play a traditional flat gong instrument called *gangsa*.

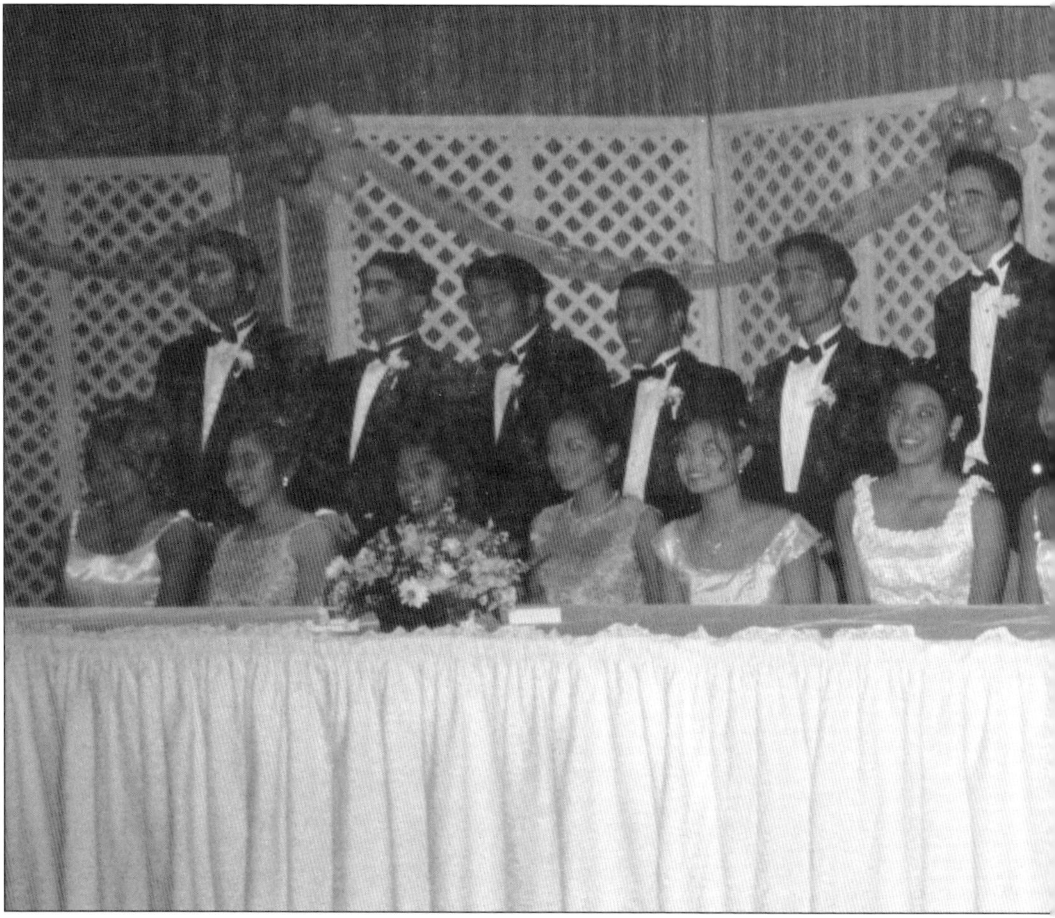

Known as a "debut" for short, debutante balls are significant events in Filipino American communities across the United States. Although past balls were held by other Filipino organizations in Boston, this photograph represents the first one organized by the Philippine Dance Company of Boston in

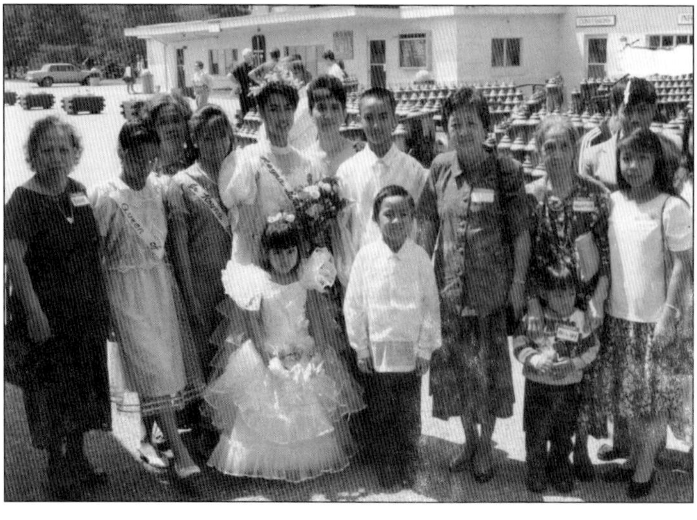

This photograph was taken in 1994 at a Santacruzan celebration at La Salette Park, National Shrine of Our Lady of La Salette, in Attleboro. Santacruzan, Spanish for "holy cross," takes place every May in the Philippines. (Courtesy of the Solar family.)

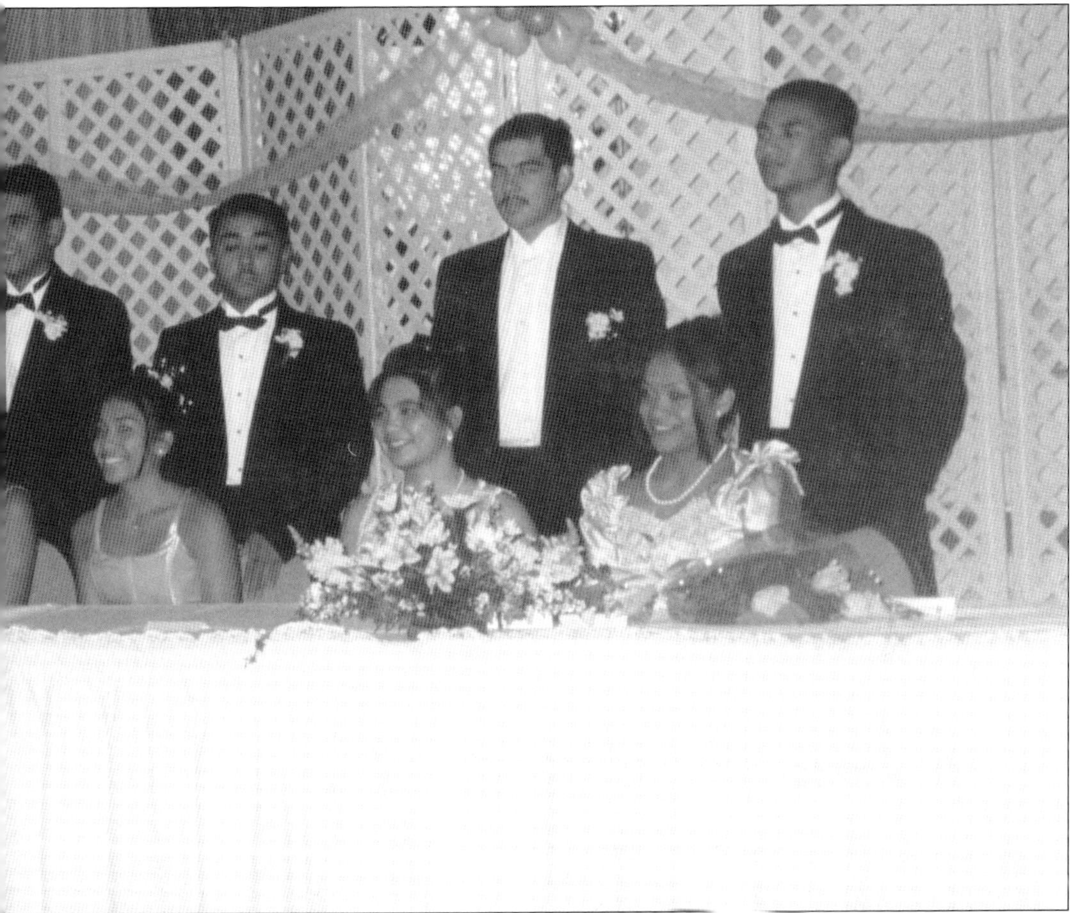

1998. A film called *The Debut* (2000), directed by Gene Cajayon, vividly depicts the lives of Filipino American youth through a debutante ball.

Members of the Philippine-American Association of New England were invited to perform Christmas carols at a private party during the 1990s. (Courtesy of Francisco Celazo.)

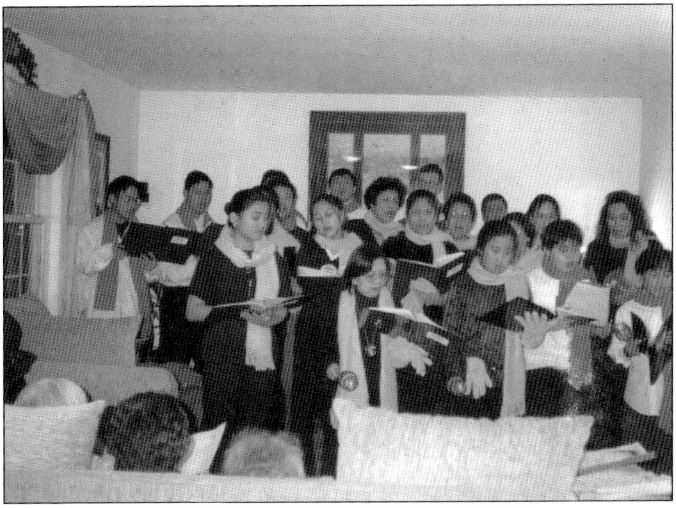

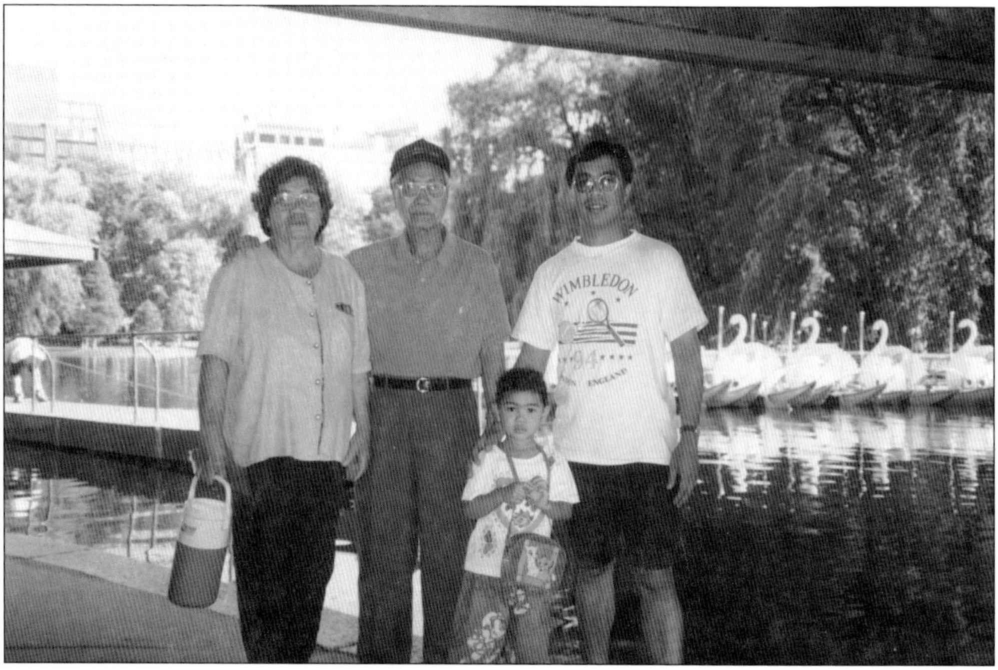

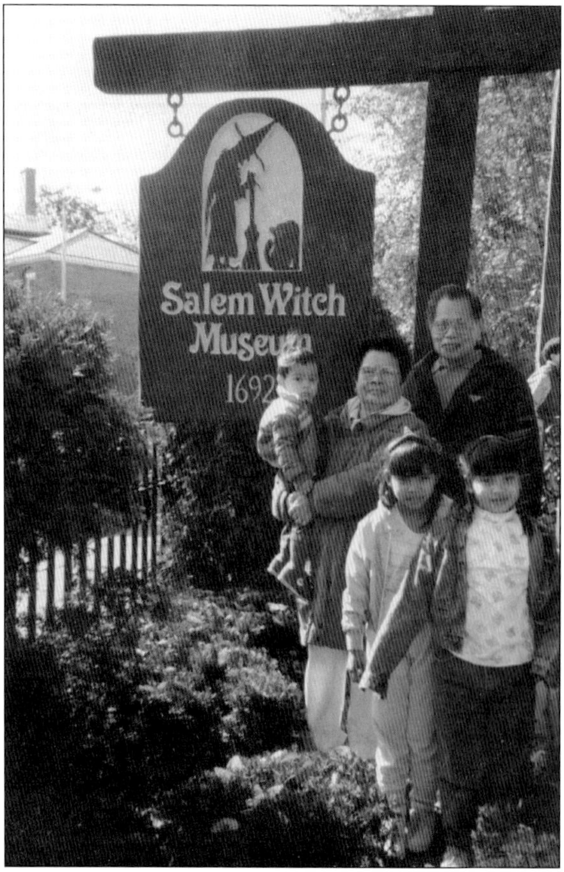

Brian Mangilog (child, center) visits the Swan Boats with his father, Ross, and grandparents at the Boston Public Garden around 1999. Brian's grandparents stayed in Boston for five years. He attended Boston Latin School and graduated from Harvard University. He plays piano with the West Roxbury Filipino Choir for masses held by the Filipino Apostolate and works for the Broad Institute of MIT and Harvard. (Courtesy of the Mangilog family.)

The Amarra children visit the Salem Witch Museum in 1990 with their grandparents, who were visiting from the Philippines. The museum provides education about the Salem Witch Trials, which took place in 1692. The museum opened in 1972 in a renovated historic church building. (Courtesy of Leila C. and Gregorio A. Amarra.)

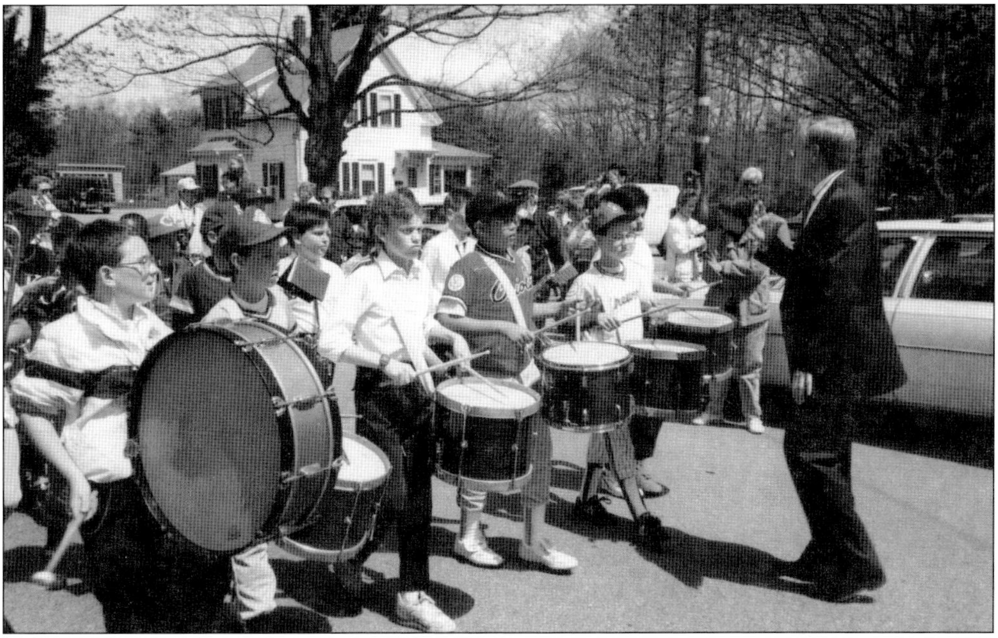

Paul Talusan (center on drums) paraded with his middle school marching band in Easton in 1991. Many of the smaller towns in Greater Boston had very few Filipino families living in them. Filipino American children participated actively in these local events in addition to celebrations held by the Filipino American community.

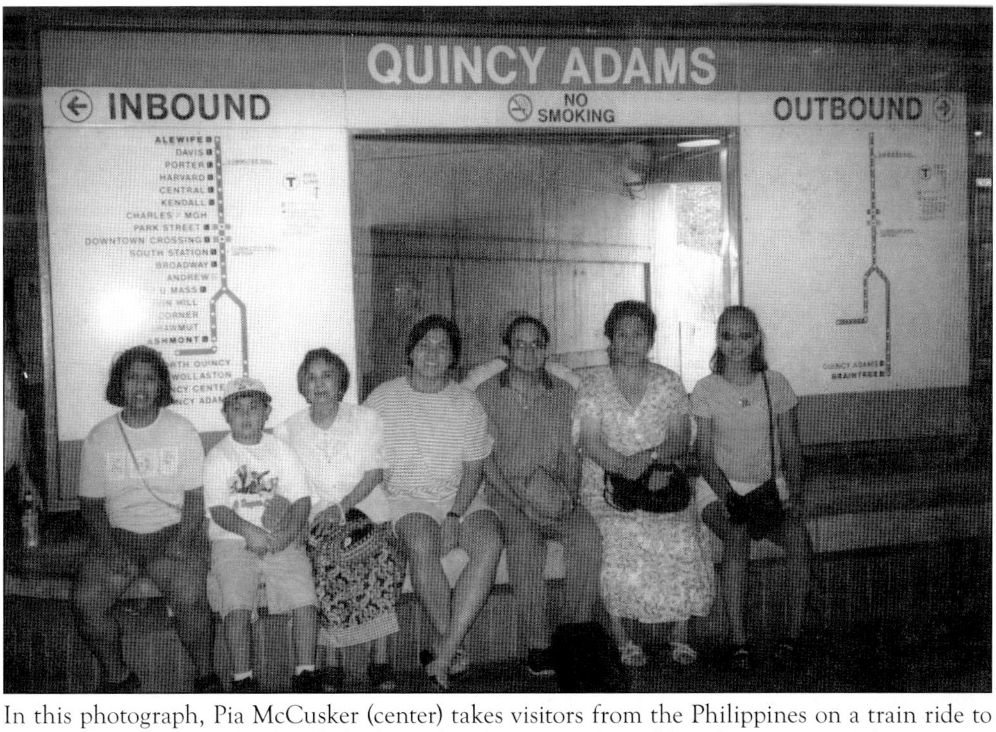

In this photograph, Pia McCusker (center) takes visitors from the Philippines on a train ride to Boston in the 1990s. They headed inbound to the city on the red line from Quincy Adams station in Quincy. Public transportation is run by the MBTA. (Courtesy of Nida Prado and Pia McCusker.)

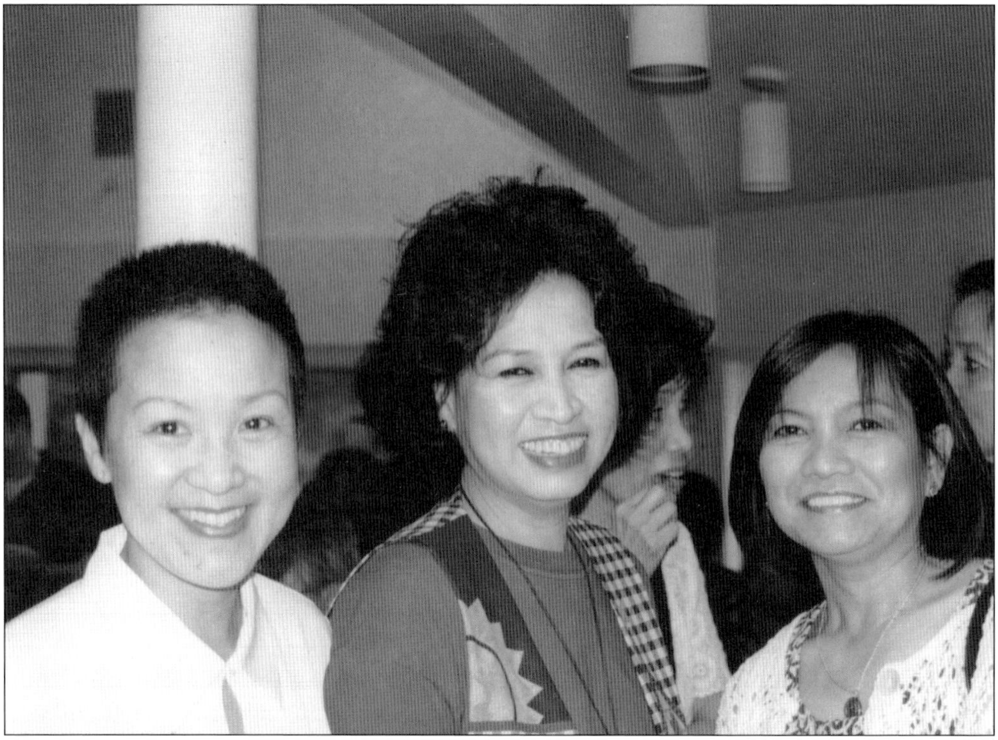

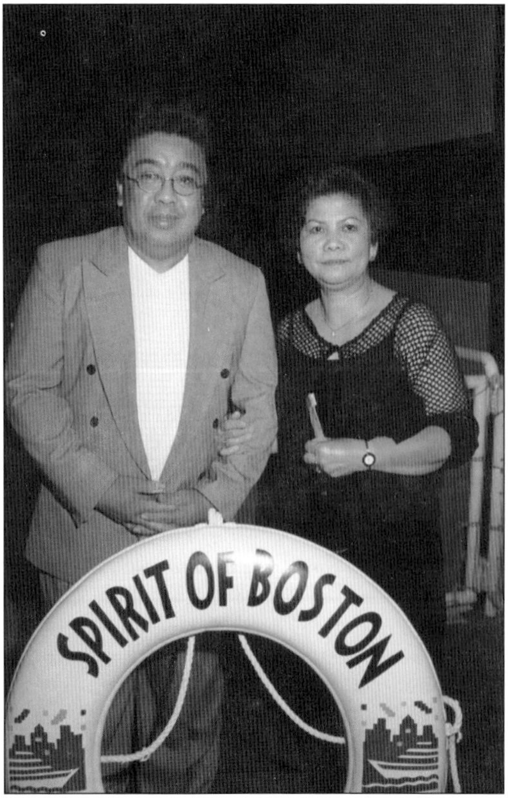

This c. 1990s photograph is of, from left to right, Miriam Villanueva, Mimi Strickland, and Arcel Talusan. Talusan established her travel agency, Flights Travel, in 1995. She has taken many Filipino Bostonians on pilgrimages over the years to Portugal, France, Rome, and Israel. She and these two friends visited Fatima and Lourdes among other holy places.

This photograph of Antonio R. and Trinidad C. Martin was taken in 1996. CPO Antonio R. Martin served in the US Navy for 23 years. The couple moved to the Boston area in 1984 when he was transferred to the Naval Academy Preparatory School in Newport, Rhode Island. Trini worked at the Turner Corporation at 855 Boylston Street as a senior project accountant. They have two children. (Courtesy of the Martin family.)

Lisa Moquite moved to Boston in 1999 when she was taken in by a couple who brought her to America. She worked at Logan Airport for 15 years and saved earnestly to buy property in the Philippines. (Courtesy of Lisa Moquite.)

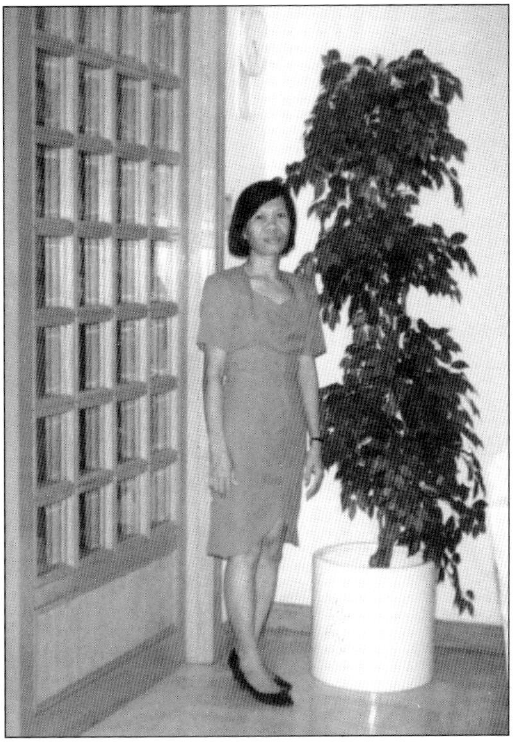

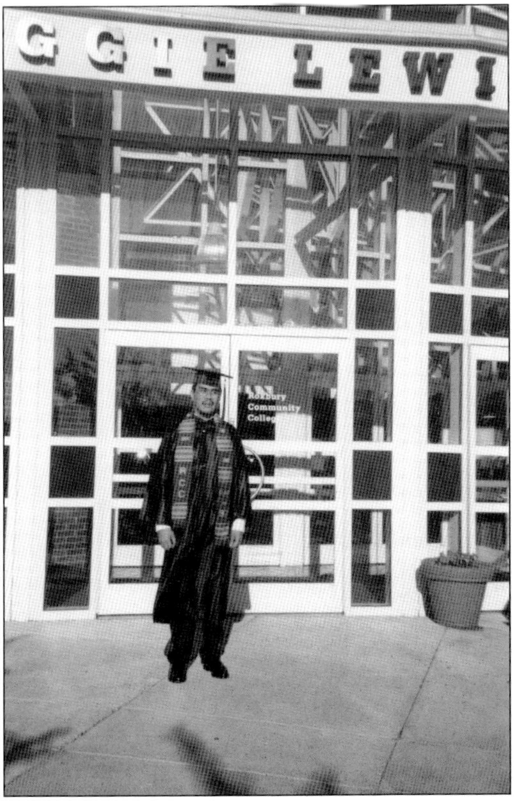

Roseller Mangilog was an engineer but shifted his career to nursing. This photograph was taken at his graduation from Roxbury Community College in 1990. His wife, Beth, worked at the Jewish Memorial Hospital and Rehabilitation Center. His son Brian graduated from Harvard University. (Courtesy of Brian Mangilog.)

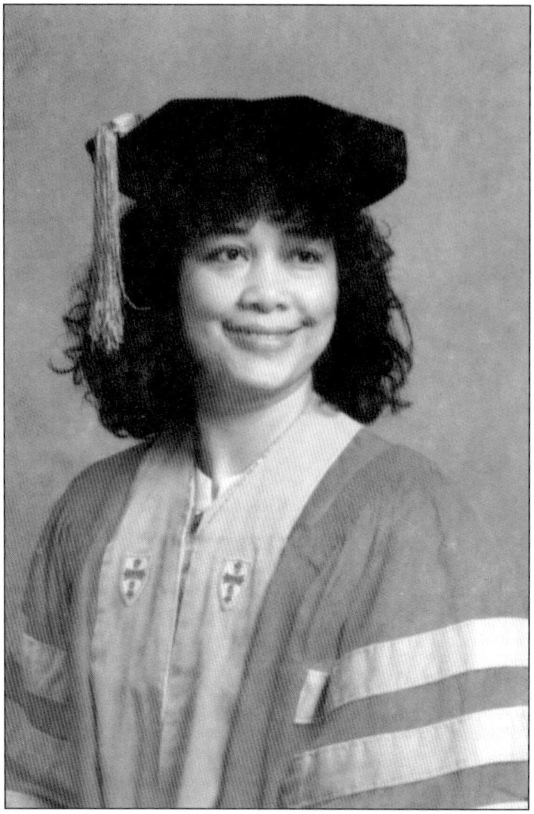

This photograph was taken in 1991 for the graduation of Dr. Ofelia Villanueva from the Henry M. Goldman School of Dental Medicine at Boston University. She married Rodolfo Villanueva in 1976. They came to Boston in 1981 with two small children and eventually had two more. They settled in Quincy, where she has a dental practice. (Courtesy of Ofelia Villanueva.)

Lina Angeles graduated with a master of science degree in nursing from the University of Massachusetts, Dartmouth. She and her husband, Gary, a psychiatrist, were born in Davao, Mindanao Island, Philippines. Lina worked at the Massachusetts Department of Corrections. She poses here at left with a friend during their commencement in the late 1990s. (Courtesy of Dr. Gary and Lina Angeles.)

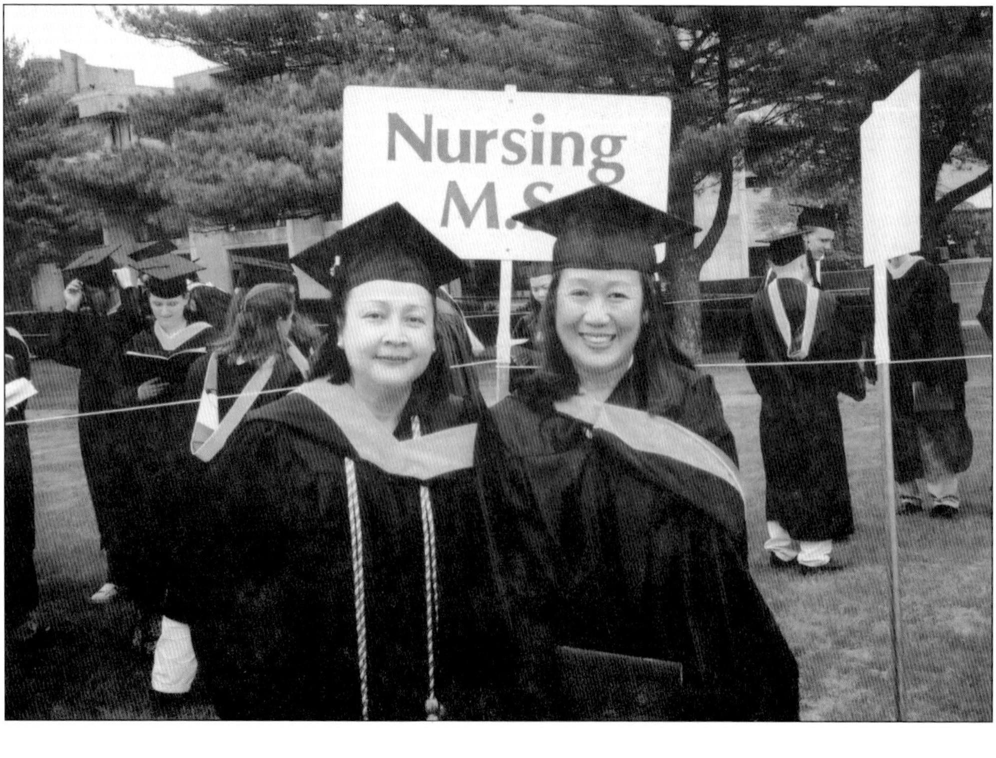

Dr. Felipe Tolentino first came to Boston in 1964 and returned in 1970 with his wife, Flora, to be part of the Retina Associates at Harvard. His crowning achievement was to do charity work with the Ophthalmological Foundation of the Philippines. He founded Restoring Sight International, a worldwide nonprofit, and the Asian Eye Institute of the Philippines. His wife, Dr. Flora Tolentino, was an anesthesiologist. They have a daughter and two sons. (Courtesy of Dr. Felipe I. Tolentino.)

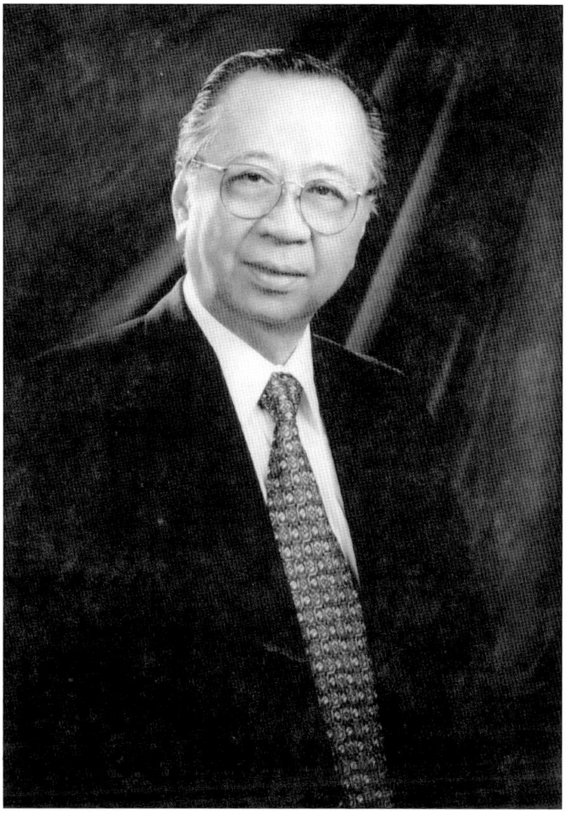

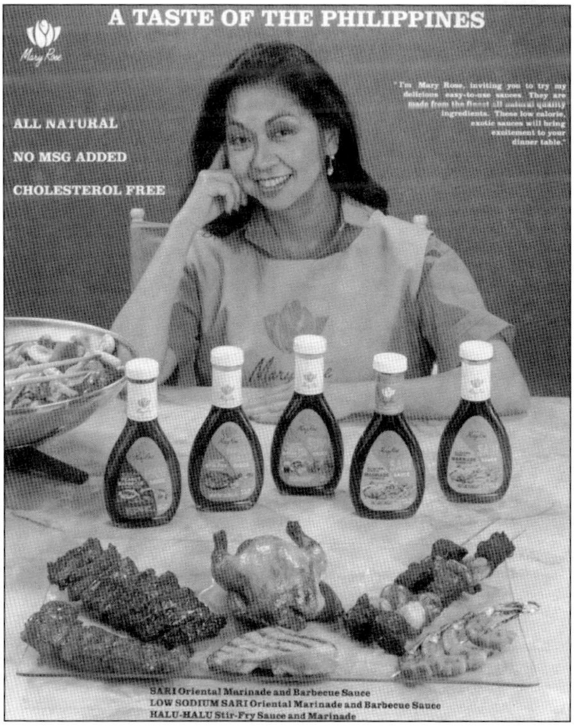

Prior to immigrating to the United States, Mary Rose Jacinto Ezpeleta starred in the popular Filipino television show *Sta. Zita and Mary Rose*, produced by the acclaimed Father Reuter. She came to the United States in 1972 with her husband, Dr. Mariano L. Ezpeleta Jr., a graduate of Harvard University. They have five children. This advertisement is for Mary Rose's Sari Oriental Marinade, which she founded in 1980. (Courtesy of Mary Rose Ezpeleta.)

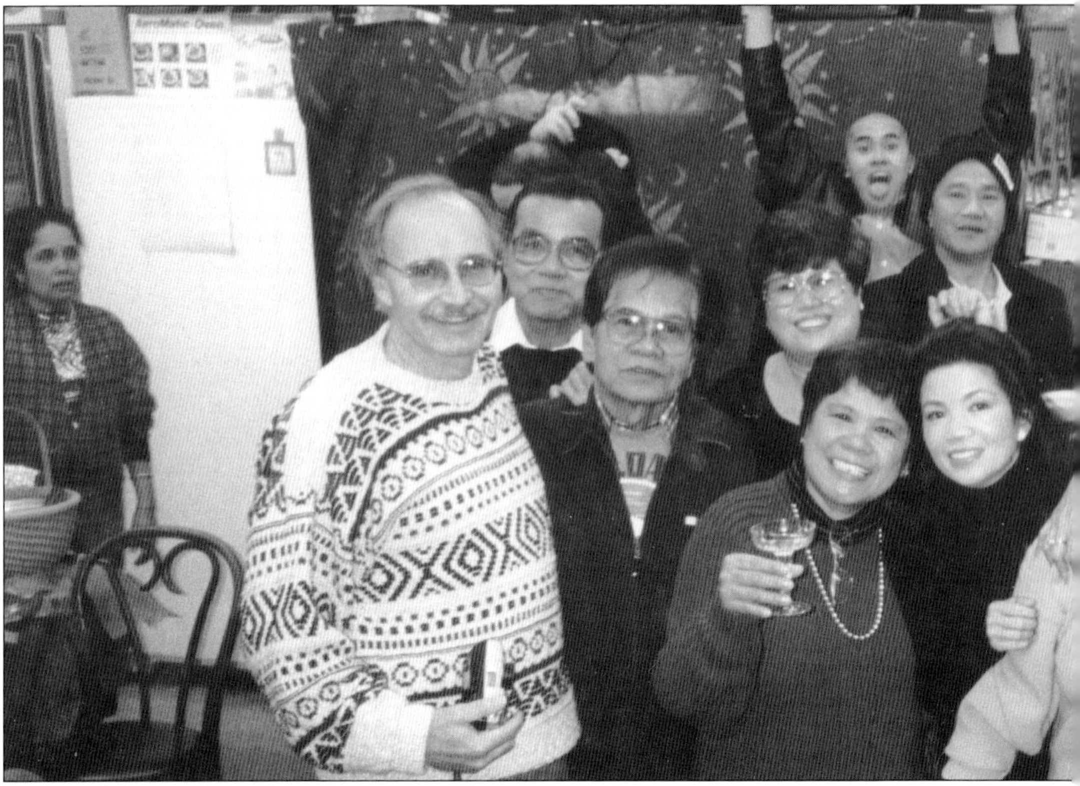

This photograph was taken on New Year's Eve in 2001 at the Shuttle Stop in Quincy, a favorite

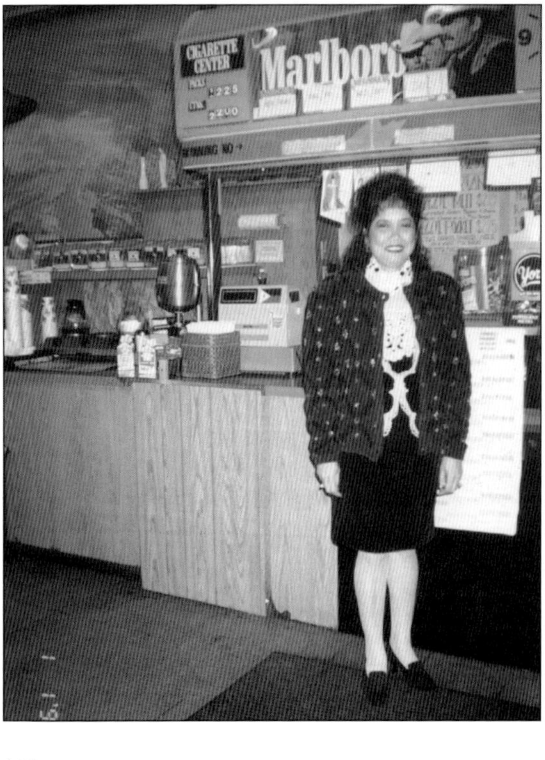

Aida Kalb opened the Shuttle Stop in 1991. At first, it was a typical deli selling sandwiches, but she also served Filipino food. She added a grocery and ran a catering business for Filipino American events. It closed in 2003. (Courtesy of Aida Kalb.)

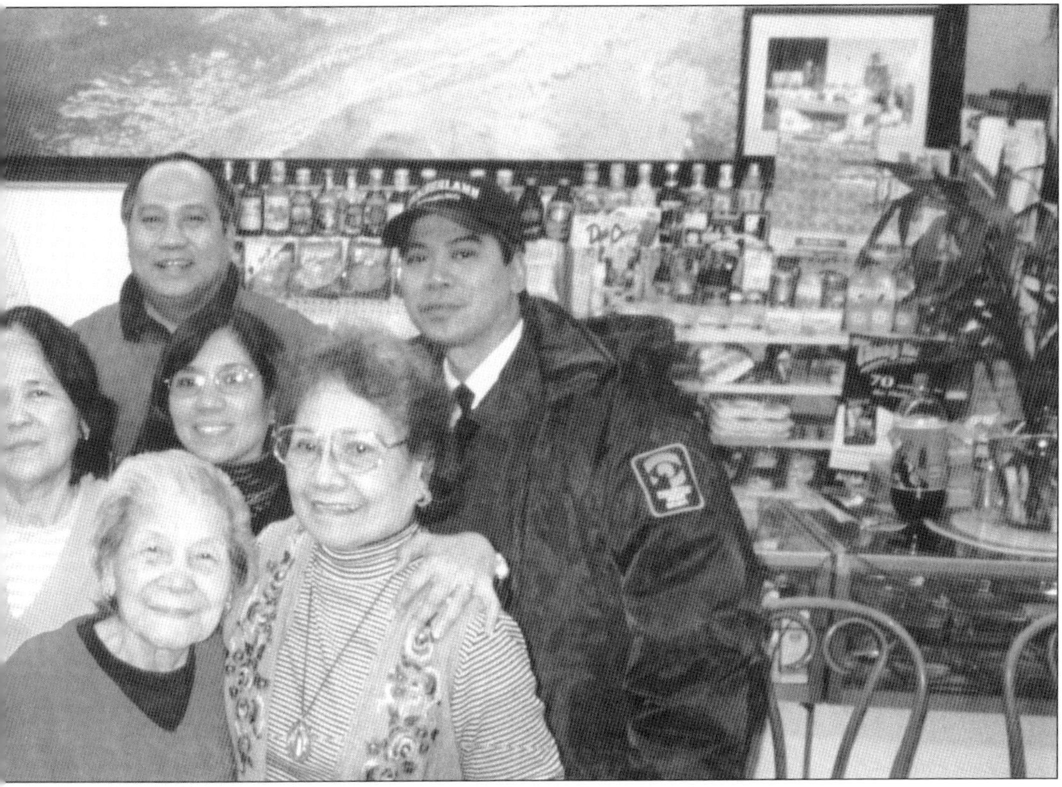

eatery among Filipinos in Greater Boston. (Courtesy of Aida Kalb.)

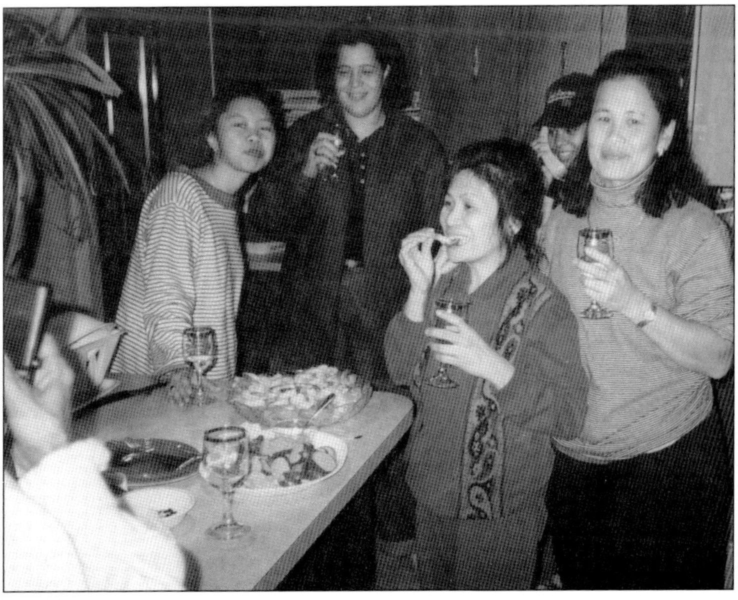

This image was captured in the 1990s during a get-together at the home of the Layug family. Margie Mateo (front) and Cresencia Colletti (right) were best friends. Colletti was a beloved Star Market employee and a dear friend of the Agular family. A mother of three and a grandmother of six, she passed away from complications due to the coronavirus in early 2020. (Courtesy of Margie Mateo.)

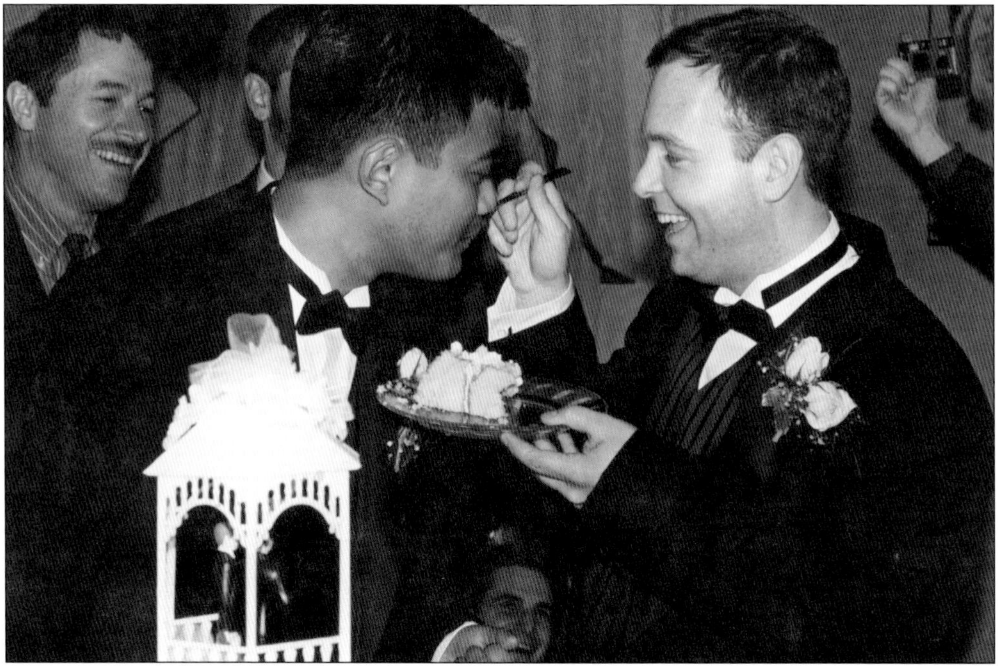

Bren Bataclan (left) and Bob L. Parlin were the first same-sex couple to have a commitment ceremony at the Memorial Church at Harvard University, Bob's alma mater, in 1998. Below, the couple poses with Bren's mother, Fe, and Bob's parents. Bren is an artist who has been featured on CNN and other news media because he gives his paintings away to "spread happiness and joy." He wrote a recent graphic memoir entitled *Fe: A Traumatized Son's Graphic Memoir.* (Both, courtesy of Bren Bataclan.)

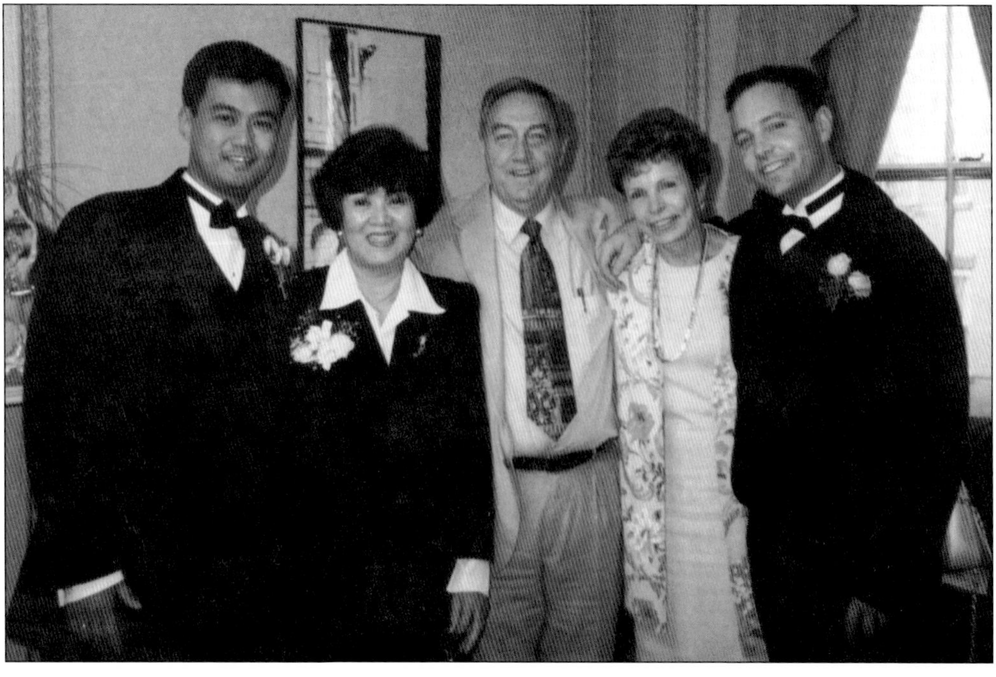

Seven

New Immigrants and Continuing Traditions 2000s

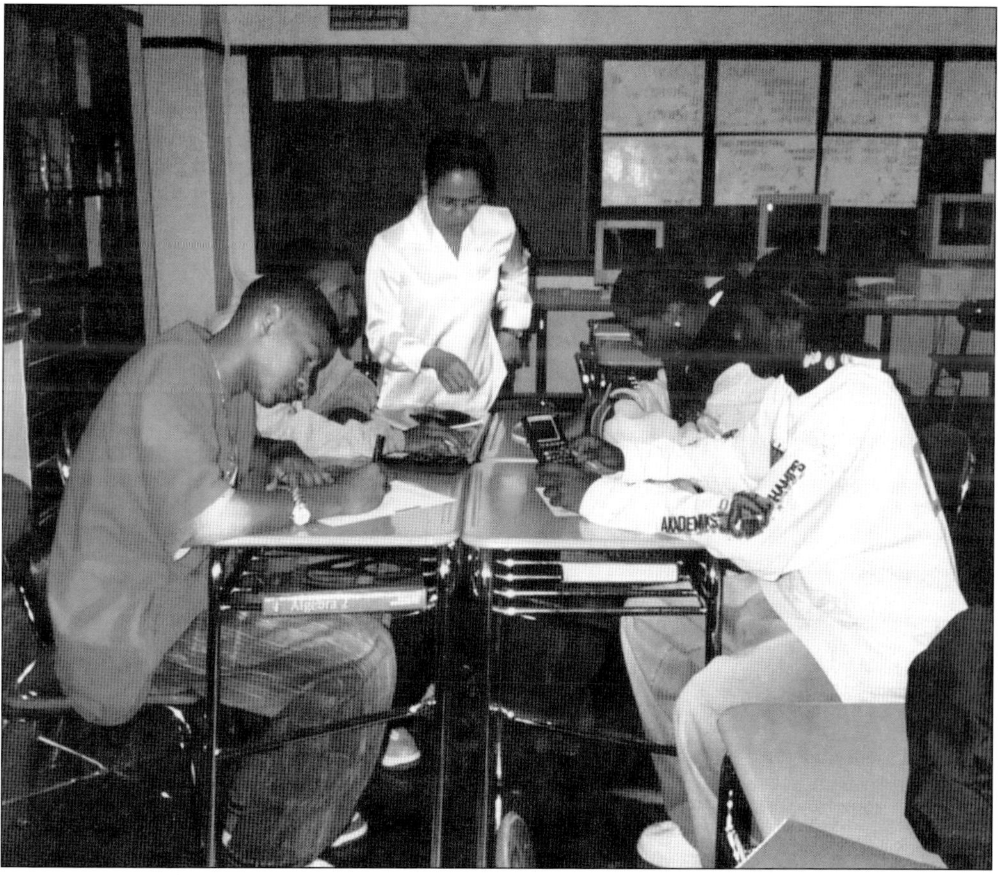

In 2000, the United States faced a nationwide teacher shortage, especially in math and science. According to a *Boston Herald* article published on August 21, 2001, some 200 teachers were recruited from the Philippines. Nine teachers came to Boston from the island of Cebu to start the 2001 school year. They appeared on television and were featured in Boston newspapers. In this photograph, Noemi Famador teaches students at a Boston public school. (Courtesy of Noemi M. Famador.)

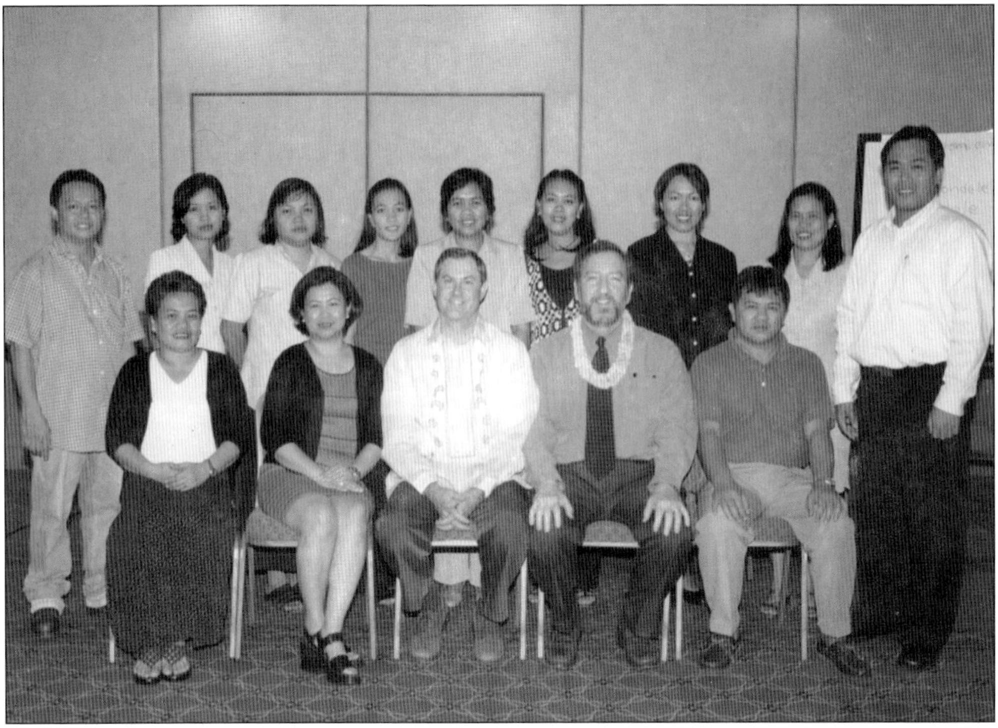

Boston Public Schools senior program director for secondary math Ed Joyce (first row, second from right) visited the island of Cebu to recruit qualified teachers. He interviewed 65 teachers and chose the nine standing in the second row; from left to right are Ramil Dagondon, Michelle Gaco Galac, Ledilla Fedillaga-Bokas, Johanna Badayos-Arrazola, Aurora Pacho, Alma Pilapi-Minoza, Amy Cortez, Noemi Famador, and Joel Minoza. When they first arrived, the teachers all stayed at a Quincy apartment complex. Members of the Philippine-American Association of New England and other Filipino Americans welcomed them warmly into the community at a party in Viking Hall in Quincy on September 1, 2001. Below, the teachers reunite with Ed Joyce (center) in a Boston restaurant three years after they arrived. He regularly checked in with teachers until he retired. (Both, courtesy of Noemi M. Famador.)

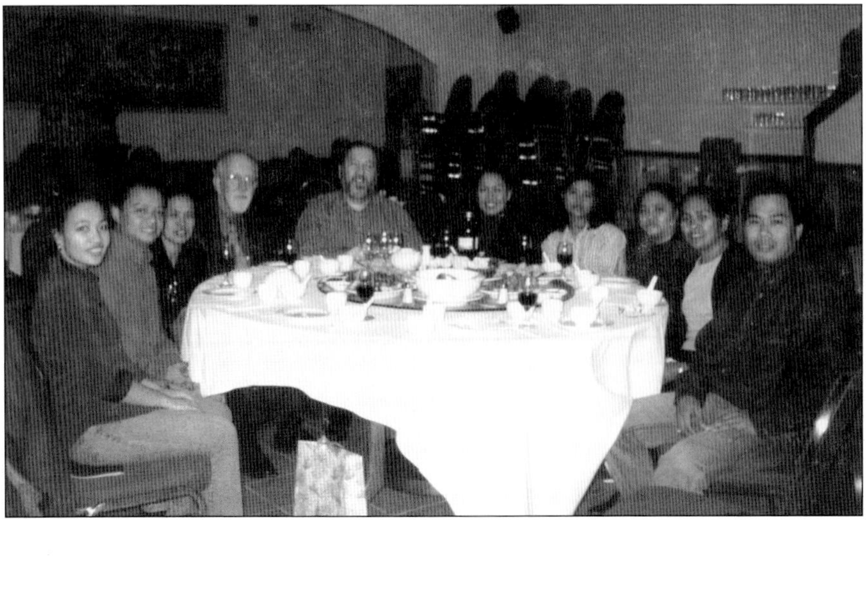

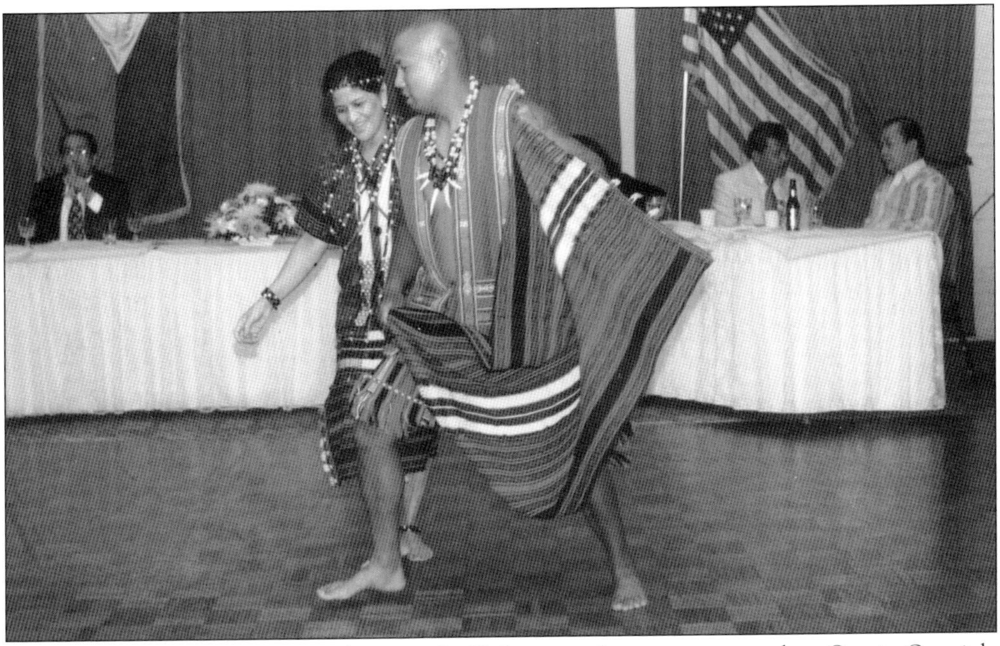

To demonstrate the diversity of cultures in the Philippines, dance troupe members Gracita Orquiola "Teng" Chiefe and Cesar Emmanuello perform Salip for a Philippine-American Association of New England formal event in 2000. This dance originates among the Kalinga people of the Cordillera mountains and displays beautiful woven traditional attire. (Courtesy of Aida Kalb.)

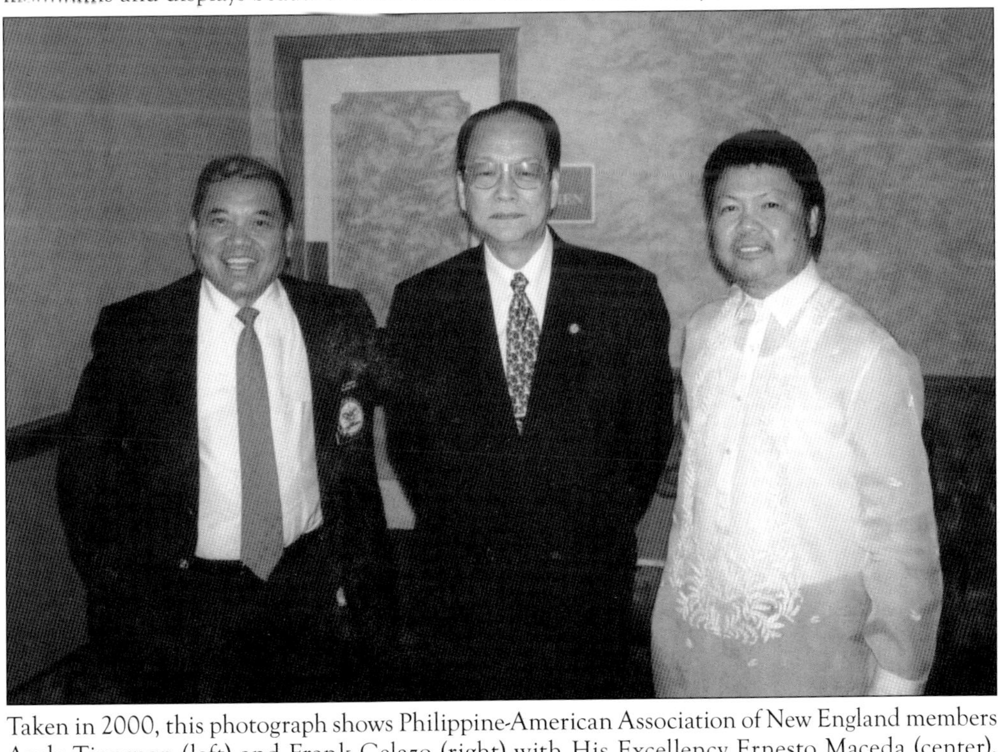

Taken in 2000, this photograph shows Philippine-American Association of New England members Andy Tiongson (left) and Frank Celazo (right) with His Excellency Ernesto Maceda (center), Philippine ambassador to the United States from 1998 to 2001. (Courtesy of Aida Kalb.)

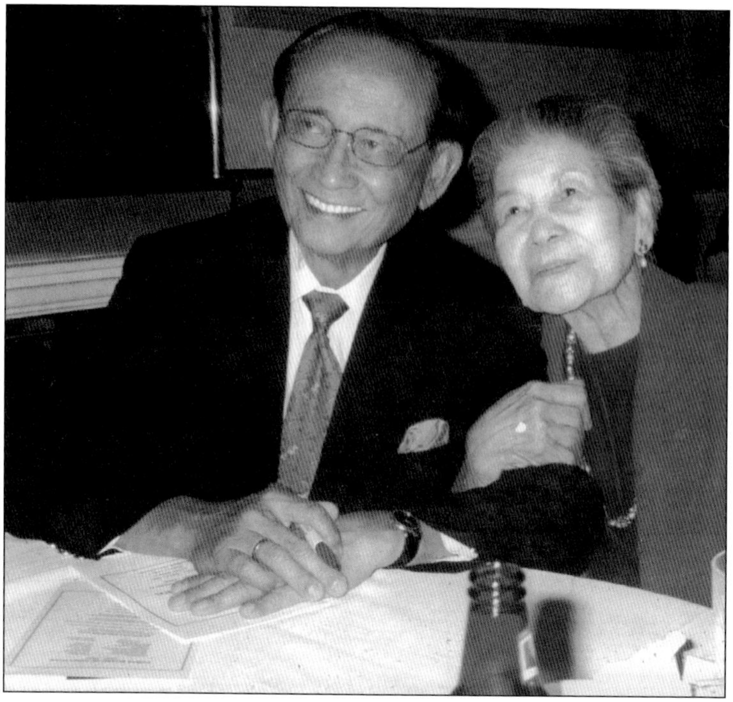

In April 2001, former Philippines president Fidel V. Ramos delivered the keynote address at a conference on corruption and good governance held at the Fletcher School at Tufts University and spoke at Harvard Kennedy School of Government. He poses here with Amanda "Aida" Kalb's mother, who lived until she was 101 years old, at an event held in his honor by the Philippine-American Association of New England. (Courtesy of Francisco Celazo.)

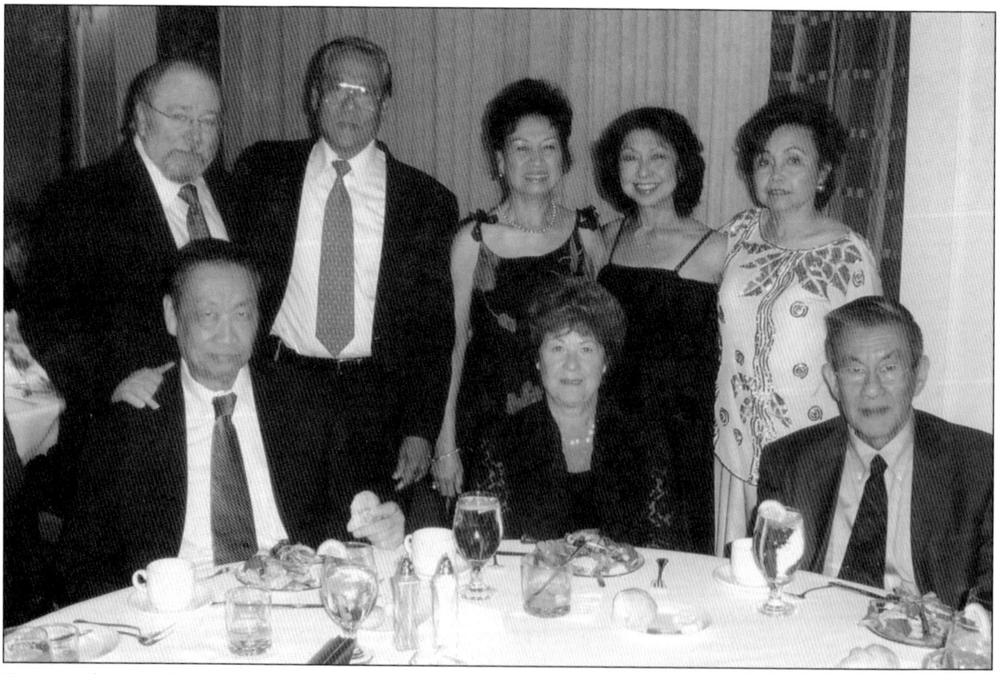

During the 2000s, the Philippine Medical Association of New England opened membership to all medical professionals including dentists and nurses. From left to right are (sitting) Dr. Antonio "Tony" Layug, Carolyn Angeles, and Dr. Mariano L. "Jun" Ezpeleta Jr.; (standing) Robert "Bob" Strickland, Dr. José "Pong" Angeles, Dr. Remedios "Mimi" Strickland, Mary Rose Ezpeleta, and Dr. Alicia Layug.

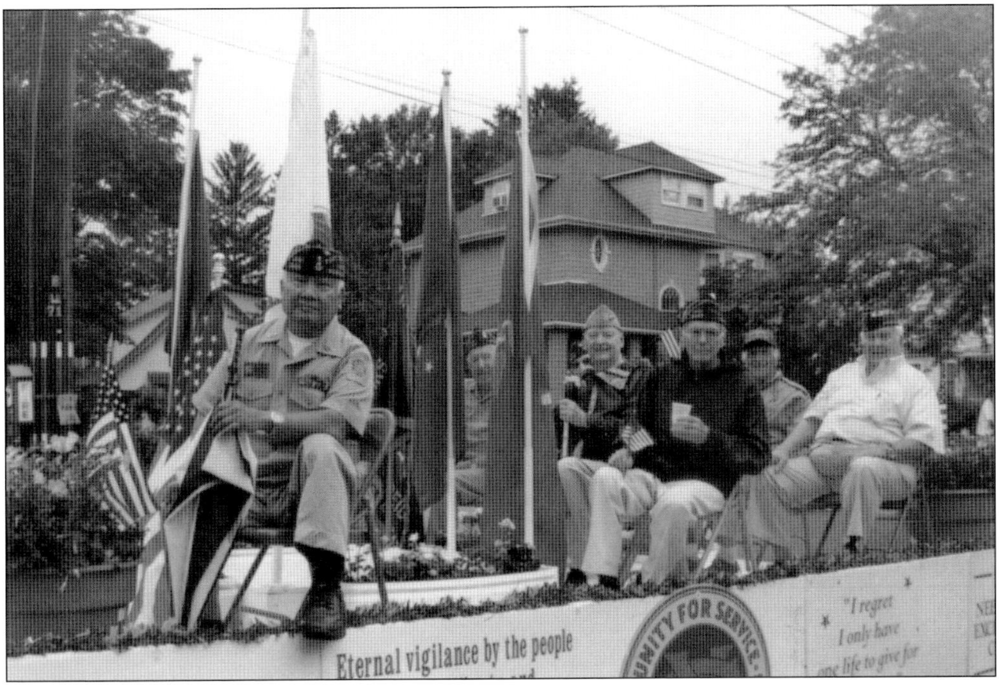

Rudolph "Rudy" Hermosa sits at the head of a Veteran's Day parade float in 2003 with fellow veterans. He was the post commander of the Veterans of Foreign Wars (VFW) Post 2498 in Needham from 2002 to 2004. (Courtesy of Rudy Hermosa.)

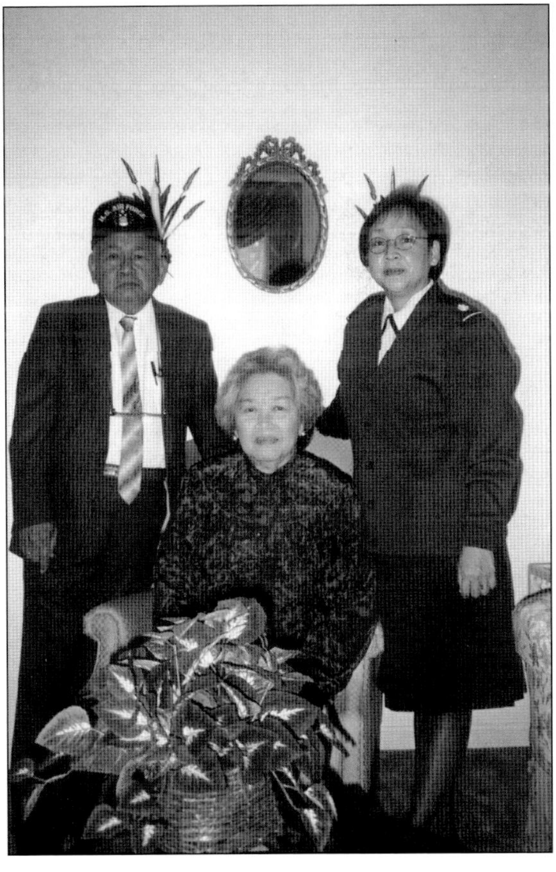

Lina Angeles (standing right) served in the US Air Force from 1980 to 2000. She is pictured here upon her retirement with the rank of lieutenant colonel. She went on to nursing school at the University of Massachusetts, Dartmouth, and worked at the Massachusetts Department of Corrections. She and Dr. Gary Angeles have five children—Liana Marie, Edgardo Luis "Chino," Kristina Marie, and Joseph Abelard Manuel—whom they raised in Easton. (Courtesy of Lina Angeles.)

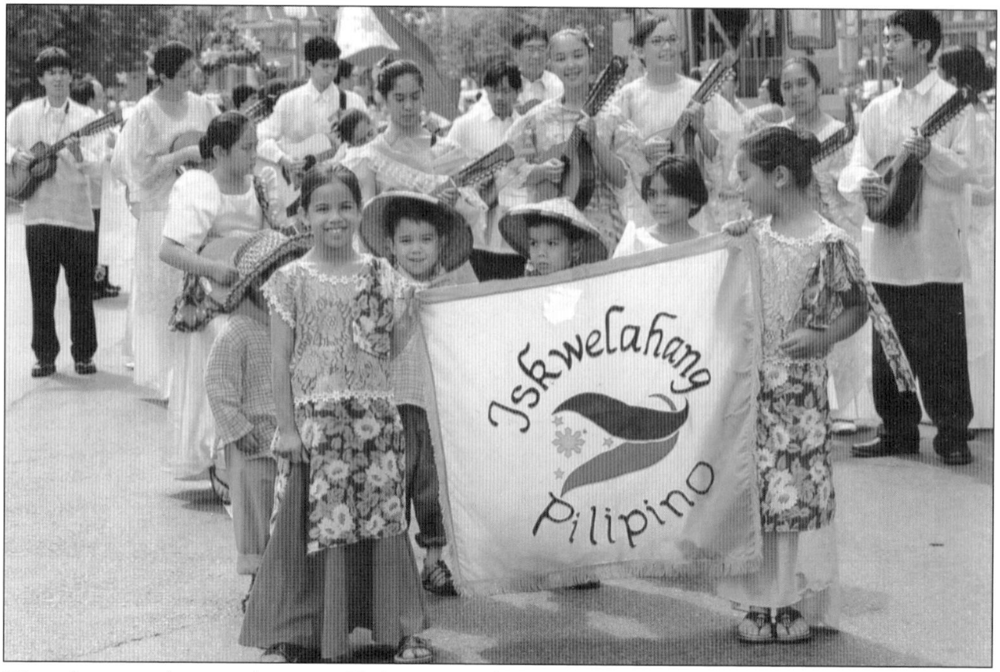

This photograph was taken at a Philippine Independence Day parade in June 2007. Students of Iskwelahang Pilipino march proudly, displaying their organization banner in front of the IP Rondalla Ensemble. They are wearing traditional Filipino attire. (Courtesy of Myra O. Liwanag.)

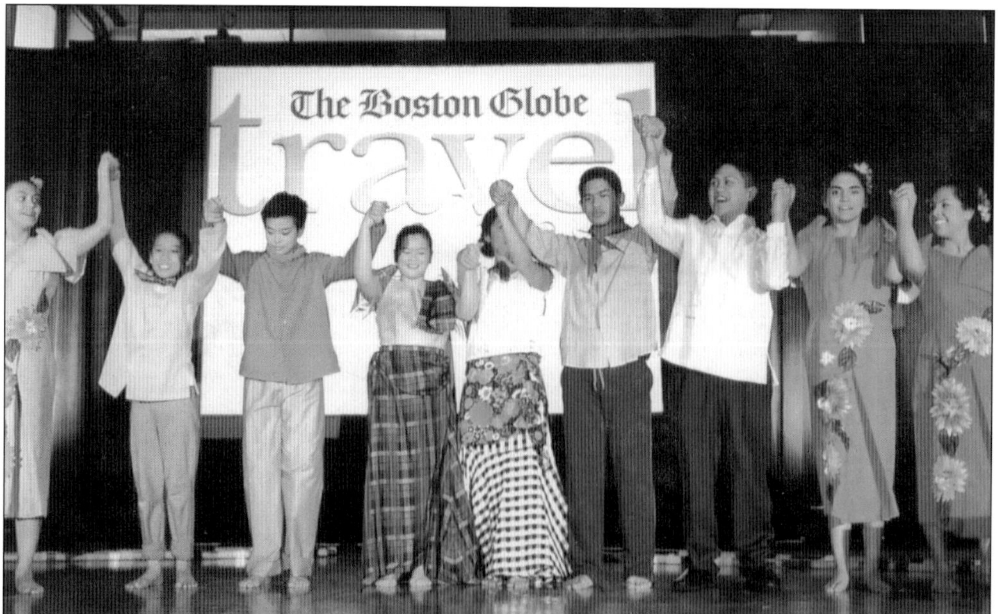

This image is from the last time that Iskwelahang Pilipino participated in the Boston Globe Travel Show, a travel expo held at the Seaport Hotel Convention Center in Boston, on February 11, 2017. They performed Tinikling, a traditional dance that features gracefully jumping between clapping bamboo poles, and other folk dances. (Courtesy of Myra O. Liwanag.)

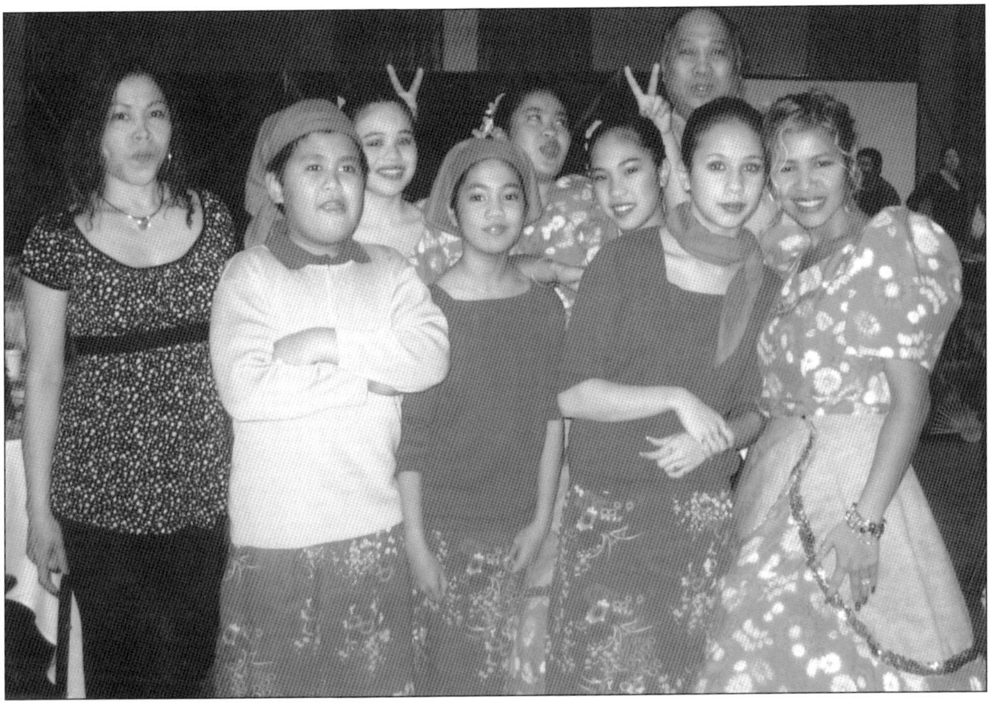

Young Filipino Americans of the Philippine-American Association of New England perform cultural dances at Bridgewater State College in 2007. Below is a close-up of Jessamyn Celazo dancing Pandanggo sa Ilaw, balancing a candle in a glass on top of her head. (Both, courtesy of Aida Kalb.)

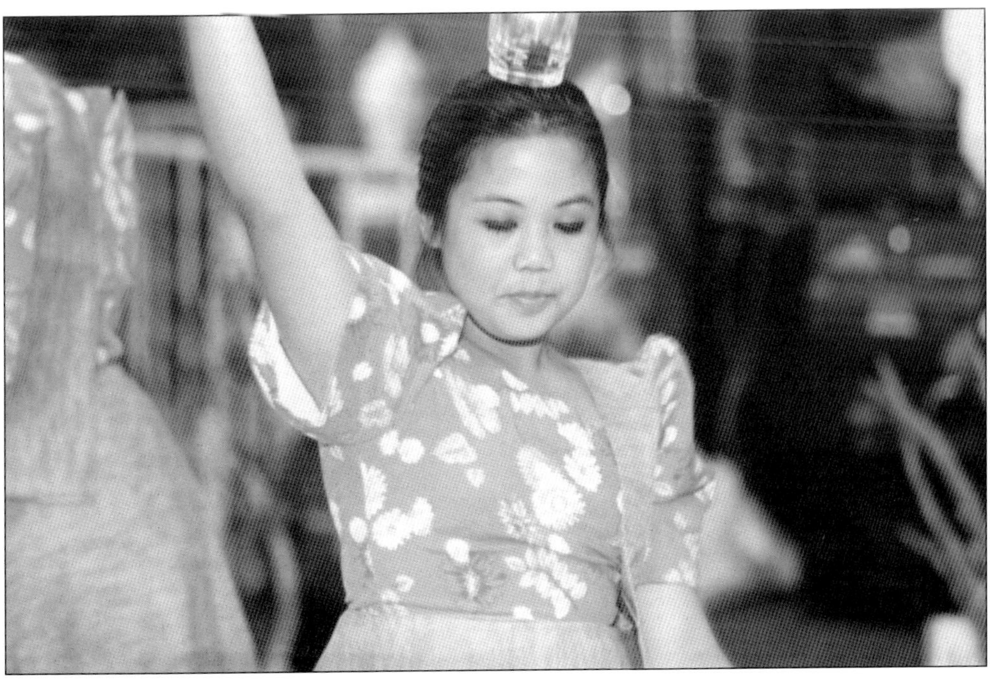

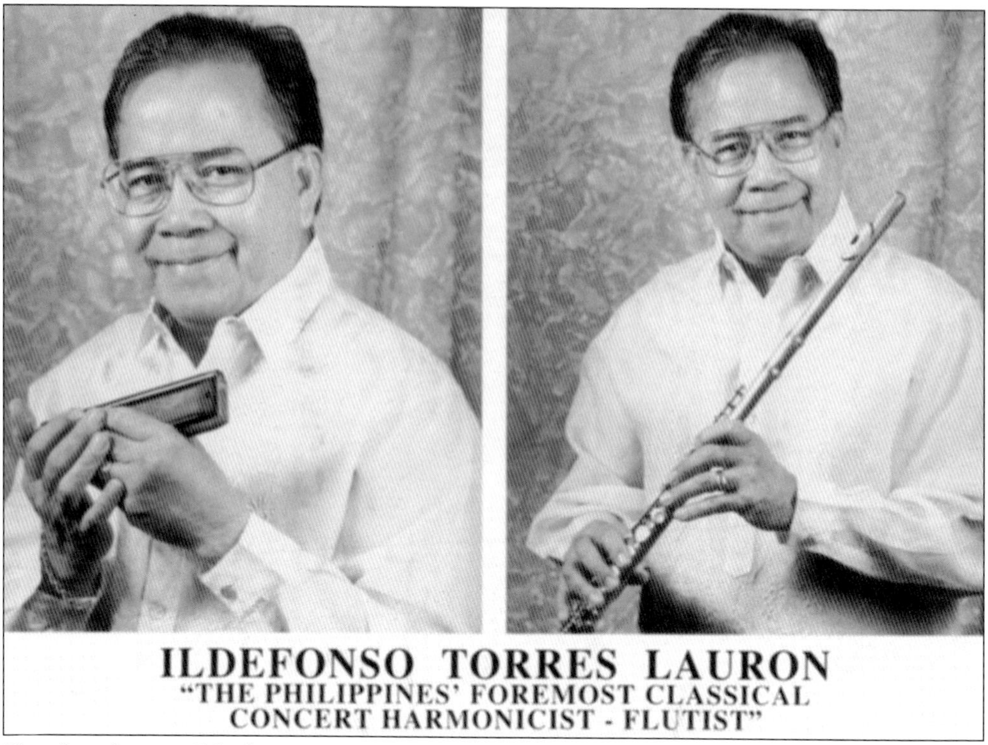

This flyer features Ildephonso Torres Lauron, who played the flute for the Boston Pops. On June 10, 2000, he featured two songs in a concert at Boston Symphony Hall in honor of Philippine Independence Day: "Ang Bayan Kong Pilipinas" ("My Country, Philippines") and the Philippine national anthem, "Lupang Hinirang" ("Chosen Land"). The anthem's lyrics were written by José Palma, and the music was composed by Julián Felipe. (Courtesy of the Lauron family.)

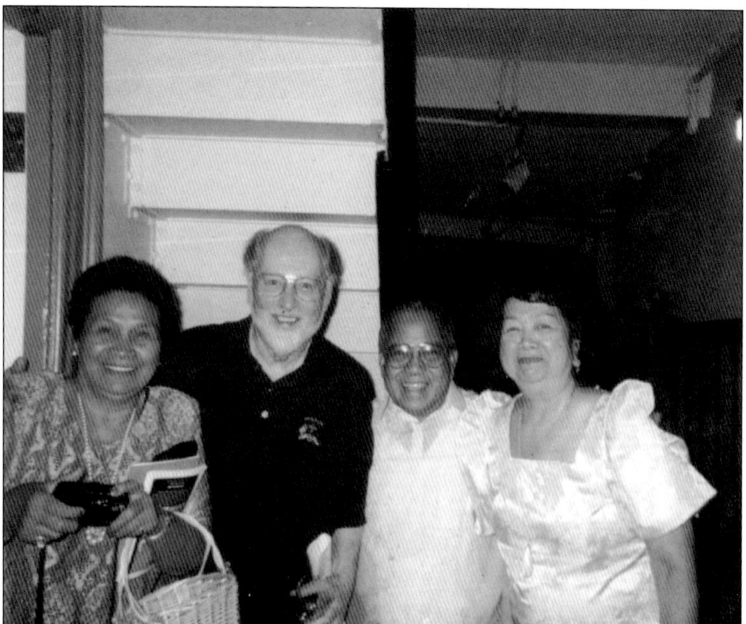

This photograph was taken backstage at a Boston Pops concert at Boston Symphony Hall on June 10, 2000. Flutist Ildephonso Torres Lauron (third from left) played two Filipino songs to celebrate Philippine Independence Day. Nida Prado (left) and Lauron's wife, Lucy (right), pose with maestro John Williams (second from left). (Courtesy of Alfreda Prado and Pia McCusker.)

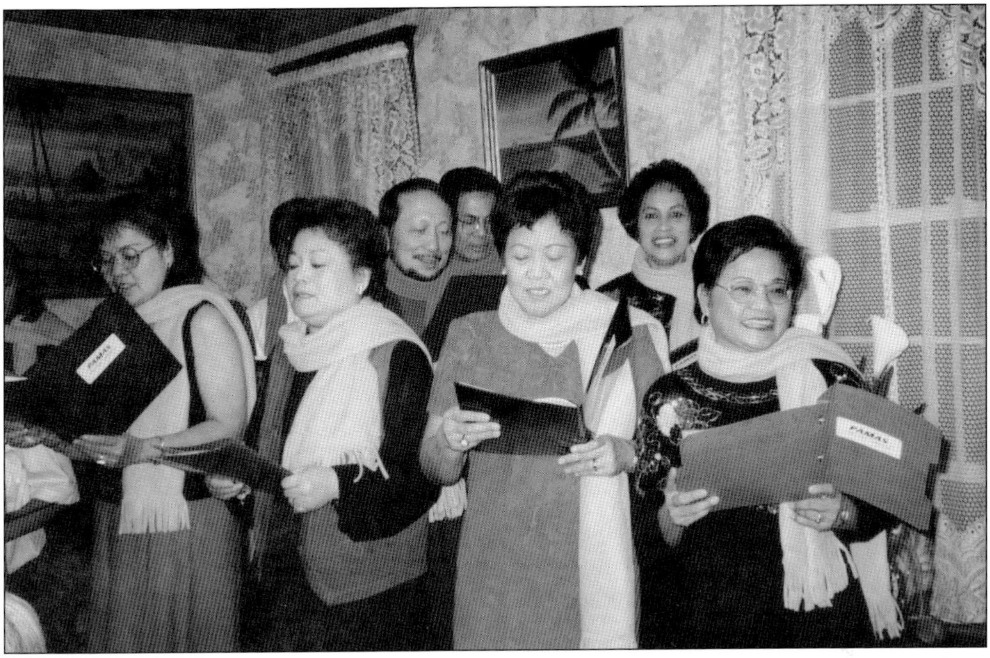

Christmas traditions are very important in the Filipino American community. These singers from the Philippine-American Association of New England are caroling at a private party in the 2000s. (Courtesy of Leila C. and Gregorio A. Amarra.)

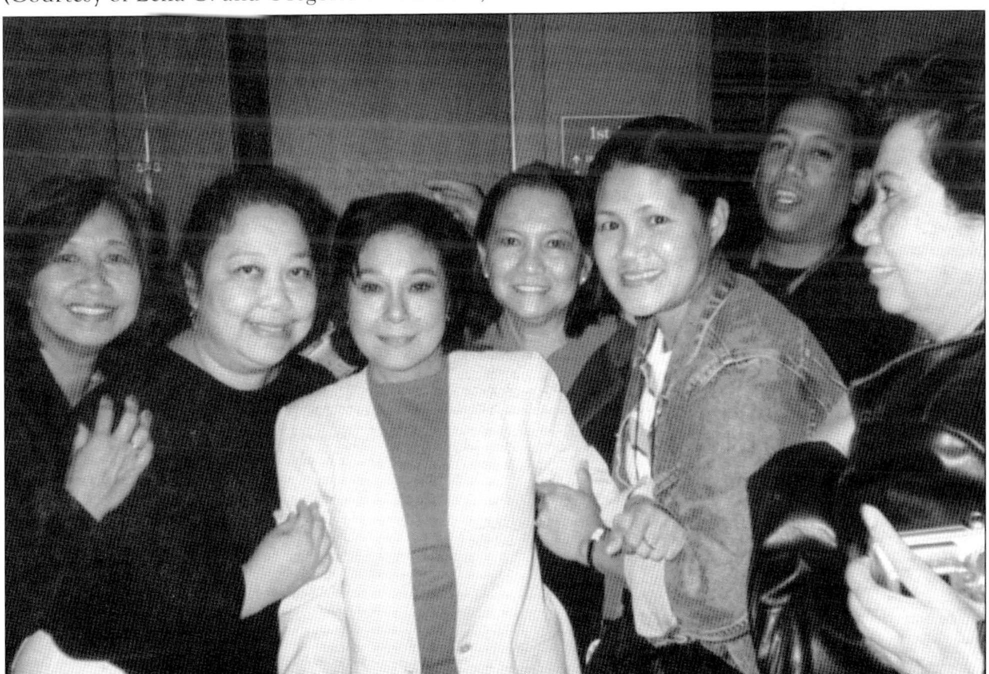

This photograph shows members of the Boston Filipino community posing with the acclaimed actress and singer from the Philippines Nora Aunor. According to a major Philippine network, ABS-CBN, Aunor came to Boston in 2012 for a throat operation. She is well-known for her movie and television roles as well as her work as a recording artist and film producer.

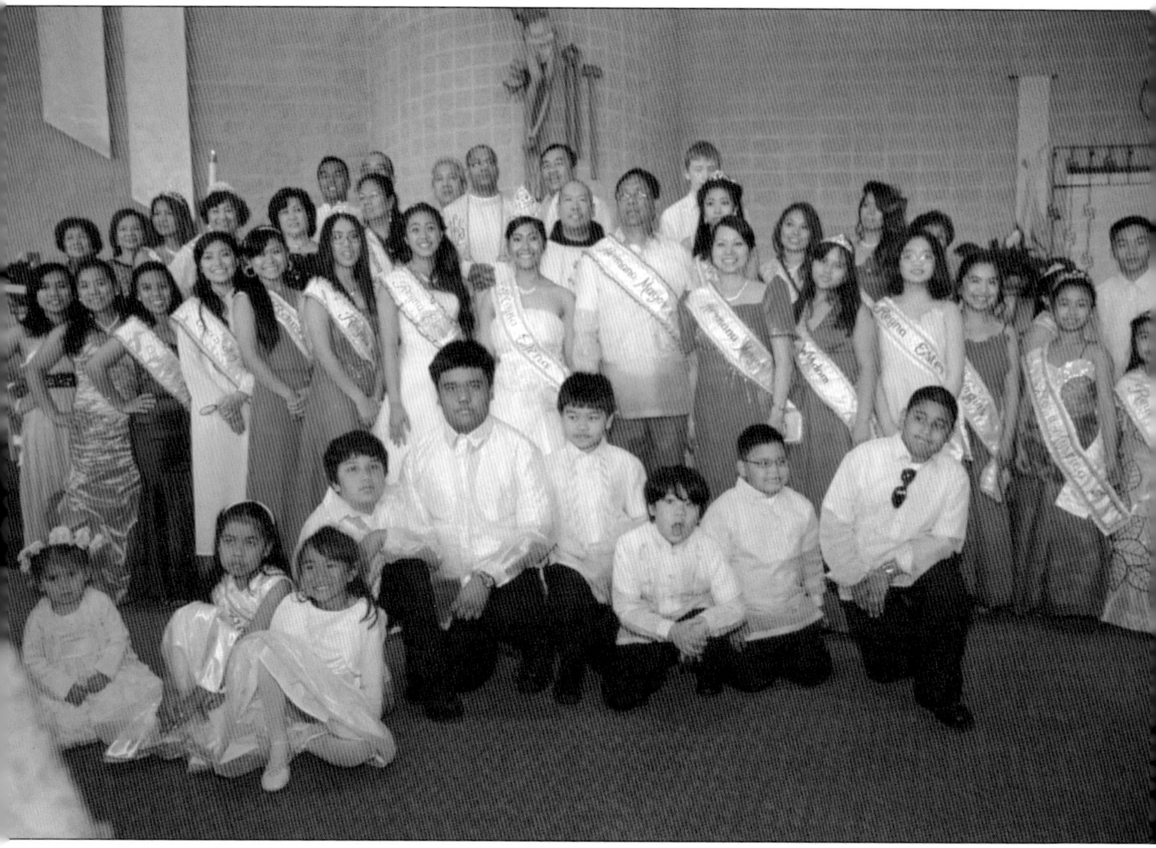

This Santacruzan was celebrated at the National Shrine of Our Lady of La Salette in Attleboro in May 2013 by members of the Filipino Apostolate of Boston. (Courtesy of Rev. Fr. Cyriac Mattathilanical.)

Joebell Manuel (right), who was the Reyna Elena for the 2013 Santacruzan parade, poses with Fr. Cyriac Mattathilanical (second from left) and her parents, Johny and Belinda Manuel. Father Cyriac was born in India but was ordained to the priesthood in Cavite, Philippines. He was assigned to the National Shrine of Our Lady of La Salette in Attleboro in 2006 and appointed as chaplain of the Filipino Apostolate. (Courtesy of Rev. Fr. Cyriac Mattathilanical.)

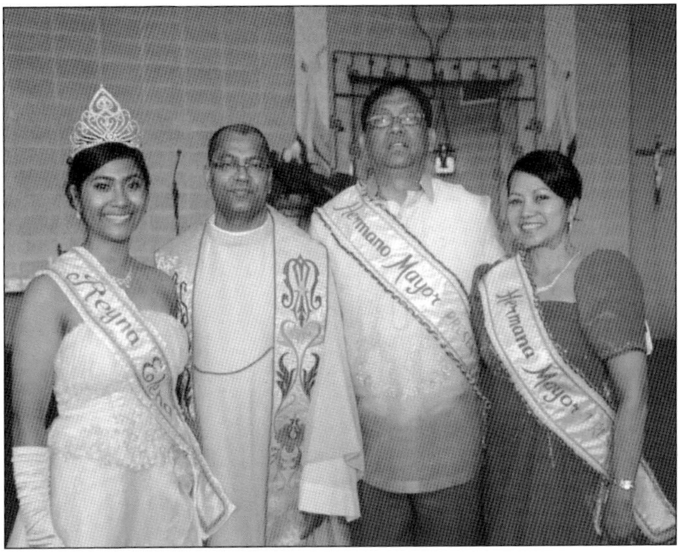

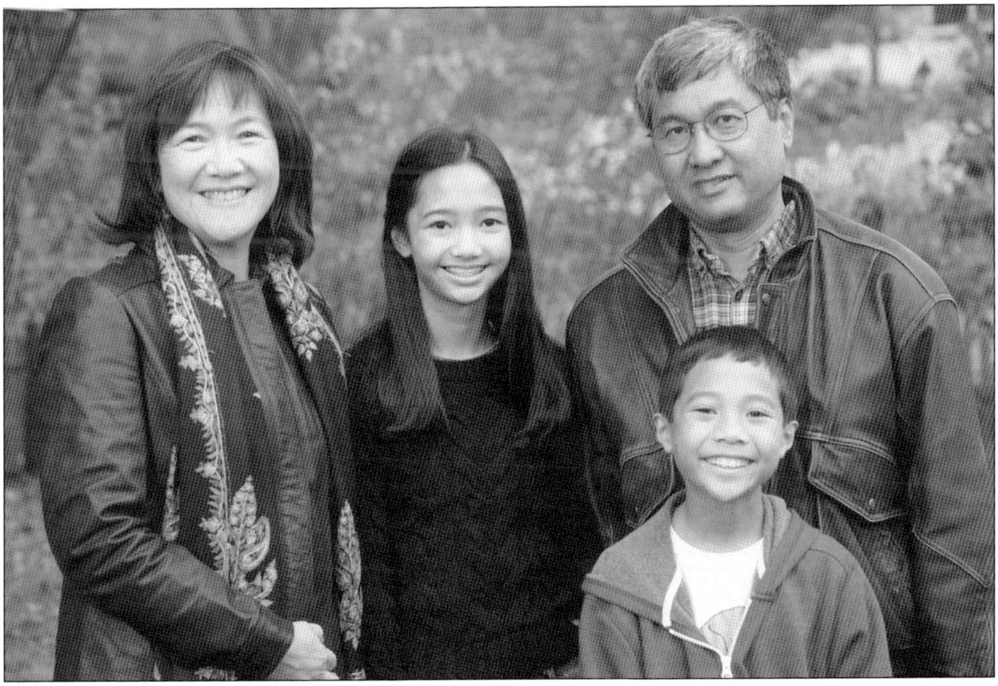

Jesus N. Vallasenor (right), a research scientist at MIT Kavli Institute for Astrophysics and Space Research, came to Boston in 1984 as a graduate student, around the time his wife, Agnes Quisumbing (left), was a postdoc. She is a senior research economist at the International Food Policy Research Institute. The picture was taken around 2010 with daughter Cecilia and son Lucas. (Courtesy of Vallasenor family.)

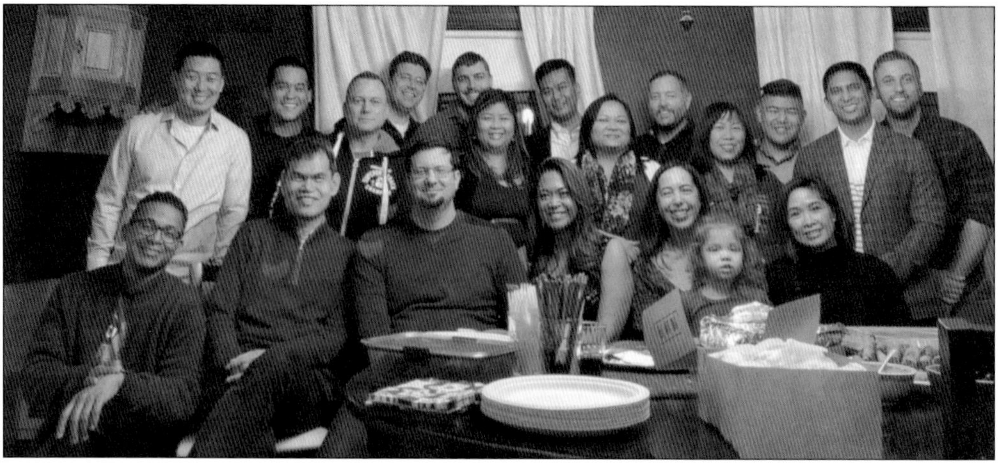

The Boston Filipino American Book Club was founded in 2007 by artist Bren Bataclan as a social club to buy, read, and discuss books written by Filipino American authors. Authors often join the meetings for an intimate discussion of their work. In this photograph, BFAB members celebrate New Year's Eve 2018 at the home of Bren and Bob L. Parlin in Cambridge. (Courtesy of Alonso Nichols and Grace Talusan.)

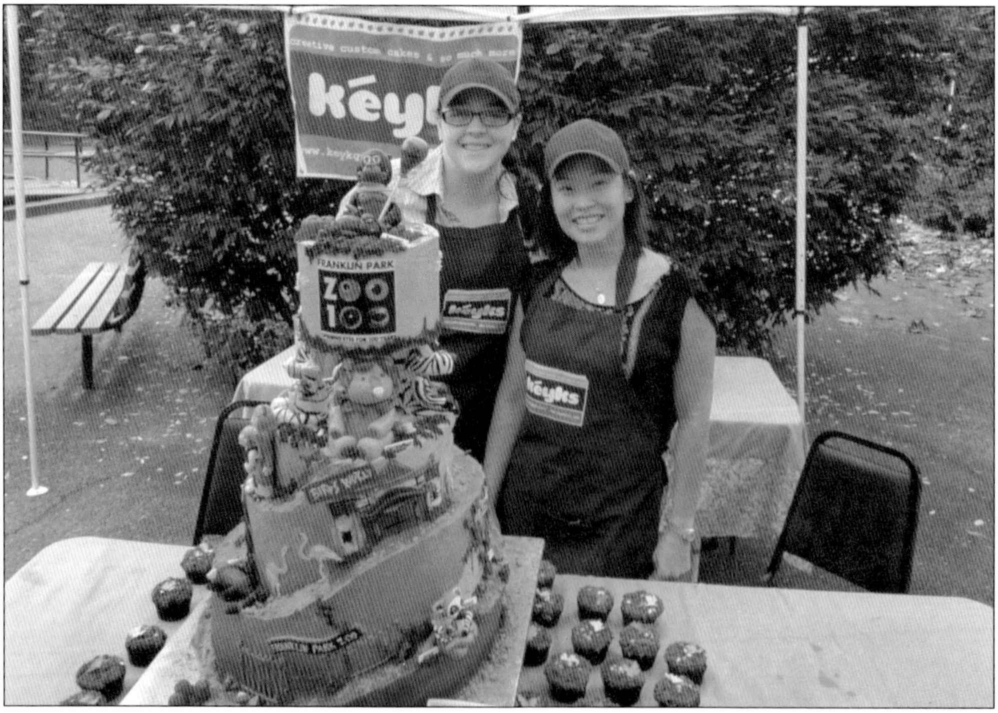

Rowena Sy-Santos (right) is the owner of Kéyks Bakery in Chelmsford. Along with popular flavors such as German chocolate and red velvet, Sy-Santos features Filipino favorites such as *ube* (or purple yam), mango, and *ensaymada*, a buttery pastry. In this photograph, she displays a cake that won "guests' favorite" at the birthday cake competition in 2012 during Franklin Park Zoo's centennial celebration. (Courtesy of Rowena Sy-Santos.)

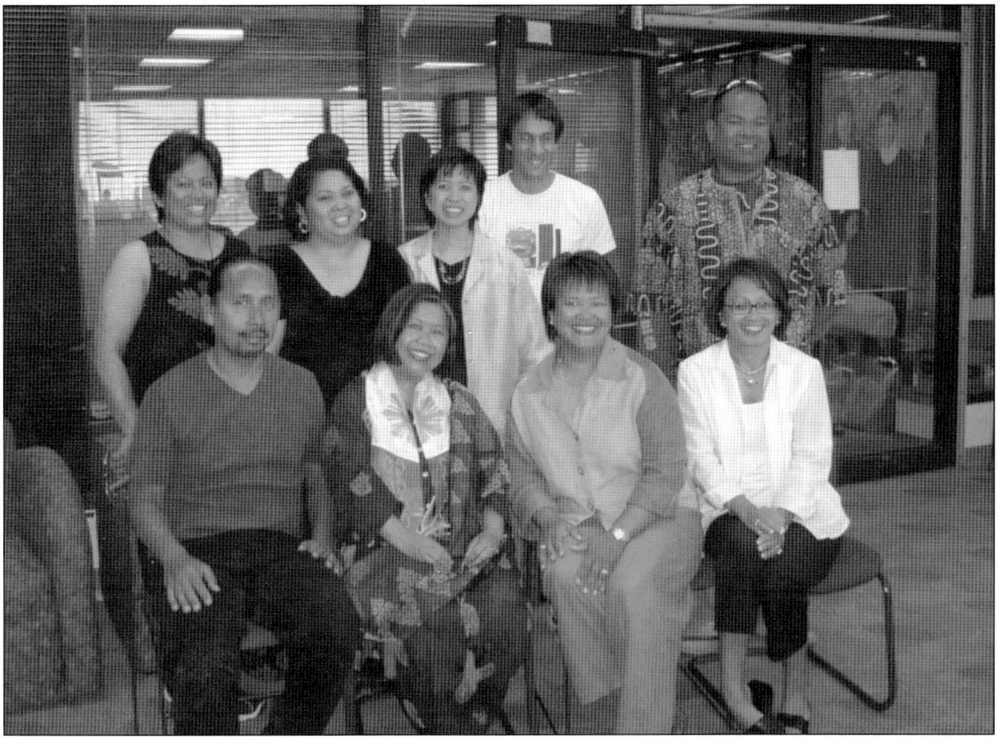

The Filipino American National Historical Society New England chapter's conference at the University of Massachusetts, Boston, in 2004 featured leaders of Filipino American National Historical Society (FANHS) chapters from across the United States. From left to right are (first row, seated) Alexis Canillo, Dr. JoanMay Cordova, Evelyn Casuga, and Debra Louie; (second row, standing) Edwina Bergano, Dr. Dawn Bohulano Mabalon, Emily Lawsin, Dr. Peter Kiang, and Dr. Allan Bergano. (Courtesy of JoanMay T. Cordova.)

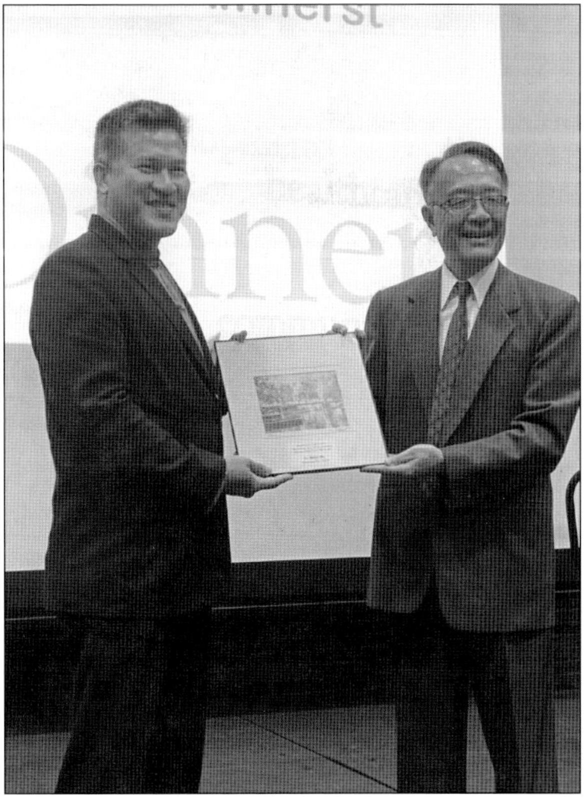

Dr. Richard Chu (left), a professor at the University of Massachusetts, Amherst, received a 2018 Community Hero Award from the Commonwealth of Massachusetts Asian-American Commission at Boston University. In 2007, he published a study about Filipino Americans in Massachusetts. (Courtesy of Richard Chu.)

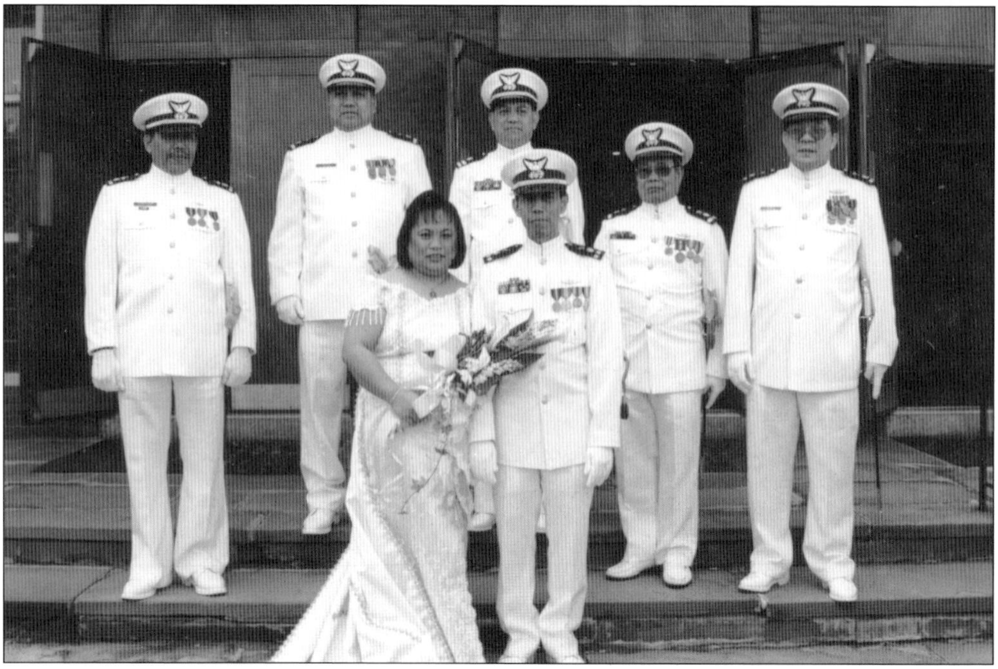

Above, Fracel Somera and Isabelo Sistoza Solar, commissioned chief warrant officer, celebrated their silver wedding anniversary in 2002 surrounded by retired Coast Guard friends, all from Greater Boston. In the back row, from left to right, are commissioned chief warrant officers Felix Atienza and Antonio Mateo, Lt. Bienvenido Manzano, and commissioned chief warrant officers Felimon Servino and José Jacin Marmol. Below, another photograph from the celebration was taken inside the venue in Dedham. (Both, courtesy of the Solar family.)

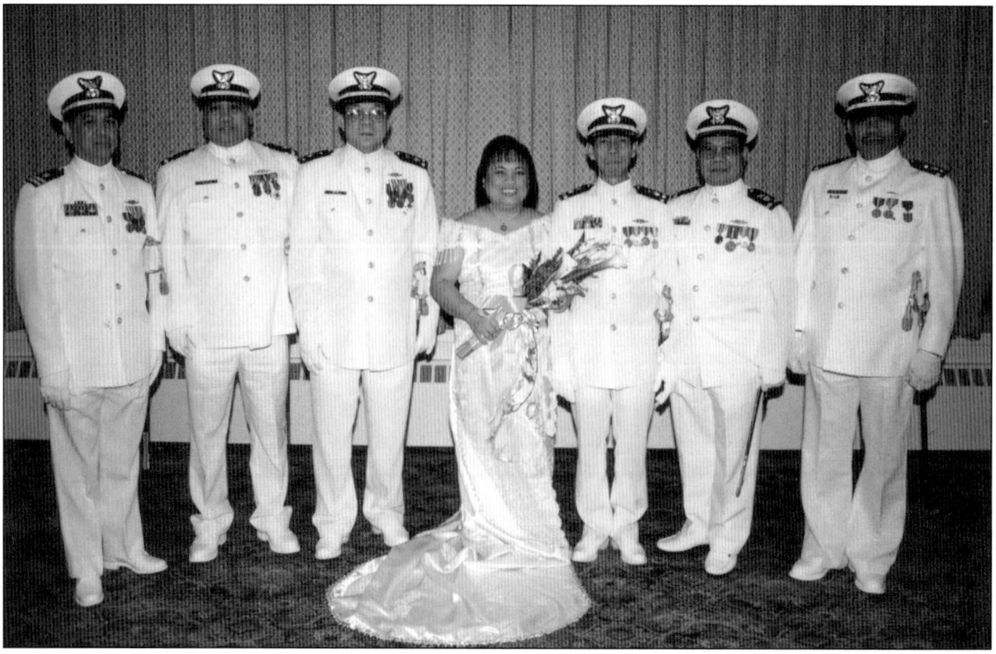

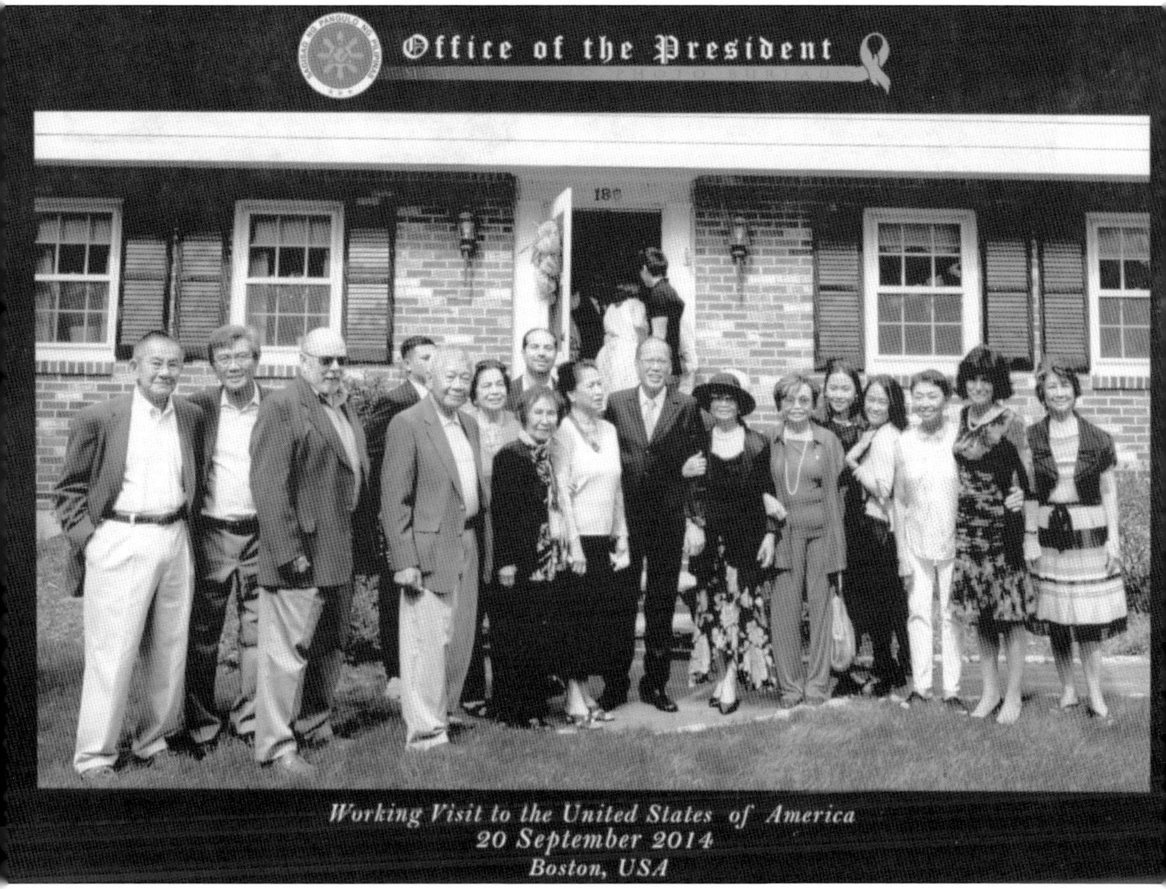

President of the Philippines Benigno S. Aquino III (center) poses with members of the Filipino American community at the home of the Bucal family in Sudbury on September 20, 2014. This was his first time in Boston since his family left in 1983. He visited the house in which his family lived in exile on Commonwealth Avenue and gave speeches at Boston College and the Kennedy School of Government at Harvard University. (Courtesy of the Agular family.)

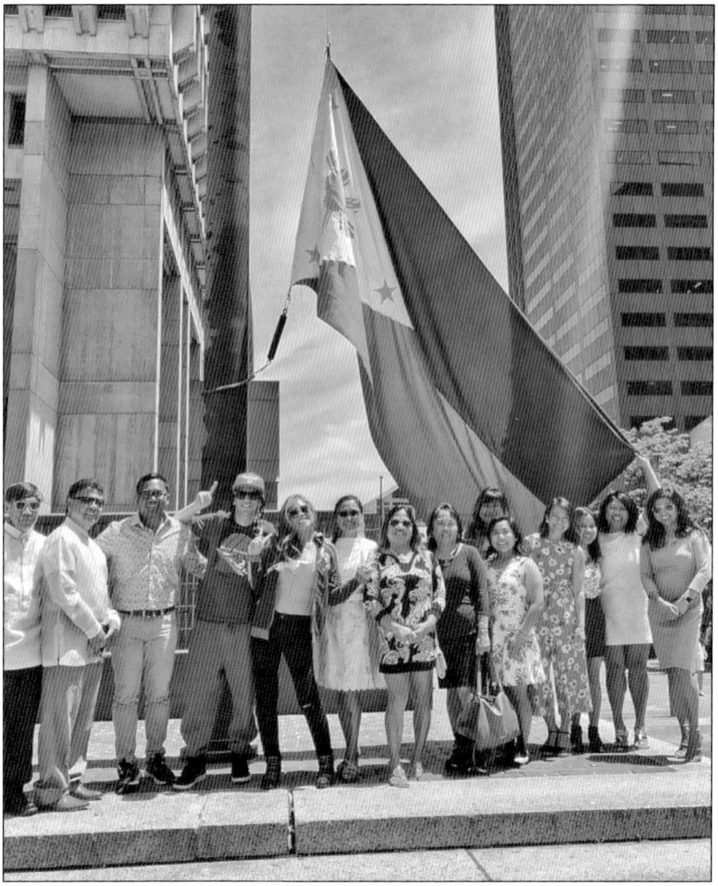

These photographs were taken at the 119th Philippine Independence Day celebration in 2017 at Government Center, spearheaded by the Philippine-American Mainstream Advocacy for Nonpartisan Association. The celebration creates visibility for Filipinos in the United States and celebrates pride in their heritage from the Philippines. (Both, courtesy of the Solar family.)

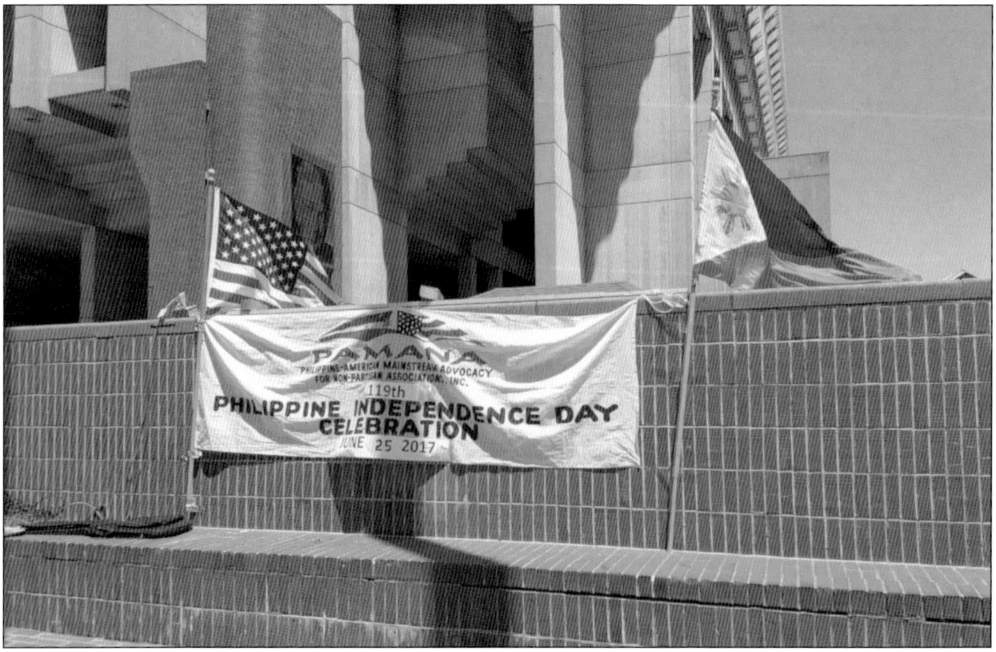

BIBLIOGRAPHY

Bayog, Rogelio D., executive ed. "Highlights of the Benigno S. Aquino Memorial Foundation." *Benigno S. Aquino Memorial Foundation Newsletter*, vol. 6, Special Edition, 1989.

Chu, Richard. "Profiles of Asian American Subgroups in Massachusetts: Filipino Americans in Massachusetts." *Institute for Asian American Studies Publications* 9, 2007.

Cullinane, Michael. *Liberty and American Anti-imperialism: 1898–1909*. London: Palgrave Macmillan, 2016.

De Leon, Sylvia M. *The Patriarch, Marceliano R. Montemayor*. Novato, CA: S.M. De Leon, 1986.

Enriquez, Nestor Palugod. "Filipino Veterans of the US Civil War." philusnavy.tripod.com/fabroscw.htm.

Fung, Cornelia Lichauco. *Beneath the Banyan Tree: My Family Chronicles*. Hong Kong: CBL Fung, 2009.

Javier, Lourdes A. *Montage*. Boston: Filipino Association of Greater Boston, Inc., 1982.

Ilacqua, Joan. "Dr. Fe del Mundo." Center for the History of Medicine at Countway Library, November 27, 2018. cms.www.countway.harvard.edu/wp/?p=15381.

Mercado, Monina A. *People Power: The Philippine Revolution of 1986*. Manila: The James B. Reuter S.J. Foundation, 1986.

Mercene, Floro L. *Manila Men in the New World: Filipino Migration to Mexico and the Americans from the Sixteenth Century*. Quezon City: University of the Philippines Press, 2007.

Santiago, Teodoro V., Jr. "How the Tragedy of the 'Great Raid' Fosters a Lasting Friendship." *Manila Times*, May 19 ,2021.

Schirmer, Daniel B. *Republic or Empire: American Resistance to the Philippine War*. Cambridge, MA: Schenkman Publishing, 1972.

Sides, Hampton. *Ghost Soldiers: The Forgotten Epic Story of World War II's Most Dramatic Mission*. New York: Doubleday, 2001.

Storey, Moorfield, and Marcial Primitivo Lichauco. *The Conquest of the Philippines by the United States, 1898–1925*. New York: G.P. Putnam's Sons, 1928.

Talusan, Mary. *Instruments of Empire: Filipino Musicians, Black Soldiers, and Military Band Music during US Colonization of the Philippines*. Jackson: University Press of Mississippi, 2021.